GRIDIRON UNDERGROUND

GRIDIRON UNDERGROUND

Black American Journeys in Canadian Football

JAMES R. WALLEN

DUNDURN
TORONTO

Cover images: John Williams Sr. photo courtesy of Scott Grant (upper right); Bernie Custis photo courtesy of the Hamilton Public Library (upper left); Johnny Bright photo courtesy of the Canadian Football Hall of Fame (upper middle); Chuck Ealey photo courtesy of the Canadian Football Hall of Fame (bottom); author photo: William L. Armstrong.
Printer: Webcom, a division of Marquis Book Printing Inc.

Library and Archives Canada Cataloguing in Publication

Wallen, James R., author
     Gridiron underground : Black American journeys in Canadian football
/ James R. Wallen.

Includes bibliographical references and index.
Issued in print and electronic formats.
ISBN 978-1-4597-4321-2 (softcover).--ISBN 978-1-4597-4322-9 (PDF).--
ISBN 978-1-4597-4323-6 (EPUB)

     1. Football players--Canada--Biography. 2. African American football players--Canada--Biography. 3. Canadian Football League--History. I. Title.

GV939.A1W34 2019   796.335092'2   C2018-906007-7
                                          C2018-906008-5

1 2 3 4 5   23 22 21 20 19

Conseil des Arts du Canada | Canada Council for the Arts | Canada | ONTARIO ARTS COUNCIL / CONSEIL DES ARTS DE L'ONTARIO / an Ontario government agency / un organisme du gouvernement de l'Ontario

We acknowledge the support of the **Canada Council for the Arts**, which last year invested $153 million to bring the arts to Canadians throughout the country, and the **Ontario Arts Council** for our publishing program. We also acknowledge the financial support of the **Government of Ontario**, through the **Ontario Book Publishing Tax Credit** and **Ontario Creates**, and the **Government of Canada**.

Nous remercions le **Conseil des arts du Canada** de son soutien. L'an dernier, le Conseil a investi 153 millions de dollars pour mettre de l'art dans la vie des Canadiennes et des Canadiens de tout le pays.

Care has been taken to trace the ownership of copyright material used in this book. The author and the publisher welcome any information enabling them to rectify any references or credits in subsequent editions.
     — J. Kirk Howard, President

The publisher is not responsible for websites or their content unless they are owned by the publisher.

Printed and bound in Canada.

VISIT US AT

dundurn.com | @dundurnpress | dundurnpress | dundurnpress

Dundurn
3 Church Street, Suite 500
Toronto, Ontario, Canada
M5E 1M2

For Bernie C. and Bruce S. and those long remembered for their exploits on the gridiron and those sadly forgotten.

Every time I go out and speak to someone or go to an event, there's someone who comes up to me with a story about Varsity Stadium back in the day. Ulysses Curtis was playing. Or they have stories about when Pinball [Michael Clemons] played. And man, that really means something. If someone can hold on to a memory, "I remember this day when I was sitting in Varsity Stadium, it was freezing cold, and I was sitting there with my dad and we got two hotdogs." I sit back and I say, "You know this is embedded in a lot of peoples' hearts." I think this game was here before the NFL existed. Even though hockey is the number one sport here, the CFL has a place, and I understand the importance of it.

— Chuck Winters, motivational speaker and former CFL player

CONTENTS

FOREWORD

Flipping through a dated scrapbook was a pretty common activity for my twelve-year-old self. Sometimes I'd read the headlines but mostly I'd just be mesmerized by the black-and-white photos. For as long as I could remember my father's press clippings had captivated me. Images of #23 flying through the air, striking fear into the hearts of all the wide receivers that dared line up across from him. The psychedelic purple-and-red scrapbooks were as familiar a sight to me as the grade-school photos of my sister that adorned the side of the refrigerator. And like distant relatives, they would show up unexpectedly on holidays or family gatherings. If I was questioned by any of my friends regarding my dad's exploits on the football field, the books served as tangible evidence — physical proof that my dad played, and that he did so at the highest level. As a kid, convincing others of your father's toughness was, and probably still is, part of the neighbourhood bragging routine.

But then one time, as I flipped through the press clippings and photos I had seen hundreds of times, a certain headline caught my attention:

"A Black Player Wants To Coach."

As children we don't always understand the hardships and adversities, the highs and lows, the constant sacrifices that so many of our parents and ancestors endured, all to make it possible for us to live the lives we do. This particular article was in no way written to suggest that a "black player" could not coach; rather, it was written to shed light on the fact that the coaching ranks and front offices remained, as the author put it, "remarkably pale." In the forty-two years since that article was written, I have learned a great deal about my father and so many others just like him. Because behind the black-and-white images we see in scrapbooks and in old highlight reels were men who endured the kind of racism that my generation could only begin to imagine. And yet despite this they thrived, making lives and careers for themselves as family men, coaches, educators, and community leaders.

As a co-producer on the film version of this book, I experienced an awakening of sorts. Throughout the sometimes long, drawn-out, tedious process of making a documentary, I felt as though I was taking my own journey. Just as many of the men in this story uprooted their own lives and moved to another country in the hope of realizing a dream of something greater than just a sport, I began to feel as if I were riding right alongside them aboard the Gridiron Underground. With every thought they had, I had the same one. With every experience they went through, I wondered what I would have done in that same situation, whether being refused a meal with the rest of my teammates or being unable to drink from a water fountain because it was designated "whites only." The latter was my own father's experience growing up in the 1940s, '50s, and '60s in Denton, Texas, where the heat could reach ungodly temperatures in the summer. With each of these stories, these stops along the route to our destination, I was learning more about myself.

Out of all my time with the Toronto Argonauts, the 2004 Grey Cup game particularly stands out. Not just because we won but because there was something happening that was much larger than football. There was Michael "Pinball" Clemons becoming the first black coach to win a Grey Cup. We had Damon Allen at quarterback, a position that to this day still draws a large amount of attention, especially in the States, particularly if the man playing it has a certain skin colour. And finally, there was me, a son playing in the same game his father came to play in this country some thirty-two years before. Even the halftime show was headlined by the legendary Gord Downie, a man who some years down the line would bring national attention to the horrors of the residential school system with his album *Secret Path*. There was just something about that night that made it seem larger than football — we were breaking down walls.

When we look at the current state of professional sports, we see the re-emergence of the kind of athlete-driven activism that occurred in the 1960s, from individuals like Muhammad Ali who drew support from the Cleveland Summit, a collection of the best black professional athletes across all sports in 1967, to iconoclasts like John Carlos and Tommie Smith, who are remembered for raising their fists in protest at conditions in their own country for Black Americans. (What many people don't know or remember is that John Carlos played one season in the CFL with the Montreal Alouettes.) Current crusaders such as Colin Kaepernick, Michael Bennett, Lebron James, and others have shown that they want to create a legacy larger than any on-field accomplishments and that they're willing to sacrifice their careers and financial sponsorships to speak out about the injustices happening around the world.

As a second-generation CFL kid, I sometimes feel as though I am the product of not just a country but also a league. My father came to Canada for an opportunity, and he found it. Not just to play a sport but to live a life, meet a woman, raise a family, and give back to a game that provided him so much.

Since that article I discovered as a twelve-year-old kid, Black Americans have made advances in the coaching ranks. And yet in the NFL, where 70 percent of the players are black, there is still no black representation in ownership. In university athletic departments across North America, women and people of colour still remain underrepresented in leadership positions.

So where does this leave us? We all still ride that train, and each of us may face some of the same ups and downs our ancestors experienced on our individual journeys. But, like those passengers who came before us, it's up to us to ensure that the next generation's ride is a little smoother.

— John Williams Jr.
November 2018

INTRODUCTION

I grew up in the border town of Sarnia, Ontario, situated at the mouth of the St. Clair River directly across from Port Huron, Michigan, and less than an hour's drive from Detroit. In my youth, Sarnia was famous — some might say infamous — for a number of things, including being known as "the Chemical Valley of Canada." As monikers go, it sounded a lot cooler back then, before the argument of jobs versus the environment became a matter of social concern. As a result of that particular (now) ironic epithet, our citizens enjoyed the highest per capita income in Canada. The local football team, the Sarnia Imperials, won two Grey Cups in 1934 and '36 when teams from all over the country could compete for football's highest prize. In those days the team was sponsored by Imperial Oil, the largest of the petrochemical industries in town, and the team was able to attract better players by providing jobs in the local plant during the off-season. In the 1930s, there was no greater perk than a guarantee of employment.

But an even greater boasting point than two Grey Cups for the Sarnia football fan was the fact that Carlton Chester "Cookie" Gilchrist played football for the Imperials in 1954 before finding fame with the Hamilton Tiger-Cats and the Toronto Argonauts, and then attaining stardom with the Buffalo Bills of the old American Football League. Cookie arrived as a teenager in Sarnia with a deep-rooted grievance at the core of his being, which defined him and ruled his actions throughout his controversial career and post-football life. If he could have only rid himself of this bilious mix of distrust and resentment, his career and life after football might have run a lot smoother. Instead, his querulous nature damaged his reputation, his business efforts, and his prospects for entry into either the NFL's or the CFL's Hall of Fame. He was his own worst enemy and not even a sojourn in Canada could lighten the burden of bitterness he carried.

Cookie Gilchrist was an eighteen-year-old phenom playing high-school football in Brackenridge, Pennsylvania, when the Cleveland Browns of the NFL offered him a contract for $5,000 to play professional football for them. That was more money than anyone in his family had ever seen. Art Rooney, the owner of the Pittsburgh Steelers, got wind of the deal, and he didn't like the fact that Paul Brown, owner and head coach of the Browns, had swooped into his territory and scooped up this high-school wunderkind right from under his nose. Rooney complained to the powers-that-be in NFL headquarters and they, in turn, declared Cookie ineligible to play professional football for a period of four years, presumably the length of time it would take for him to complete his college football career. This decision, however, carried unintended consequences. Having signed a professional contract, Cookie was ineligible for a university football scholarship in the States regardless of the fact that he had never received any of the money promised. This was devastating for a kid who had more than a hundred universities lined up offering a full scholarship.

Did Cleveland ownership feel remorse for taking away his only chance at an education? Did they regret leaving him penniless and in a state of limbo as far as his football career was concerned? Did Art Rooney lose any sleep over the fate of a black teenager? Doubtful. He had achieved his goal of preventing a rival football team from stealing a prime asset. To paraphrase Michael Corleone in *The Godfather*, "It's nothing personal, Cookie. It's strictly business." And so Cookie did what other Black Americans had been doing since Herb Trawick first pulled on a red Montreal Alouettes jersey back in 1946.

He came to Canada. But he never forgot and he never forgave.

Cookie would only last a year in Sarnia. He simply outgrew the place. Plus, the Imperials could never hope to match the financial offers he received elsewhere: Kitchener, Hamilton, Toronto, Buffalo, and finally Denver. Cookie was one of the first true superstars of the game. He was a man before his time, a twenty-first-century athlete stuck in a conservative age where there was no room for outspoken athletes with oversized egos bringing excessive contract demands to the table. Canada had given him a wife and two children and a number of business opportunities but it could never give him peace of mind. There was, throughout his life, the overriding sense that he was owed something, that something precious and rare had been stolen from him and he could never get it back. It haunted him until the day he died.

November 18, 2007. The four remaining Canadian Football League teams were set to play the Eastern and Western semifinals for the right to vie for the Grey Cup to be held at the Rogers Centre in Toronto. The early game had Toronto against Winnipeg in the Eastern final with Damon Allen at quarterback for the Argonauts and Kevin Glenn at the helm of the Blue Bombers. The Western final had the B.C. Lions featuring Jarious Jackson at quarterback against the Saskatchewan Roughriders, who were led by their own star quarterback, Kerry Joseph.

All four quarterbacks for those remaining teams were Black Americans. There was nothing in the coverage even hinting at the historical significance of four black quarterbacks vying for the right to play in the Grey Cup game. Maybe no one was commenting on it because in the Canadian Football League it wasn't exactly earth-shattering news. Had this been the National Football League, the American media would have fallen all over themselves in a self-congratulatory frenzy in honour of this singular event. Such a rare phenomenon as four black quarterbacks vying for the NFC and AFC conference championships would have been held up as an illustration of just how far Black Americans had come after only *one hundred and fifty years* of freedom.

In contrast to the CFL, of the final four QBs in the playoffs that year leading to the Super Bowl, none were black. Of the final eight teams in the playoffs, there was only one black quarterback. Of the twelve teams that entered the playoffs, which included wild card teams, there were a grand total of two black starting quarterbacks. Two. In the land where football has been elevated to the level of both industry and religion.

Back in 2003, Rush Limbaugh, no stranger to controversial or offensive statements — he once accused Michael J. Fox of faking his Parkinson's symptoms to promote stem cell research — declared on national television that the Philadelphia Eagles' quarterback, Donovan McNabb, was at best a mediocre quarterback and that the media had been so "desirous that a black quarterback do well" that they had, in essence, conspired to create the illusion that McNabb was an elite quarterback. Limbaugh was promptly fired from ESPN, but the damage had been done. It was McNabb's reputation that took the biggest hit, not Limbaugh's. The conservative shock jock had his syndicated radio show and legions of right-wing sycophants waiting in the wings to cushion his fall from the lofty heights of liberal television. In an age of "alternative facts" and "fake news," the truth is just another lie and vice versa.

Kevin Glenn is still playing football today. At thirty-nine years old, he is a reserve quarterback for the Edmonton Eskimos. He has the bizarre distinction of being the only player in the history of the CFL to have had his rights owned by every team in the league. Back on November 18, 2007, he was one of the four black quarterbacks looking to lead their teams to victory and the right to play for the Grey Cup a week later. On that day, Glenn led the Winnipeg Blue Bombers to a 19–9 victory over Damon Allen and the Argos in the Eastern final. (The Bombers were going on to play in the Grey Cup game but Kevin Glenn was not. He had broken his arm during the fourth quarter against Toronto and would be forced to watch his understudy, Ryan Dinwiddie, take the field in his place.)

Meanwhile in the Western final later that day, Kerry Joseph, who'd been named the CFL's Most Outstanding Player for the season, led the Roughriders to a 26–17 win over the favoured B.C. Lions. Thus, the stage was set for the Grey Cup game, Saskatchewan against Winnipeg. It marked the first time in history that these two teams had met in a Grey Cup final, the obvious reason being that Winnipeg had traditionally been a Western team but had been relegated to the weaker East division to provide balance to the league. Most CFL fans, and most certainly Rider fans, remember that particular Grey Cup as it marked the first Grey Cup victory (23–19) for Saskatchewan in eighteen years. (For any CFL team, eighteen years in the wilderness is a long time, but in Saskatchewan, where Rider years are like dog years for the disappointed faithful, it approaches infinity.) Rock fans might remember the 2007 Grey Cup more for Lenny Kravitz's blistering rendition of *American Woman* (originally recorded by Winnipeg band The Guess Who) during the halftime show. One for the ages.

When you add together the number of seasons that those four East and West finalist quarterbacks — Damon Allen, Kevin Glenn, Jarious Jackson, and Kerry Joseph — played in the CFL, you come up with a staggering total of fifty-nine. Now, add in Henry Burris, whose Ottawa Redblacks won the Grey Cup in 2016 but whose Calgary Stampeders team lost in the Western semifinal to Jackson's B.C. Lions that 2007 season, and you end up with a mind-boggling seventy-seven years of football in Canada. That is what you call a commitment to a game and to the country that provided the opportunity to ply their trade.

A film producer I worked with on several historical documentary projects, including two critically acclaimed series on Canada during the First and Second World Wars, watched the rough cut of my film *Gridiron Underground*, the basis for this book, and said, "What you have here is a love letter to Canada from these players." During the production of the film, the athletes interviewed agreed on one thing: that it was time a film like *Gridiron Underground* was made. It mattered to them. They had left their country, friends, families, and hometowns behind and made real commitments to a new league, new teams, a new community, and a new country. For that they rightly felt a desire to be recognized not only for their exploits on the football field but for their contributions to the cultural mosaic of Canada. This book is a continuance of that recognition so richly deserved.

Chapter One

SOMEONE ALWAYS HAS TO GO FIRST

October 4, 1946. The Montreal Royals, champions of minor-league base-ball's International League, were hosting the Louisville Colonels, champions of the American Association, at Delorimier Stadium in Montreal. The hometown Royals led the Little World Series — the minor-league version of its big brother, the World Series, which was contested by the best of the American and National Leagues — three games to two. A record crowd of 19,171 was there to watch their beloved Royals vanquish the despised Colonels from Kentucky. One more win and the Royals would accomplish the ultimate victory: good over evil, enlightenment over ignorance, love over hatred, and, finally, equality over racism.

Montrealers did not throw around terms like "karma" back then but they knew about payback. Their star player that year was none other than Jackie Robinson, who led the International League in batting average and runs scored and was second in stolen bases with forty. The stolen base in particular appealed to Montrealers, who liked their sports figures to display a dash of élan like hometown hockey hero Maurice "Rocket" Richard, whose famous glare as he broke in on goal had backed down many a defenceman and frozen goalies where they stood. They also loved an underdog, and no one had faced a greater uphill battle in his career than Jackie Robinson, who would go on to become the first black Major League Baseball player, playing with the Brooklyn Dodgers the following year.

But this year Jackie Robinson belonged not just to the Royals, a Brooklyn farm team, but to them — the people of Montreal. When Branch Rickey, president of the Brooklyn Dodgers, signed Robinson in 1945, he knew what he was doing by sending him to Montreal. There were teams and cities in the United States that would not exactly open their arms to a "Negro" ballplayer living and plying his trade in their midst. It was expected that Robinson would have an easier time in a foreign country. Hector Racine, president of the Royals, had gone on record as claiming that Montrealers were not racially biased and would judge Jackie Robinson on his play alone.

Unfortunately, not every game during the long season and the playoffs would be played at home. Jim Crow laws were still in effect in America, particularly in the South, and though Kentucky was considered a border state — the Mason-Dixon Line passes right through it — most of its inhabitants would probably have considered themselves Southerners. And that's where the trouble in this series started, right in Louisville, during the opening three games.

"I had been booed pretty soundly before, but nothing like this," wrote Robinson in his autobiography, *I Never Had It Made.* "A torrent of mass hatred burst from the stands with virtually every move I made."

The extreme vitriol was enough to throw him off his game as he had only one hit through the first three games. The Royals returned to Montreal down two games to one. The Montreal fans had read and heard about the way Robinson had been treated in Kentucky and, through the first two games in Montreal, they let the Louisville players know it every time they came to bat. The Royals won those first two games; momentum shifted to the home side.

"I felt a jubilant sense of gratitude for the way the Canadians expressed their feelings," Robinson wrote. "When fans go to bat for you like that, you feel it would be easy to play for them forever."

But even the Montreal fans knew that Jackie would not be satisfied with playing in the minor leagues forever. They knew of Brooklyn's plans for Robinson and the role he would play in the making of history south of the border. They were, however, determined to give him a send-off befitting a player — and man — of his stature.

In the bottom of the first inning in that sixth game, Robinson stroked his first hit of the day and would eventually come around to score. That would prove to be the winning run as veteran pitcher and former National League All-Star Curt Davis pitched a shutout for Montreal. The final score was 2–0. When the final out was recorded, Montreal fans swarmed the field. They hugged and kissed Robinson before he broke away and beat a hasty retreat to the dugout and dressing room. He had to catch a plane to Detroit where he was set to join a barnstorming tour of the States. But the fans refused to leave until Robinson made another appearance.

"Finally I had to take a chance. I passed my bag to a friend, hunched my shoulders and plunged smack into that throng."

Robinson forced his way through the crowds, who slapped him on the back, hugged him tightly to their breasts, sang his praises to the skies, and kissed him on both cheeks as French Canadians do. At last, he managed to squeeze through the gates and into the street before breaking into a sprint with hundreds of Montreal fans in hot pursuit. Residents emerged from their homes to see what all the ruckus was about. A passing car pulled up and someone shouted, "Jump in, Jackie!" So he did, landing right onto a strange woman's lap. Jackie shouted instructions and the car sped off. He caught his flight to Detroit that night.

Credit for the most famous description of the riotous post-game celebration and Robinson's desperate efforts to escape his adoring fans goes to Robinson's writer-friend Sam Maltin, who wrote in the *Pittsburgh Courier*: "It was probably the only day in history that a black man ran from a white mob with love instead of lynching on its mind."

Someone who watched Robinson's success on the field and his popularity with the fan base with a keen interest was Lew Hayman, the newly installed general manager and coach of the latest addition to the Interprovincial Rugby Football Union (a.k.a. the Big Four), the Montreal Alouettes. The Alouettes had been reborn from the ashes of a succession of failed Montreal efforts to sustain a professional football team, under various names: Indians, Cubs, Royals, Bulldogs, and most recently, Hornets. Montreal had won a Grey Cup in 1931 as the Winged Wheelers over the Regina Roughriders. Hayman, together with local businessman Leo Dandurand and financier Eric Cradock, formed a partnership to bring a Montreal franchise back to the Big Four.

Hayman was the football mind. He had come to Toronto in 1932 as an assistant coach for the University of Toronto basketball program. He had been a standout athlete at Syracuse University in basketball and baseball, winning All-American honours in his senior year as a high-scoring forward on the Syracuse Orangemen basketball team. While coaching basketball at U of T in '32, Hayman looked around for something to do in his spare time. He heard about the local football team, the Argonauts, and managed to swing a meeting with the head coach, Buck McKenna. McKenna was impressed with this brash, young Jewish-American from New York City and offered him a position as assistant coach. When McKenna fell sick partway through the 1932 season, Hayman was appointed interim head coach. The next year, Toronto management dropped the "interim" title and made Hayman the full-time coach. In his first full year as head coach, he led the Argos to a Grey Cup victory, and he followed that up with two more Grey Cups in back-to-back years, 1937 and 1938.

When the war came, both the IRFU and the Western Interprovincial Football Union (WIFU) suspended play for the duration. Hayman enlisted in the RCAF and was stationed in Toronto. When the war ended, seeing a void in Montreal, he hooked up with Cradock and Dandurand to form a football team. Dandurand, as the homegrown connection to the French media, no doubt pointed out to both Hayman and Cradock that it wouldn't hurt to have a symbolic name that appealed to the Québécois populace and cultural imagination. Thus, the Alouettes were born.

Montreal at that time was the most cosmopolitan city in Canada and, with the exception of New York, in all North America. It had achieved a reputation as a pleasure capital, the "Paris of North America," with jazz clubs, strip joints, gambling dens, and hundreds of brothels where tourists and inhabitants alike could indulge their every desire without fear of arrest. When Hayman saw the popularity that Jackie Robinson enjoyed in Montreal and the buzz he helped to create around the Royals, he figured he could duplicate that success and at the same time get a jump on the rest of the league by integrating the Alouettes. Hayman knew it was only a matter of time anyway before someone else accomplished the feat. He wanted to be the man who did it first. And Montreal was the place to do it.

Canadian teams were limited in the number of import players (Americans) they were allowed to have on a team. In 1946 that number was five. Since most Canadian teams were either managed or coached by Americans, no one in this group had been eager to break the unwritten code prohibiting the signing of black players that had existed in the National Football League since 1933. Prior to 1933, there had been a number of black players in the NFL. But these were the Depression years and the feeling shared by most American owners was that employing black football players would take jobs away from more-deserving white ones — "more deserving" by virtue of being white, that is. The owners may have actually believed their own rhetoric that by prohibiting black athletes from joining the professional ranks they were doing a great service to the nation during those troubling economic times. Black players were slowly and not so subtly encouraged to find greener pastures elsewhere until none remained in the league. After 1933, it was understood throughout the NFL that there would be no more black signings.

Most historians attribute much of the NFL ban against black players to the influence of George Preston Marshall, the owner of the Washington Redskins, which was the last team in the NFL to integrate (and when it finally did in 1962, it was only through government intervention). While it seems only natural that the owner of a team with the most racially insensitive name in professional sports, then and now, would promote a racist ideology when it came to black athletes, he openly encouraged the employment of Native Americans as a promotional tie-in to what today we would call his "brand." In defending the continued use of the offensive term "Redskins," Washington's current owner, Dan Snyder, has argued that Marshall was honouring the legacy of the Redskins' first coach, William "Lone Star" Dietz, an Oglala Sioux.

(The factual problem with that argument was that fourteen years before Marshall and Dietz had come up with the name "Redskins" in 1933, Dietz had been tried in Spokane, Washington, for avoiding the draft in the First World War by falsifying his identity and posing as the son of an Oglala Sioux mother. He pleaded "no contest" and received a sentence of thirty days in jail. This minor setback did nothing to discourage Lone Star in his endeavours and he continued with his charade for the rest of his life.)

Just as Branch Rickey had conducted an intensive search of the Negro leagues and minor leagues to find the right ballplayer to be the first black player in the majors, Hayman searched for the right football player. Hayman took a more cautious approach. He chose not to go for a big signing, an offensive dynamo with the potential pizzazz to equal or surpass that of Jackie Robinson. Instead, Hayman set his sights on a defensive lineman out of Ohio State University, Bill Willis, who had graduated in 1944 and, with nowhere to play professionally in 1945, had taken a coaching position at Kentucky State College for Negroes, an all-black school in Frankfort, Kentucky. (The school would drop the title "for Negroes" in 1952 and eventually earn status as a university in 1972, becoming Kentucky State University with a student body today that is 51 percent non-black.)

Willis was set to accept Hayman's offer to play in Montreal when he received an invitation to try out for the Cleveland Browns of the fledgling All-America Football Conference. The Browns were led by Willis's former coach at Ohio State, Paul Brown, the man who had coached the Buckeyes to a national championship in 1942. Willis decided to sign with his old coach. Lew Hayman now had to adjust his plans. Willis recommended a former Kentucky State College lineman named Herb Trawick who was, according to Willis, even better than he was. Trawick was also a veteran of both the European and Pacific theatres of the Second World War, which, combined with the Willis stamp of approval, Hayman took as a testament to Trawick's ability and character. Plus, Trawick fit the bill as a blue-collar kind of player, the guy in the trenches, someone who would never get to touch the football unless he fell on another man's fumble.

Trawick was small by today's standards, only five feet ten inches tall and weighing in at 230 pounds. In today's game he would be a fullback, the last line of defence against onrushing Goliaths intent on ripping the head off David, the team's puny stone thrower. He was also quick, the first tackler downfield on kicks ready to separate some unsuspecting receiver from his senses as well as the ball. Trawick had a reputation for being tough as nails, a reputation he'd earned while playing football at Kentucky State.

Trawick was a three-time black All-American in college. He left in 1942, before graduating, to join the army. When he was overseas in Fordingbridge, England, serving in the medical corps attached to the 183rd Combat Engineers, the white officers warned the locals they would be well-advised to watch out for and keep their distance from the "Negro soldiers." In a November 10, 1956, *Maclean's* magazine article by writer Trent Frayne, Trawick recalled how one officer went so far as to tell the townsfolk that the black soldiers "had tails" as if, being British and non-American, they were anatomically ignorant or gullible enough to swallow tales of bogeymen hiding in their closets. Instead of breeding fear in the people of Fordingbridge, the warnings had the opposite effect. The townspeople held a dance and made sure they invited all the American soldiers, not just the white ones.

"They saw that a lot of our boys could sing and dance, and I guess they figured we must be human beings." And with a certain satisfaction and perhaps a bit of the old nudge nudge, wink wink, Trawick added, "We had a good time at Fordingbridge."

After the war, he returned to Kentucky State in order to graduate before going on to Ohio State to study for his master's. And that's when Lew Hayman reached out to him.

"I was just out of college and needed bread," Trawick told Frayne. "Lew offered me $1,500 that first year and I accepted. I must have been pretty hungry. I was disappointed but I knew if I made good I would get more money. So I put football ahead of everything else."

Before Hayman's offer to come play in Montreal, Trawick had never played against white football players. He was naturally a bit hesitant to start now, especially in another country and in a city where French was the predominant language. But by this time, everybody knew that Montreal was the current address of Jackie Robinson. So when Trawick came to Montreal, he and Robinson hooked up and became fast friends. They shared the anxieties and experiences that come with being ground-breakers. But Trawick conceded that Robinson's roadmap contained the bumpier terrain.

"I've never run into discrimination on the football field," he told Frayne, "although I must say it's the only place I haven't. Jackie ran into it everywhere, probably more of it on the field from other players than off it."

Although Jackie played for a team that was located in Montreal, Canada, his sport was not played by Canadians at that level. Professional baseball, outside the Negro leagues, remained a game played exclusively by white Americans, a huge percentage of whom came from the rural South and thought that black people were inferior. Black athletes, to a great degree, were shielded from the worst excesses of racism on the playing fields in Canada by the rule preventing teams from having more than five American imports on the roster. Teams were therefore limited in the number of players they could have that had been raised in hotbeds of Southern racism.

Before the 1946 season had even begun, Lew Hayman heard from two of the teams competing in the Big Four, Ottawa and Toronto. Toronto's owners, who had chosen not to sign any American players despite the new rules allowing imports, said they were particularly incensed that Hayman was planning to play league games on Sundays, citing unwritten ethical and moral standards for operation, and concluded that "we simply did not use black players." Hayman replied that he "couldn't find anything in the rules against either one." Undeterred, Ottawa and Toronto responded that if he intended to go ahead with his plans, they would boycott games against Montreal. Hayman told them to go ahead, "because if they forfeited, it would be the easiest two points I'd ever pick up." As Hayman had figured they would, both teams meekly capitulated.

It is only natural that when athletes in any sport come into a new environment, they want to make an impression on the coaching staff, their teammates, and the fans. They want to prove to the coaches that they're dependable. Their teammates just want to know that new players have their backs and won't put their own needs above those of the team. And the fans just want to see a player who will bust through brick walls for the logo on their chest. In Montreal, they had the Rocket. They had Jackie Robinson. And now they had Herb Trawick. All three were wall busters.

"Trawick's irrepressible bounce on the field has endeared him to Montreal fans," wrote Frayne. "He has a habit, when the Alouettes are kicking off, of jumping straight up and down as the Montreal kicker starts forward to boot the ball. This brings a rising roar from the crowd that reaches a crescendo as Trawick churns downfield under the kick and barrels his bulk at the player who catches the ball."

In 1951, now playing for the defending Grey Cup champion, the Toronto Argonauts, former Alouette Billy Bass settled nicely under a punt one day only to have the human tank that was Herb Trawick bring Billy's participation in that afternoon's game to a sudden and terrible end. As Bass lay there on the turf like a deflated balloon and the Argo trainers dutifully sprinted out carrying a stretcher, Trawick stood over Bass's crumpled body, not pounding his chest or trash-talking in the manner of today's more self-aggrandizing players, but gently coaxing his friend to get up.

"C'mon, Billy, get up. My wife bought a roast and we're expecting you for dinner at our place right after the game."

Billy Bass would have to skip dinner that night at the Trawicks' house. He had a broken bone in his back and would have to return to Toronto for medical treatment. The two had become good friends during the 1948 season, Bass's lone season with the Alouettes. Black players enjoyed the companionship of other black players on their teams and were drawn even closer because of their estrangement from the white players. It was that closeness that drew Herb Trawick to the Montreal train station that night to see his friend Billy off to Toronto.

Herb Trawick would last twelve seasons with the Alouettes; in eight of those years he was a true "sixty-minute man," playing offence, defence, and special teams. He never left the field. He was rarely injured badly enough to miss playing time. (*Concussion protocols? What are those?*) Trawick suffered four broken bones in his back and four broken ribs, and yet missed only three games in his career. In 1951, his teammates named him captain, the first black team captain in professional football. Herb Trawick was a man his teammates knew they could depend on.

Perhaps his greatest moment on the gridiron occurred in the 1949 Grey Cup game against the defending champs, the Calgary Stampeders. The Stamps had come into that game believing it would be a cakewalk, led by their own black stars, Woody Strode (of later Hollywood fame) and Kentucky State alumnus Ezzrett "Sugarfoot" Anderson. The field conditions, as they often were in November in Varsity Stadium, the home of the Grey Cup game, were hideous, mud swamps broken by islands of iced-over turf. The Alouettes began the game strong and leaped out to an 11–0 lead but the Stampeders closed the gap to 11–7 near the end of the first half and they had the ball again. The Stamps' quarterback, Keith Spaith, dropped back to pass — he never saw Trawick coming. Trawick slammed into him and the ball came loose. Trawick trampled the poor quarterback into the muck as he scooped up the loose fumble and rumbled thirty-five yards for the touchdown.

Herb Trawick had done what Lew Hayman had never signed him to do: stolen the show on the biggest stage in Canadian sports, the Grey Cup game. The Alouettes won that game, 28–15. Trawick would play in three more Grey Cup games, the three classic matchups in a row against the Edmonton Eskimos from '54 to '56; Edmonton would win all three. The most bitter of the three straight losses was the first, the 1954 Grey Cup, which is remembered for Jackie Parker's ninety-yard touchdown run after he recovered a Chuck Hunsinger fumble in the dying minutes, tying the score at 25–25. The Alouettes claimed Hunsinger had been in the process of passing and the play should have been whistled dead, negating Parker's touchdown. The referees stood by their call. The Esks would score a single point shortly afterward, bringing the final score to 26–25 for Edmonton.

Though much beloved by Montrealers during and after his career with the Alouettes — he had a park in Montreal named after him in 1997, Parc Herb-Trawick on Avenue Lionel-Groulx — life was not always easy for Trawick away from the gridiron. As Frayne reported in his article, Trawick never felt "social discrimination" in Canada but he did feel a certain "economic discrimination." In those days, football front offices would find jobs for many of their players during the off-season to help supplement their income. The many revenue streams teams have today to boost their finances did not exist back then; what the team took in at the gate was all it could pay its players. Thus, a good job arranged by the team was, more or less, a benefit package. Trawick was offered the job of doorman at a popular Montreal restaurant.

In his view, other players — *white* players — seemed to have fared much better, landing more rewarding jobs that promised future positions if they were inclined to pursue them. It wasn't a question of money because, as a celebrity doorman at a local hot spot, Trawick made a lot of money in tips. It was the nature of the job: there wasn't much of a future in doormanship. He had a degree. To him it was menial work with undertones of racism. Nevertheless, he took the job and together with his income from football managed to put away enough money to start a shoe-manufacturing business in the late '40s. The business thrived for a year until Trawick and his partner had a falling out. Trawick tried to sell his end of the business but could not find any takers at the price he wanted. It wasn't long before the animosity between the partners led to a decline in business and eventual bankruptcy, leaving Trawick with a heavy debt load.

So, he went back to being a doorman. Once again, pooling his resources from tips and wages along with his football salary, he managed to save another $6,000 and opened his own restaurant in close proximity to two popular nightclubs, Rockhead's Paradise and Café St-Michel, located at the intersection of Rue Saint-Antoine and Rue de la Montagne, which was known to the citizens of Montreal as simply The Corner. The broader neighbourhood, including The Corner, housed the vast majority of Montreal's English-speaking black community in a pocket known as Little Burgundy. Oscar Peterson was born in Little Burgundy and was a semi-regular at Café St-Michel along with a number of Black American bebop jazz musicians, like Art Farmer and Sonny Rollins.

But change was in the air in 1950s Montreal as city officials looked to crack down on the criminal influence and seedier aspects of Montreal nightlife. It was during this period that both Café St-Michel and Rockhead's Paradise "were closed down," according to Frayne. Whatever the reasons behind the closures, no longer was The Corner drawing crowds to the neighbourhood. With the decline in drop-in traffic, Trawick's modest restaurant suffered a slow and quiet death.

With another failed business under his belt, Trawick decided to try his hand at professional wrestling. Why not? He had the build for it. Other pro footballers had had success making the transition to wrestling, perhaps none bigger than football legend Bronko Nagurski, who won three NFL titles with the Chicago Bears in the 1930s. Besides, wrestling was a big attraction in Montreal during the '50s with hometown boy and fan favourite "Mad Dog" Vachon capable of drawing 14,000-plus to the Forum. But, as Trawick soon discovered, the big money went to either heroes or villains, and unfortunately for him he did not fit either category. That experience lasted a year and a half, both during and outside of football season. With expenses coming out of his own pocket, he was barely breaking even. Hardly the supplemental income he had hoped it would be. He needed a less physically demanding job than wrestling, one that wouldn't put his football career at risk through injury.

When the *Maclean's* article came out in 1956, Herb Trawick had found success in a printing business, which he ran until he retired from football in 1957. While he may have struggled off the field to find career opportunities in an age when football amounted to a decent but not high-paying part-time job, his on-field performance over a twelve-year career ranks among the very best in Canadian football. His jersey number, 56, is one of only seven jersey numbers retired by the Montreal Alouettes since the team's inception. But it wasn't just the Alouettes who recognized his contribution to the game. Trawick was named an Eastern All-Star seven times and appeared in four Grey Cup games, winning one and losing three heart-breakers in a row to the magnificent Edmonton Eskimos team of the 1950s. He was the first black captain of a CFL football team and was elected to the Canadian Football Hall of Fame in 1975. Had he played a far more flashy position, like Tom Casey had out in Winnipeg — Casey was the first black player inducted into the Hall of Fame, in 1964 — Trawick would have been knocking at the doors to the Hall of Fame long before. At his induction ceremony, Lew Hayman, the man who had brought Trawick to Montreal thirty years before, paid him the highest compliment anyone could about a football player of that day.

"He was the best two-way player I ever coached."

Herb Trawick was being recognized for an accomplishment that transcends the sport itself. Like Jackie Robinson in professional baseball, Herb Trawick was the first. Always a humble man, Trawick might have said he was just in the right place at the right time or that sooner or later it would have been somebody else. And he would have been right. But history chose him. And he was there to answer the call.

Chapter Two

"IF I HAVE TO INTEGRATE HEAVEN, I DON'T WANT TO GO"

Jackie Robinson is remembered for his exploits on the baseball diamond and for breaking the colour barrier in Major League Baseball. Today, major leaguers wear his number, 42, on their jersey sleeves every year on Jackie Robinson day (April 15) as a tribute to his legacy. What isn't generally known about Robinson is that in 1939 he was part of an offensive football juggernaut at UCLA, sharing a backfield with the great Kenny Washington, then in his senior year. Another senior on that team was end Woody Strode, future breakthrough black action film star. He was "the body" long before Schwarzenegger's extreme pumped-up android hit the screen. If Woody were around today, he'd give Dwayne "the Rock" Johnson some serious competition.

Woodrow Wilson Woolwine "Woody" Strode was born in a predominantly black neighbourhood of Los Angeles known as Furlong Tract, today considered part of the notorious South-Central Los Angeles. Woody's parents had come west in 1900 to escape the severe racism in Louisiana, where slavery had existed only a single generation before. In areas like Furlong Tract, they could own businesses catering to a growing black community or find jobs of a more menial nature in the broader white landscape. Compared to what his parents had experienced in Louisiana, Woody never felt the same sting of racism, cushioned as he was by a growing black community in California.

"The racism out here was very subtle," wrote Strode in his autobiography, *Goal Dust*. "A restaurant wouldn't have a sign saying 'Whites Only' like they would in the South. They'd have a sign saying, 'We reserve the right to refuse service to anyone.'"

But even within the greater Los Angeles area, some communities were more racist, or certainly more openly racist, than others. Strode wrote that during the 1940s black people could not walk through Inglewood after dark. There was nothing subtle about the signs in Inglewood, which boldly declared: "No Jews and no coloureds are welcome in this town." Even as late as 1960, there were no black children enrolled in any Inglewood school.

Strode got into UCLA on the basis of his athletic prowess, not just in football but in track and field as well. This prowess and his legendary physique, sculpted by his daily ritual of a thousand push-ups, a thousand sit-ups, and a thousand squats, led to one of Strode's oddest and more famous encounters. Leni Riefenstahl, the German filmmaker responsible for the infamous Nazi propaganda film *Triumph of the Will*, was preparing to make her masterpiece on the 1936 Olympics in Berlin, *Olympia*. Somehow she had seen photographs of Strode's magnificent physique and she journeyed to Los Angeles with a German artist in order to paint the athlete for the official Olympic Art Show.

"You have the greatest physique of any athlete we have ever seen," she told the young athlete as her artist circled and studied and took measurements. When Hitler saw the paintings he was astounded by Strode's physical perfection and he sent Riefenstahl back to Los Angeles to film Woody engaged in vigorous physical pursuits connected to his track specialty, the decathlon. Riefenstahl wanted to take Woody up to Carmel and film him "against all that beautiful white scenery." By this time, however, Woody's friends had put him wise to the nature and goals of the Nazi party. He politely refused to take part in further activities with Riefenstahl. Still, he couldn't help wondering why they had such interest in him.

"I've often thought that if Hitler had won the war," he wrote, "they would have picked me up and either bred me or dissected me."

Before Jackie Robinson joined the UCLA backfield, Strode and Kenny Washington were huge star athletes, capable of drawing crowds in excess of 100,000 to the Los Angeles Memorial Coliseum, 40,000 of whom were black. The only celebrities bigger than Washington and Strode in town were movie stars, and that depended on who they were and how their last picture had done at the box office. The press labelled them "the Goal Dust Twins," a play on the advertising campaign by Fairbank's Gold Dust Washing Powder that featured Goldie and Dusty, "the Gold Dust Twins," two black, bald-headed, genderless twins doing dishes and other household chores. The slogan was "Let the twins do your work."

Naturally, when Jackie Robinson came along and joined that dynamic duo at UCLA, the press leaped at the opportunity to expand their repertoire of nicknames. Thus, Strode, Washington, and Robinson became known as "the Goal Dust Trio." Now you could "let the triplets do your work." Jackie was the only UCLA athlete to ever letter in four varsity sports: track, basketball, baseball, and football, all that same year. In Woody's estimation, baseball was Robinson's weakest sport. In 1939, Jackie averaged twelve yards every time they handed him the ball. Of course, it helped that the defences of the time had to split their concentration across all three offensive threats.

That year, UCLA and USC were both undefeated going into the final game of the season, and the winner would be guaranteed a berth in the prestigious Rose Bowl. This game was the hottest ticket in town with 103,500 fans filling the seats, an all-time attendance record. It's hard to believe from these two teams with such high-quality players on both sides of the ball, but they wound up tied 0–0. UCLA had a chance to win right at the end of the game. The Bruins were sitting on USC's four-yard line, with just enough time on the clock to run one more play. The team could kick a field goal and win, or they could try to rush or pass the ball over the goal line for a touchdown. The coaches on the sidelines left the decision to the players in the huddle. They were the ones who had given the favoured USC team everything it could handle on the field that day, both defence and offence. The players, including Robinson, Washington, and Strode, voted to go for the touchdown. No one wanted the game to end on a simple kick.

Unfortunately for UCLA, the pass fell incomplete in the end zone and the game ended in a scoreless tie. In the *Los Angeles Times*, sportswriter

Dick Hyland wrote a moving tribute to Strode's performance on the field: "When a man does all he is supposed to do on every play, when on top of that he does things no one can fairly expect him to do, that man is playing great football. Woody Strode was great Saturday; he climaxed a fine football career and from now on he can think, if things ever seem tough, I did my part once."

UCLA had to win the game to go to the Rose Bowl. In tying powerhouse USC, they proved to themselves, to their fans, and to the sportswriters across America that they belonged on the same field as USC. But a tie was as good as a loss. By virtue of entering the game ranked higher than UCLA, it was USC who was invited to play in the Rose Bowl game on January 1, 1940. Woody reflected later that "football is so much like life. Every time you get knocked down, you wonder if you want to get up. Sometimes, you wonder, 'Is this worth it?' But you pick yourself up, dust yourself off, and keep on going."

As the doors to the NFL were closed to black players, both Strode and Kenny Washington played semi-pro football for the Hollywood Bears of the Pacific Coast League. There were five other teams in the Pacific Coast League: San Diego, Fresno, Salina, Los Angeles, and Phoenix. At that time, there was no athlete more popular in the Los Angeles area than Kenny Washington. League games were advertised as "the Hollywood Bears with Kenny Washington" against whoever the other team happened to be. Nobody cared. The crowds came to see the great Kenny Washington play. He was paid $200 a game plus a percentage of the gate — taking home $500 a week in all — when one of the top NFL players was making $175 a week and no percentage of the gate. Even Woody was making roughly $300 per week, more than any comparable NFL player.

Following the Japanese attack on Pearl Harbor, Woody was recruited to play with a West Coast air force team, the March Field Flyers, which, like other service teams, also played against university football teams. For many top athletes of the day, this was a way of serving in the military without seeing action overseas. He played three years of service football before being sent to the Pacific Theatre of the war, where he quickly learned what an easy time he and his fellow ballplayers had enjoyed in California while others had been fighting in places like Okinawa. He was there about three months before atom bombs were dropped on Hiroshima and Nagasaki and the fierce Pacific war came to a sudden and silent finish. When Woody returned to California, the Hollywood Bears were practically waiting at the docks for him. The Bears had a game coming up against the San Francisco Clippers. Kenny Washington, who had been rejected by the armed forces following a succession of knee injuries, was with the team. The coach told Woody he'd had his old uniform hauled out of mothballs, just waiting for him. So Woody Strode stepped off a boat from the Pacific and into his old number, 17. He played forty minutes in his return to the gridiron.

Daniel Reeves was a young New York stockbroker who came into a fortune when his father sold a chain of grocery stores to supermarket heavyweight Safeway in 1940. In 1941, Reeves shopped around for a football team to buy and settled on the Cleveland Rams, which he purchased for $135,000 from a local Cleveland ownership group. In 1945, the Cleveland Rams won the National Football League championship at home in −22 degrees Celsius. Reeves celebrated that frigid victory by announcing that he was moving his team from Cleveland to sunny Los Angeles. Until then, there hadn't been any major professional sports teams located on the West Coast. This was more than a decade before the New York Giants baseball team took up residence in San Francisco and the Brooklyn Dodgers in Los Angeles, breaking the hearts of hundreds of thousands of New Yorkers. (Cleveland football fans, however, would be spared a lengthy mourning period for the loss of their Rams as that same year, 1946, would see the birth of the All-America Football Conference, a new league, with a franchise in Cleveland, the Browns, named for their first head coach and part-owner, Paul Brown.)

The Los Angeles Rams expected to play in the Los Angeles Memorial Coliseum, which was already the home of both the USC Trojans and the UCLA Bruins, and though neither team was anxious to share their digs with a professional football team, they really had no say in the matter. The Coliseum was publicly owned, and permission to lease the facility for Sunday football games would have to come through the Los Angeles Memorial Coliseum Commission. When a number of black sportswriters, led by Halley Harding of the *Los Angeles Sentinel*, learned of the Rams' lease application, they demanded that the commission make its acceptance conditional on the signing of black players by the Rams and, in particular, that one of those players be Kenny Washington. It didn't matter that Washington's best days were behind him. This was about honouring the greatest black sports figure on the West Coast.

The commission listened to an impassioned address by Harding about the contribution Black Americans had made to the war effort and to the original NFL before black players had been systematically squeezed out. Harding and the other black writers found an unexpected ally in commission member Roger W. Jessup, who told the Rams' representatives at that meeting, "I just want you to know if our Kenny Washington can't play, there will be no pro football in the Los Angeles Coliseum." The commission decided to grant a three-year lease to Reeves on the condition that he sign Kenny Washington to play for his team.

Reeves and the Rams organization were backed into a corner. He'd already committed the team to the move and no other football venue on the West Coast could fit 100,000 fans. And so he agreed to sign Washington who, in turn, requested that the Rams also sign his best friend and Hollywood Bears teammate, Woody Strode. Washington did not relish the idea of being the lone black player on an all-white team in an all-white league. And, as far as the Rams were concerned, well, someone had to room with the black guy; why not another black guy?

What is truly fascinating is that three players from the same 1939 university team broke the colour barrier in two major professional sports in the United States: Robinson in baseball, Washington and Strode in football. It took eight years for Robinson and seven for Washington and Strode, who, by the time they signed with the Rams, were shadows of their former selves. Robinson, at twenty-seven, was entering his prime as a baseball player. Washington was only twenty-eight but he had a lot of wear-and-tear on his knees, including off-season surgery. Woody was thirty-one, still an amazing physical specimen but older, slower, wiser, and more protective of his body. Woody did not play much that season, riding the bench for the majority of games.

Woody had never been keen on carrying the weight of expectation that came with being a racial ground-breaker. He intended to live as a free bird. He fully embraced a California laid-back lifestyle before most Californians even knew one existed. Breaking the colour barrier in the NFL would never bring the kind of glory that Jackie Robinson's ascension to the Dodgers would in 1947. Professional football, at that time, had none of the history, popularity, or American mythology attached to baseball. Woody also never faced the same animosity on the gridiron that Robinson faced on the diamond.

For one thing, in a physical sport like football, unless someone notified you ahead of time that they were going to inflict extra punishment on you because of the colour of your skin, how would you know the difference? During one Rams game, when Kenny Washington was lying on the turf, an opponent went to kick him in the head. Washington caught sight of him at the last second and managed to move his head out of the way. When one of his white teammates mentioned the incident in the locker room, Washington just shrugged.

"It's hell being a Negro, Jim," he said.

For Robinson, every act of aggression on the diamond sent a message that said, for the most part, "We don't want you here." No one was more surprised than Woody Strode when Jackie kept it together in the face of all that animosity. Strode could hit back. Jackie Robinson could not; he'd made a promise to Branch Rickey. Years later, Strode famously said, "If I have to integrate heaven, I don't want to go."

The next year, Woody was cut by the Rams. Too old, they said. At thirty-two he was in better shape than anyone on the team, but no matter. The Rams wanted him gone. He thought he might give pro wrestling a try. He had done some professional wrestling back in 1941 after getting out of school. Then a former teammate with the Rams, Les Lear, called to offer Woody a contract with a team called the Calgary Stampeders up north in Alberta, Canada. The Stampeders were offering $5,000 for the season plus $100 a week for living expenses. That was more than he had been making with the Rams. Hell, it was close to what the Rams were paying their star attraction, Kenny Washington.

Les Lear and Woody had become friends during the one season they were together in Los Angeles. After spending the 1947 season

with the Detroit Lions, Lear had been approached by Calgary's owners and offered the position of player-coach with full control over the
on-field personnel. Lear was as close to a homegrown Canadian as they
come. He had grown up in Winnipeg and played for the hometown
Blue Bombers, winning two Grey Cups, in '39 and '41, before joining
the Cleveland Rams. He was exactly the kind of prototypical head
coach the league desired (but has never yet consistently developed):
Canadian-bred, experienced in the Canadian game but knowledge-
able of the American game, and familiar with American talent and
American football ingenuity. With only five spots available for imports,
Calgary was counting on Lear, with his experience in the NFL, to fill
those positions with the best available bang for the buck. Les Lear had
gone up against Strode in practice day after day for a year. He was well
aware of what Woody Strode brought to the table: size, speed, strength,
and devotion to fitness.

Les Lear had warned him that he'd better bring his old shoes and
pads because he doubted that the team could find any to fit him. Just
because they could pay him a decent salary didn't mean they could
afford to outfit him. There were three other American imports with
Woody that year: Keith Spaith, Pete Thodos, and Rod Pantages. Spaith,
a quarterback, had played college ball at USC and played the 1947 season with the Hawaiian Warriors of the Pacific Coast Football League.
He then tried out for the Rams but was cut, and Lear grabbed him to
lead the Stamps' offence. Lear planned to use a stripped-down version
of the complex Los Angeles Rams offensive playbook, and both Spaith
and Strode had a working understanding of its nuances and its emphasis
on the forward passing game.

The Stamps played their home games out of Mewata Stadium
(Mewata means "O be joyful" in Cree), a 10,000-seat stadium. The stadium was much smaller than Woody was used to playing in, but the field
was wider and longer, allowing runners and receivers more room on the
outside. With his size, Woody tended to stand out on the field no matter
how large its dimensions; off the field he was like a magnetic pole drawing attention everywhere he went. Because he had Native-American
blood on both sides of his family, Strode was very popular with the
Indigenous people around Calgary. According to Strode, he did not need

to broadcast his racial makeup to the First Nations community; they just saw it in him. Members began to show up at his downtown hotel, bringing gifts of wild game and traditional clothing on a regular basis.

That first year in Calgary for Woody, the Stamps went undefeated during the season and remained so in the two-game, total-points semi-final, winning by a combined score of 21–10. The Calgary Stampeders were off to the Grey Cup game in Toronto. That year marked the beginning of what would become a Canadian football tradition: the great migration of fancy western-dressed football fans to the East via rail, hooting and hollering, drinking and dancing, creating the greatest moveable party on the continent.

The train east contained thirteen cars. One car carried a dozen horses and a chuckwagon. On arrival, the revellers invaded Toronto City Hall, cooking flapjacks and bacon in front of the building and handing them out to hungry Torontonians, who were fascinated by this unrestrained display of Western *chutzpah*. The Calgary Stampede had come to Ontario's staid capital, not just to show support for their football team but to create a buzz about their hometown tourist attraction. In so doing, they revolutionized the way Canadians viewed the Grey Cup. It was transformed from a single game into a week-long national celebration, long before the NFL copied the template for its Super Bowl, an annual two-week orgy of hype and overkill.

The Stampeders wisely took an earlier train to avoid the party and get in a little practice in the eastern time zone. Every time the train stopped, Lear had the players outside doing calisthenics or running laps around the train, regardless of the weather, even in knee-deep snow. The team stayed in Oakville and practised on a football field at Appleby College, six hours a day, including time spent watching game film of the Ottawa Rough Riders, an unusual practice at the time. They watched their opponent with interest, a team known for its "sleeper" play where an on-field offensive player did not return to the team huddle and instead might linger near the sidelines behind the line of scrimmage, hopefully unnoticed by the defence. At the snap of the ball, he would suddenly come to life and dash downfield uncovered to await a pass from the quarterback. This play was eventually outlawed, like the spitball in baseball, because it was stretching the rules and nature of sportsmanship. But it would be Calgary in the 1948 Grey Cup game that would turn the tables on Ottawa.

The game itself was a tightly contested affair. With a minute left in the first half, Spaith dropped back and hit Woody Strode with a pass that took the ball down to the Ottawa fourteen-yard line. One Stampeder, receiver Norm Hill, did not return to the huddle after that particular play, instead lying on the field close to the sidelines as if he'd been injured on the previous play. No one noticed — no one except Pete Thodos, who returned to the huddle wondering where his teammate was. He was quickly shushed and told that Norm was "sleeping."

"You've got to be joking," he said.

The referee was hovering nearby and Spaith asked him to avoid looking toward the sidelines if at all possible. On the snap of the ball, Hill jumped to his feet and took off for the end zone. Spaith let the ball fly. Hill juggled the ball in the end zone and it popped up in the air just as he was knocked flat by the defensive back. Hill hit the ground and sat up. The ball fell into his lap. Manna from heaven. He secured the ball for the touchdown. It wasn't pretty but it counted; it would gain a degree of infamy as the "sitting touchdown."

Strode would put his stamp (so to speak) on the game in the second half. The quarterback for the Rough Riders threw an overhand lateral pass that his receiver missed. Everyone on the field assumed it was just an incomplete pass and stopped playing; everyone except Woody, that is. With teammates on the sidelines screaming "Pick it up!" Woody grabbed onto the loose ball.

"An official got out of the way as I picked it up. That's how I knew I could run."

And run he did. For a ways. Then he lateralled the ball to a teammate who took it down to the ten before getting tackled. On the very next play from scrimmage, Pete Thodos ran the ball in for the winning touchdown. In Woody's autobiography, he never lateralled the ball, and neither was he or anyone else tackled short of the goal line. According to him, he ran the ball in himself for the winning touchdown and left the field on his teammates' shoulders with a bottle of rye whisky in his hand. Now, he may very well have left the game on his teammates' shoulders. He had, it could be argued, made the deciding play of the game by picking up the fumble and taking it downfield. So that part could be true. But by the time he wrote his book he had been a Hollywood star for forty years, so why not embellish. It's not like anyone in Hollywood was ever going to check the facts regarding a game played over forty years before in another country.

When the game ended in victory for Calgary, the western celebrants descended upon the Royal York Hotel in the heart of conservative Toronto. On November 29, 1948, sportswriter Jim Coleman reported in the *Globe and Mail*: "The football game for the Grey Cup was contested officially in the stadium and was continued unofficially in the hotel lobby. At 5:01 p.m. the goalposts were borne triumphantly through the front doors and were erected against the railings of the mezzanine. At 5:02 p.m. two platoons of bellboys circumspectly removed the potted palms, flower vases and anything that weighed less than three thousand pounds."

The bellboys were presumably attempting to limit the damage. According to legend (and Woody's memoirs), Strode burst through the front doors of the Royal York astride a pure white horse, wearing "a white linen cowboy-type suit, reddish lizard-skin boots, and a navy blue silk scarf around my neck." He paraded the horse around the lobby, once again clutching a bottle of Canadian rye whisky in one hand (along with the reins) and waving his ten-gallon hat in the other. The horse reared up and Woody let out a war whoop to applause and encouragement from the hotel guests. As the police closed in to restore order, Woody charged out of the hotel and into the night aboard his magnificent steed.

Did Woody really ride a horse into the Royal York lobby? It's doubtful. But it makes for a good story. And the story that someone had ridden a horse into the Royal York lobby had existed for years before Woody claimed credit in his autobiography.

On the return train to Calgary, Woody and the rest of the team joined the fans, the cowboys and cowgirls, the horses, and the chuckwagon for a continuous two-thousand-mile-long party.

At the beginning of the next season, Woody sustained an injury that limited his effectiveness. He suggested to Les Lear that a good insurance policy might be to sign a former teammate of Woody's from the

Hollywood Bears, Ezzrett "Sugarfoot" Anderson. Together, Lear and Strode embarked on a recruiting trip to Los Angeles where they found Anderson on the set of *Everybody Does It,* starring Linda Darnell and Paul Douglas.

"Woody told Les Lear I was the greatest tight end in the world. So they talked me into coming to Calgary," said Anderson years later.

Anderson was twenty-nine at the time and making a living playing bit parts in Hollywood films in a time when black parts were mostly domestic servants, slaves, porters, Tarzan extras, or simply wide-eyed comic caricatures. He had gotten his membership in the Screen Extras Guild and the Screen Actors Guild in 1947 while playing with the Los Angeles Dons of the All-America Football Conference. The owners of the team were Hollywood heavyweights Don Ameche (thus the name "Dons"), Bob Hope, and Bing Crosby, and they helped him supplement his income in an era when West Coast football stars were every bit as popular as Hollywood stars in Los Angeles. His first big "small" role was as a stable hand and horse-walker named Walkin' Murphy in the film *Seabiscuit,* Hollywood's first attempt to bring the story of America's beloved, indomitable racehorse to film.

Anderson was a natural for films. He lived his life in dramatic fashion, dressed well, wore lavender perfume, and played football with an exaggerated air of showmanship. There was no such thing as an easy catch for Sugarfoot. According to Strode, with Ezzrett every catch appeared far more difficult than it really was. If he made a tackle, he was the last to emerge from a pile, lifting his body from the turf like Lazarus rising from the dead, ensuring that every set of eyes in the stadium recognized the magnificence of his achievement. He played the game as if at death's door until it was time to spring into action, on offence or defence. In the home of Hollywood, his ability to grab the spotlight played well with the fans. It remained to be seen how it might play in Calgary.

Woody Strode and Ezzrett Anderson bookended Calgary's front line, both offensively and defensively. They also shared a hotel room in downtown Calgary.

"We had a suite with a jukebox and all our favourite records," wrote Strode in his memoir. "We didn't need an icebox; we'd just sit a case of beer outside the window and five minutes later we'd have ice-cold beer."

Anderson claimed that he loved Calgary from the moment he arrived and that once, no doubt after a few of those weather-chilled beers, he confessed to Strode that he prayed both to God and to Woody. Strode wondered why in the world anyone would pray to him. Anderson's answer was direct: because Woody was responsible for bringing him to Calgary. He told Woody that his mother had picked cotton when he was a child, and that she used to pull him through the fields on a sack because she couldn't leave him while she worked and she couldn't afford not to work. Woody, who had enjoyed a much easier upbringing in California, envied his friend's total embracement of Canada.

"You're getting more out of this than I am," he admitted.

Woody's life waited for him back in California. He was never ungrateful for the treatment he received in Canada or the lifestyle he was able to enjoy, but he missed his family and the California vibe. Ezzrett, on the other hand, would commute to Los Angeles for three years, taking small film roles during the off-season, before finally moving his family up to Calgary full-time in 1952. To his kids, he might as well have moved them to the Arctic Circle, it seemed such a cold and remote existence. But he remained confident that they would come around in the end, and they did, growing up playing the winter sports so foreign to their former Southern California life.

In 1949, the Stampeders were favourites to repeat as Grey Cup champions. Sportswriter and editor Tony Allan with the *Winnipeg Tribune* gave the most obvious reasons: "As if it wasn't bad enough last year trying to figure a means of stopping Spaith and Strode — and nobody did, by the way — the problem is worse this season with Sugarfoot Anderson operating on the other flank."

Once again, the Stampeders were the dominant force in Canadian football during the season except for one minor hiccup, a 9–6 loss to Saskatchewan preventing them from achieving two unbeaten seasons in a row. Keith Spaith, with Strode and Anderson as his two bookends, formed a potent passing attack that few defensive backs could cover completely because of their size and strength. For the second year running, Spaith would be named the Most Valuable Player in the WIFU. Sugarfoot led all receivers with thirty catches for 539 yards and five touchdowns.

Sometimes during pre-game workouts, the three would give the fans a highly entertaining aerial display of circus catches, with Spaith as straight man firing passes to Strode and Sugarfoot, a gridiron version of the Harlem Globetrotters or the Kansas City Monarchs (who played rapid-fire shadow-ball infield drills without a baseball that would have fans gasping at the illusion). These were the moments when these black athletes demonstrated their true prowess, not just as skilled players but as entertainers capable of connecting with an audience.

The Western semifinal that year was a two-game, total-points affair between the Stampeders and their archrivals, the Saskatchewan Roughriders, the only team to beat them during the regular season. While Strode and Anderson were treated like royalty in Calgary, Les Lear warned them that Saskatchewan's Taylor Field might not top the list of most racially tolerant environments. Roughrider fans were known to give a rough ride to all visiting players regardless of their ancestry, but Lear feared Strode's and Anderson's size and colour might make them particularly enticing targets. In fact, according to Sugarfoot, Lear flat-out told them "to keep our helmets on when we were on the sidelines to avoid getting hit on the head by bottles thrown by the fans." Lear grew up playing football in western Canada so the two star players presumed he knew what he was talking about. They kept their helmets on.

Calgary won the first game of the semifinal, 18–12. Sugarfoot caught six passes for ninety yards and one touchdown. But Woody separated his shoulder and required freezing at halftime. By the end of the game he was in such pain that further medication was necessary. This time, however, he decided to opt for more traditional Canadian methods of pain management.

"The doctor came to see me. He said, 'Woody, do you want me to give you a shot for the pain?' 'No!' I said, 'Give me some whiskey!' And the Canadian boys brought me some of their finest rye whiskey, emptied half the bottle, and filled it up with beer. I drank that and they picked me up and carried me to the train."

The second game of the semifinal was played on Calgary's home field, Mewata Stadium. As time was winding down on the game, Saskatchewan had the ball deep in Calgary territory with the score

8–4 in their favour. They lined up for what should have been a routine field goal that would give them an 11–4 win as well as an overall victory edge in total points. But the Roughrider kicker, Buck Rogers (for real), missed. As the Stamps, leading the two-game semifinal in total points, were about to let loose in celebration, the referee whistled for an offside penalty. *No!* And the offender was none other than playing-coach Les Lear, the man the players called Lord Lear or just "the Lord" for his tough, no-nonsense attitude. Sugarfoot, who was captain of the team, confronted Lear, a story he clearly relished telling some seventy years later on a video clip for the Alberta Sports Hall of Fame and Museum: "And I walked up to him and I said, 'Lord, this year I'm playing with you for the first time and everything, but if you ever jump offside like that again, I'm going to choke you.' And he looked at me and said, 'I'll never do it again, Sugar.'"

There was much laughter in the retelling, but one can only imagine what a humbling moment it must have been for a tough-nosed head coach to be called out for such a potentially costly mistake. The ball was moved five yards closer to the goalposts. This time, Saskatchewan opted for a different kicker, Del Wardien, in hopes he could succeed where Rogers had failed. The Roughriders should have stuck with Rogers. Wardien shanked the ball low and wide of the uprights. This time, Lear and the rest of the Stampeders managed to stay onside. Calgary still lost the game 9–4, but they won the Western championship by a hair on total points, 22–21. For the second year in a row the Stamps were off to the Grey Cup in Toronto.

Their opposition in the 1949 Grey Cup game would be the Montreal Alouettes, champions of the Big Four in the East. Once again, it seemed that half the city of Calgary hopped aboard the train for the journey east and, for good measure, brought their horses. Everybody was looking for a repeat of last year's festivities. Like the year before, the participation of Calgary and its fans had generated something unusual in Canadian football — national interest in the Grey Cup game. Scalpers were reported to be getting astronomical prices for a pair of tickets. Some as high as $10.00 a pair!

Woody was in rough shape for the game. He could not raise his arm above his shoulder, which made it nearly impossible to reach for a pass over his head, taking away his height advantage. He did not practise catching passes in the run-up to the game. He didn't even want to think about what it would feel like to get hit in the shoulder. Just before the game, his teammates held him still while the team doctor stuck a metal syringe loaded with novocaine into Woody's shoulder … six times. He could feel the needle scraping against bone. And pretty soon he felt nothing. You could have driven a spike into his shoulder and he wouldn't have felt it. He was good to go.

The Varsity Stadium field, however, was not in as good shape as Woody. Whatever stadium crew existed had not bothered to cover the field the week before the game. The field was muddy in most areas, partially frozen in others, with small patches of snow spread throughout the field providing the only spots of traction available. There was no point in getting frustrated by conditions. It was the same for both sides. And so Les Lear gave the team his usual pre-game pep talk — "I'll see you at the end of the game if they don't take you out on crutches" — and sent the Stamps onto the gridiron.

With only one of his favourite passing targets functioning at anywhere near 100 percent, quarterback Keith Spaith had a miserable day. He threw for four interceptions and coughed up the football when he was hit by Montreal strongman Herb Trawick, who picked up the loose ball and carried it into the end zone. It was Trawick's second fumble-recovery of the game. Not to be outdone by Trawick's heroics, Sugarfoot also recovered a fumble and carried it downfield for a touchdown. Woody was forced to pull himself from the game with five minutes left, his arm hanging useless and throbbing at his side, the freezing worn off, the pain too much to endure. He watched helplessly from the sidelines while the clock ticked down and the Alouettes celebrated their victory.

Although the mood on the train heading west was more subdued than it had been the previous year, you wouldn't know it by the turnouts at every whistle stop along the route. In Winnipeg the team drew a thousand fans to the train station. Bagpipers led an impromptu parade. They were given the kind of reception generally reserved for conquering warriors. The players were overwhelmed by the reception they received in the West, even in hardcore Roughrider land. And there were no more popular players than Woody Strode and Ezzrett Anderson. But nothing could have prepared the team for the reception they got when they reached Calgary.

"When we came to Calgary — the population in 1949 then was a hundred and twenty-five thousand people — we had lost the Grey Cup but sixty thousand people were at the train station … which was unbelievable to me," recalled Sugarfoot, some sixty years later, with amazement.

The city council had declared a half-day civic holiday and local schools did the same so that children could attend the festivities. Almost half the city turned out to greet the Stampeders. There was a parade throughout the downtown core, beginning and ending at the train station. Woody, wearing a Hawaiian shirt, jeans, and cowboy boots, played guitar while Sugarfoot, dressed in a long fringed jacket and a white cowboy hat, serenaded the crowd, much to the fans' delight. That was Woody Strode's swan song in Calgary.

Woody returned to California and the world of wrestling. But a whole new world of opportunity opened up for him in Hollywood. He became great friends with John Ford and made four films with him, including playing the title character in *Sergeant Rutledge*. Strode is probably best remembered for his role in *Spartacus* as Draba, a gladiator slave who must fight the title character, played by Kirk Douglas, to the death in the arena. When they first meet in the film, Spartacus asks Draba his name.

"You don't want to know my name," Draba replies. "I don't want to know your name."

"Just a friendly question," says Spartacus.

"Gladiators don't make friends. If we're ever matched in the arena together, I have to kill you."

Thankfully, he was never required to go that far on the gridiron. In all, Woody Strode made seventy films. There were black stars who were bigger attractions, like Sidney Poitier and Harry Belafonte, but none were busier. He was really the first black action star. In 1980, Woody Strode was inducted into the Black Filmmakers Hall of Fame in Oakland, California. His last film, *The Quick and the Dead*, starring Sharon Stone, Gene Hackman, and Russell Crowe, was released in 1995, a year after his death from lung cancer.

Ezzrett "Sugarfoot" Anderson played five more years with Calgary before retiring. He started up a number of businesses in the city and even had his own radio show for a time, playing his favourite jazz recordings. He maintained a connection with the Calgary Stampeders for the rest of his life. He was in all respects a local legend and a proud Canadian. The man Calgarians came to know as "Sugarfoot" died on March 8, 2017. He was ninety-seven years old.

Chapter Three

CRAZY LEGS

At the beginning of training camp for the 1946 football season, Coach Jake Gaither of Florida A&M, an all-black college in the all-black Southern Intercollegiate Athletic Conference, was surprised when one of his new scholarship players — Tom Curtis from Albion, Michigan — brought his younger brother along with him.

"I appreciate you inviting me down on a scholarship," said Curtis. "I have my kid brother who's never really played a game of football but he's athletic and played basketball and baseball. You think you can give him a chance to try out for the team?"

Coach Gaither sized up the younger brother.

"What's your name, son?"

"Ulysses."

You didn't attain a master's degree from Ohio State University without knowing a bit of Homer. Ulysses was not the greatest of fighting warriors but he was the smartest, the most cunning, and, perhaps most importantly, the most ruthless. Maybe the kid brother had something. And Jake Gaither was not about to look a gift horse in the mouth. Besides, he really wanted Tom Curtis on his team so there was no point in creating an awkward situation right off the bat.

"Oh sure, I'll give him a tryout."

And so Ulysses Curtis went with the other running backs, and Coach Gaither put him through a series of gruelling drills, the kind that coaches use early to determine who will stick with the program. Ulysses ran around and between a series of pylons that directed him toward the waiting arms of different linemen at every turn. In surviving this gauntlet unscathed and untouched, he not only earned a spot on the team, he also earned himself a nickname: Crazy Legs.

There was no scholarship money available for Ulysses but that was all right with him. He had his GI Bill benefits for two years' service in the U.S. Navy. Ulysses had gone to boot camp at Naval Station Great Lakes north of Chicago when he was eighteen years old. Great Lakes was segregated, having opened its doors to the first Black Americans in June of 1942. There were separate "Negro Service Schools" to handle basic training for black recruits at Great Lakes. When he finished basic training, he was shipped to Pearl Harbor, Hawaii, where he was assigned to a munitions ship.

"The ship would come in and load up ammunition from Hawaii, and then go down to Guam, Wake, Saipan, and drop the ammunition off and then come back to Hawaii," he told me during our interview at a North York community centre where he went regularly to work out. At eighty-four years old, he still looked fit in his track suit.

After two years in the navy, much of it spent in the Pacific sitting atop millions of pounds of explosives at the possible mercy of Japanese torpedoes, Zeros, and battleships, Ulysses figured he had earned every penny of his GI Bill benefits. And he was determined that he was going to get an education out of his service to his country.

When the season at Florida A&M began, Ulysses found himself on the bench throughout a 48–0 rout of Alabama State. What was the point of going through all that work if the coach didn't have faith in his ability? Ulysses Curtis had never played a down of football in his life before coming to Florida A&M. Not in public school, not in minor organized sports, and not in high school. He had nothing to gauge his talent by. He had starred in basketball and baseball in high school and knew he had the talent to play both, but this game of football was all new to him. Was he even any good? And what was the point? Where was it all leading, if anywhere? He went to see the coach.

"You know I never played football before I came here."

"I know that."

"Maybe I should just give it up."

Jake Gaither felt a kinship with this young man that went beyond coach-and-player relations. He knew what it was like to come into a strange environment, especially the segregated environment of the South, and think, *What the hell am I doing here?* In Samuel G. Freedman's book *Breaking the Line,* the author describes the circumstances under which Gaither and his wife came to Tallahassee in the summer of 1938. Shortly before they arrived, four white men had broken into a local jail and abducted two black teenagers being held for breaking into a department store and cutting an officer with a knife as he tried to arrest them. The frightened teenagers were driven out of town by the four armed men. Once out of the vehicle, the boys were told to run. They did as they were told but did not get far. They were shot in the back, cut down like animals in sport. A sign was found next to their bodies: "This is your last warning, negros, remember you might be next."

The local newspaper, the *Daily Democrat,* attempted to put a bizarre positive spin on this shocking double murder by declaring, "As lynchings go, last night's was about as free from the usual unsavoury angles as any we have heard about. The method adopted was quiet, orderly."

Quiet? Orderly? That wouldn't have given the black residents of Tallahassee much relief. Jake Gaither, despite severe misgivings about this new home, eventually settled into his job as assistant coach with Florida A&M with great success. In 1943, Gaither took over the head-coaching responsibilities and would remain the head coach at A&M for twenty-five years, becoming a legend in black college football. But he had only been the head coach for three years when Ulysses Curtis sought him out, wondering whether he even had a future at Florida A&M.

"Oh no, lad," Gaither told Curtis. "I've been watching you and you're going to be on that bus when we go down to Tennessee this weekend. And Coach never lies so you'll be there."

It was exactly the news Ulysses had wanted to hear. He could deal with biding his time now as long as he knew that his time would come. And it did. Ulysses played four seasons for Florida A&M and in his junior and senior seasons (1948 and 1949), he was named to the black All-American team. The Los Angeles Rams, who had integrated the NFL when they signed Kenny Washington and Woody Strode, expressed interest during Curtis's senior year but never made a solid commitment.

As Ulysses Curtis prepared to move back to Albion and find a job teaching, he received a call from Frank Clair, the head football coach with a team called the Toronto Argonauts up in Canada. Well, Albion was only about ninety miles from Detroit and the border of Canada. How far could Toronto be from there? Not as far as Tallahassee was from Albion, that was for sure. But, as he often did when troubled, Curtis went to his coach, his mentor, and his friend, Coach Gaither.

"You go on up to Canada and you play a year or two and they'll get you back down in the States," Gaither told him. "Cause you have the skills to play professional football."

Whether he was looking for advice or simply seeking confirmation of something he had already decided to do, it didn't matter, because Ulysses always did what his coach told him to do.

He went to Canada.

The year 1950 was a momentous year in the history of the Toronto Argonauts. Four years earlier, team management and ownership had threatened to boycott a game against the Montreal Alouettes if Herb Trawick took the field. Toronto, the bastion of conservatism, had refused to import any Americans, white or black, even as competing teams across Canada were bringing in the maximum number allowed. But suddenly, the Argos' owners decided that having the best Canadians available didn't provide enough of an edge. Toronto, as the flagship franchise and centre of the Canadian football universe, could no longer afford to fall behind the rest of the league.

And so the team went out and hired an American coach, Frank Clair, who had once been an outstanding receiver with Ohio State and had gone on to coach the University of Buffalo Bulls football team. An associate of Clair's who had attended the all-black Alabama State University provided him with a list of 1949's black All-Americans. Figuring prominently on that list was the name Ulysses Curtis. In our interview, Ulysses recalled that the hiring of Frank Clair was not a popular move with the Argos players.

"Frank Clair became the first American coach of the Argos. A lot of the Canadian players weren't too happy about the Argos firing Teddy

Morris, who had played football for the Argos and coached the Argos. And so when they fired Teddy Morris, many of the Argo players left and went out west."

But Teddy Morris adamantly refused to play American imports; there was no point in spending big money on star players from the U.S. if the coach wasn't going to play them. The growing feeling, not just in Toronto but throughout the league, was that the American coaches coming in and remaking the game in the American image did not trust the Canadian players in key positions. That goes a long way to explaining Teddy Morris's popularity with his players. He was willing to put his career on the line for Canadians. Consequently, his departure seemed less of a firing and more like an act of martyrdom.

So, goodbye Teddy Morris, hello Frank Clair. The arrival of Curtis, however, created a new problem. Who was going to room with the coloured guy? According to Curtis, that was the whole reason the Argos traded with Montreal for Billy Bass. Now, whether Billy Bass was actually brought in from Montreal just to be Curtis's roomie is questionable. Bass was an excellent all-purpose back, both offensively and defensively. The hole in Ulysses's theory lies in the fact that the Argonauts already had another black player on the team, Marvin "Stretch" Whaley from Morgan State College, an all-black college in Baltimore, Maryland. Why not just have Stretch room with Ulysses? Because now they had another problem — who was going to room with Stretch? According to Ulysses, management "decided that one of the Smiley brothers, Doug or Rod, would become Stretch's roommate. So Billy and I roomed but Stretch had a white roommate in 1950."

When the trade with Montreal was completed and Billy Bass arrived, he became part of Toronto's reconfigured backfield alongside Ulysses.

"In those years I was the marquee running back. I ran the ball more," Ulysses assured me, in case my knowledge of his career was lacking. "Teddy Toogood was the other back and we had a 'T' formation with two halfbacks and a fullback. I played left, Teddy Toogood played right, with Billy Bass in the centre. Right and left halfbacks had the same type of plays. I would carry the ball maybe fifteen times a game. But I carried most of the load."

Winning can change a lot of attitudes, especially among disgruntled athletes coping with a new system and an unpopular new coach. The

Argonauts got off to a quick start that season, winning four of their first five games.

"Both Curtis and Bass showed to excellent advantage on Saturday as ball carriers," said an *Ottawa Journal* article on September 25, 1950. "The former who has been nicknamed 'Crazy Legs' answers that description when on the loose. He has a faculty of driving into two or three tacklers, twisting or churning away from them again at the last expected moments."

"I loved the wide field because it gave me a little more distance on sweeps," Ulysses told me. "Now [in the NFL] they sweep and they're on the sidelines."

After their early success, the team went into something of a tailspin, winning only two games the rest of the regular season while losing four and tying one. They finished second behind Hamilton in the East. In the two-game, total-points playoff, they promptly lost the first game to Hamilton 13–11 on November 11 before beating them 24–6 in the return match four days later on home turf to take the series 35–19. Three days after that, the Argos took on the winner of the Ontario Rugby Football Union (ORFU), the Toronto Balmy Beach Beachers, winning handily, 43–13. That made three games in eight days, a brutal schedule, especially for those playing both offence and defence.

The Winnipeg Blue Bombers had finished their playoffs a week earlier, giving them the advantage of rest and a chance to scout the opposition, which the Argonauts brass duly claimed was unfair scheduling. But the Argonauts had something of a distinct advantage themselves with the Grey Cup game to be played on their home field, Varsity Stadium.

The Blue Bombers were led by NFL veteran quarterback "Indian" Jack Jacobs, a full-blooded Cherokee from Oklahoma, and Tom Casey, a Black American star halfback from Ohio. After graduating from Hampton University in Virginia — with a break for service in the armed forces — Casey spent the 1948 season with the New York Yankees of the All-America Football Conference. Then he moved on to Hamilton and spent the 1949 season with the Hamilton Wildcats (of the Big Four), which would merge with the Hamilton Tigers of the ORFU the following year to form the Hamilton Tiger-Cats. In 1950, he moved on to Winnipeg where he achieved stardom as both offensive and defensive back with the Bombers, leading the Western league in rushing in his first season.

(Tom Casey would be an All-Star in all six seasons he played for Winnipeg, all while putting himself through medical school at the University of Manitoba. In the year he retired, 1956, he was named Winnipeg's Citizen of the Year for his accomplishments on the field and for his service in the community. He went on to further studies in neurology in England. In 1962, he married Mary Fuller Smith, the daughter of Samuel B. Fuller, the owner and founder of the Fuller Products Company [not to be confused with the Fuller Brush Company], a cosmetic empire based on door-to-door sales that made Fuller the richest black man in the United States and worth $18 million.

In 1964, Dr. Tom Casey became the first Black American elected to the Canadian Football Hall of Fame. At a Grey Cup dinner that year, Casey, then a staff neurologist at Cleveland Veterans' Administration Hospital, urged other black players who had come to Canada to make the most of the opportunities provided in this new country. "I cherish the education I received here," he said. "I cherish my friends and I'll stand up for Canada until the day I die.")

On the Friday before the 1950 Grey Cup game the snow began to fall. Six to eight inches were expected for the day of the game with temperatures in the twenties (Fahrenheit). University of Toronto students were clearing off stadium seats, while both teams held separate workouts on the stadium turf that Friday. The field was uncovered, at the mercy of the elements. The night before the game, the grounds crew decided to take matters in hand.

"That was almost unbelievable," Ulysses remembered. "When it snowed … snowed … snowed that Friday night and the grounds crew at the University of Toronto decided to scoop all the snow off and have a clear field but in the process rolled up boulders and mud and everything."

It was the Grey Cup dubbed "the Mud Bowl," with Toronto persevering 13–0 in one of the most boring championship games on record. Winnipeg made exactly two first downs all game. Two! Jack Jacobs had his worst-ever performance as a starting quarterback, throwing two interceptions and fumbling twice. He never did find a way to get a decent grip on the pigskin. Toronto's quarterback, Al Dekdebrun, had better success handling the ball and there was a reason for that.

"Al Dekdebrun, the quarterback that year, decided that he would tape thumbtacks on his fingers here," Ulysses told me, tapping the fingertips of his right hand with his left thumb. "And then on the cement wall file them down so they'd be just little pricks that would stick into the football. He threw fair, threw a few completions."

It brings to mind the New England Patriots and the 2015 AFC championship game against the Indianapolis Colts, now known as "Deflategate," in which footballs were deliberately underinflated to allow quarterback Tom Brady to get a better grip on the ball. Imagine the field day the media would have if Brady ever got caught wearing filed-down thumbtacks on his fingers!

The next year, 1951, the Argos ended the season with the same 7–5 record as Ottawa and Hamilton, but Ottawa was awarded first place through a tie-breaker system. Though the Argos split the two-game semifinal with the Tiger-Cats, they lost where it counted most — in total points. The Argonauts would be denied a chance to repeat as Grey Cup champions. But Ulysses Curtis would earn a degree of notoriety that year for one of the strangest single plays in the history of the CFL — one that would require changes to the rule book.

It was the last game of the season, which could affect the final standings, between the Ottawa Rough Riders and Toronto Argonauts. The two teams had a history of bad blood between them dating back to the previous season when a fight had erupted on the field. Ulysses Curtis had punched an Ottawa player, which set off a skirmish on the field of play. But the spark for the fireworks had come courtesy of an American player, Howie Turner from North Carolina, who had hurled a certain racial epithet at Curtis. Having been fingered as the instigator by the press, Turner approached Coach Clair before the next game between the two teams and apologized. Clair apparently responded that he was hardly the one Turner should be apologizing to.

"Then Clair called Curtis and *the coloured boy* [my italics] ran over toward the pair," reported the *Ottawa Journal* on October 4, 1950. "Turner stuck out his hand and Curtis grabbed it warmly. 'What I said last week was in a ball game, Ulysses,' said Turner. 'I didn't mean it and I want you to know I'm sorry.'"

Events took an even more bizarre turn on November 4, in the game between the two teams in Varsity Stadium. The Argonauts were leading

18–12 when the Ottawa quarterback threw a pass intended for none other than Howie Turner.

"Tom O'Malley was the Ottawa quarterback and 'Touchdown' Turner was out in the flat," explained Ulysses. "Frank Clair would put me in on defence in certain situations. So I sensed the pass coming from O'Malley, intercepted it, and then headed down the sidelines."

With nothing but daylight ahead of him, Ulysses sprinted for the goal line. Pete Karpuk, an Ottawa player sitting on the sidelines, suddenly threw off his parka and charged the field, looking to tackle Ulysses before he could score. He failed to tackle Curtis but slowed him down and redirected him toward a teammate who made the tackle. Pandemonium broke out in the stands. This was a new one. The officials had no idea what to do.

"So the officials got together. Okay, Ottawa will be two men short and move the ball half the distance to the goal line," remembered Ulysses. "Frank Clair wanted to take the players off the field but we convinced him, 'No, let's go.'"

Though he was prevented from scoring a touchdown on the play, it remained something of a claim to fame for Ulysses as it no doubt did for Karpuk, the man who came off the bench.

"Now what were they going to do with the rule book after this?" said Ulysses. "The Big Four got together and decided that it would have to be an automatic touchdown if an extra man came on the field. So then in the Canadian rule book it was re-written. So that was kind of a highlight of my career, having a rule book re-written because of me."

During the off-season, Curtis and his wife and first child, who was born in the year of the Mud Bowl, would return to Albion, Michigan, to stay with family while he worked for Corning Glass.

"All the Canadian players had jobs because they didn't make the money the Americans made," said Ulysses. "The Americans didn't make great money either; there wasn't that much money to be made in those years."

But like Herb Trawick, Curtis did not think that the Toronto brass made much of an effort to find work for the import players, and particularly those who were black.

"Matter of fact, they paid Americans fifty dollars a week expenses," he said, "because they didn't want the Americans to work. The Canadian players worked and played. They offered us little menial jobs around and you'd be surprised. They offered me one job, Billy Bass, my roommate and me, loading beer cases on trucks. And then an article came out in the *Telegram* that said 'Crowd Caresses Curtis but He Wishes a Boss Would.' I got very few offers to work outside football. Hockey players got the salesmen jobs and the big promotions jobs."

There were no bigger stars in Toronto than the Maple Leafs, players who were born Canadian and lived in the city year-round. Teams were not eager to create even larger divides between the haves — generally the American import players and top Canadian stars — and the have-nots (everybody else). For the vast majority of Canadian players, football was a part-time job and their real life was going on elsewhere in plants, factories, schools, and offices that simply made allowances for their football schedule. Ulysses, like Herb Trawick, was looking to find a position locally that might grow into full-time employment upon his retirement, not just a job as a doorman or loading beer cases onto the back of a truck.

In 1952, Ulysses enjoyed his finest season in Canadian football. There were no statistics kept in the East before 1954 regarding yards gained rushing or receiving, but he did score sixteen touchdowns that season, the most in the league. The Argonauts finished with a 7–4–1 record, good for second place in the East behind the Hamilton Tiger-Cats. In a period of twelve days, beginning on November 15, the Argonauts played four post-season games, a ridiculously draining schedule. Three of those games were against Hamilton, with the third game necessary because the teams were deadlocked in total points after the first two games. On November 26, the Argos played against the winner of the ORFU, the Sarnia Imperials, with the Argos winning 34–15. Four days after the game against Sarnia, the Argos were back at Varsity Stadium for the Grey Cup match against the Rollie Miles and Normie Kwong–led Edmonton Eskimos. But the extended playoffs had taken their toll on Ulysses.

"I remember the season more than the Grey Cup. I got off to a tremendous start and scored sixteen touchdowns. Toward the end of that season, I was limping a bit going into the Grey Cup game because the knee was acting up. But I had a season that I'll never forget. The trainers knew I was injured. When season starts until it's over, you're always banged up and bruised all over. Every football player realizes that you're going to be hurt and it carries throughout the season."

In the first Grey Cup ever televised live — by CBLT in Toronto — the Argonauts prevailed over Edmonton, 21–11.

"I didn't have a good game in the 1952 Grey Cup," admitted Curtis. He was hobbled by the knee injury that plagued him throughout the playoffs.

Ulysses underwent surgery on his knee during the off-season but by the beginning of the next year knew that he had lost a step or two. He never got back to his pre-surgery form, and he played only two more seasons before hanging up his cleats for good.

"After football the big question was what would I do? I had a university education so I applied to the Catholic School Board but I wasn't Catholic and back in those days ..." He shrugged without finishing the statement. "I applied for a job at Corning Glass back in Michigan where I worked during the off-seasons, and nothing."

He knew by this time that he wanted to stay in Canada. He had another daughter, born in 1952, and the family was comfortable living in Toronto.

"After five years here I felt a warmth. I had been successful in sports here. I did feel that rather than go back to tiny Albion, Michigan, that I would stay here."

And that's when a friend, Ray Lewis, entered the picture.

(Raymond Gray Lewis, nicknamed "Rapid Ray" Lewis, was born in Hamilton, Ontario, in 1910, the grandson of runaway slaves who had followed the Underground Railroad to freedom in Canada. As a high-school athlete, Lewis won seventeen national championships in track. He briefly attended Marquette University in Milwaukee but grew homesick for Hamilton and returned after a single semester. Unable to find more meaningful employment, he signed on with the railway as a porter, and he worked that job for twenty-five years. Legend has it that he used to race alongside the train during stretches on the Prairies. He joined the Canadian Olympic sprint team, and, as a member of the 4 x 440-yard sprint relay team at the 1932 Olympics in Los Angeles, he became the first Black Canadian to win an Olympic medal, taking home a bronze. Shin splints would prevent Lewis from taking part in the 1936 Olympics in Berlin. In 2001, Lewis would receive the Order of Canada from then Governor General Adrienne Clarkson, who said, "This should have happened a long time ago.")

"Ray said, 'I hear you have to go back to the U.S.' and I said yes, and he said, 'Look, after I was a porter I started a cleaning company and I've had it for a number of years. I'll teach you all the techniques, strategies, and pricings and such and maybe you'll want to stay in Canada and try the business.'"

So Ulysses Curtis went into the building maintenance business. But after eight years he'd had enough. He went back to school in the Faculty of Education at University of Toronto and entered teaching.

"That was a life-saver for me, after working for eight years with my own business."

Curtis spent thirty years working for the North York Board of Education as a teacher, a guidance counsellor, a race-relations supervisor, and a coach. He was elated to see the changes in opportunities presented to black players after their football careers ended, so different from his time, "when black players couldn't buy a job." In 2005, he was named to the list of all-time greatest Toronto Argonauts for his achievements wearing the colours of the "double blue." Sixth in career touchdowns with forty-seven. Fourth in rushing with 3,712 yards. Second in most yards in a single game with 208. And third in most 100-yard games rushing with twelve. These stats reached in what amounted to a short career, a mere five years long.

"Canada represented a new life for me," he confessed toward the end of our interview. "As a matter of fact, when I came to Toronto I was twenty-four years of age. And it's been a real buggy-ride, I tell you. It's been great to take out a Canadian citizenship, and when I go to Michigan I say well, we'll be going home on Monday … they say 'Home?' Because they can't really figure out why Toronto is home when I was born and raised in Michigan."

Ulysses Curtis did make one final trip home. On October 6, 2013, he passed away from natural causes in Toronto. He was buried alongside family members in Albion, Michigan.

Chapter Four

"CAN YOU IMAGINE?" – THE BERNIE CUSTIS STORY

The player was being pelted with baby bottles. His teammates surrounded him in an act of solidarity, protecting their most valuable player from further damage. Bottles bounced off shoulder pads and helmets. These were not the lightweight plastic bottles of today but Pyrex bottles that could crack heads open. They arced through the air like arrows launched from distant battlements.

He wondered if there was some significance that he was missing. That the throwing of baby bottles represented a statement about the colour of his skin. Baby bottles hold milk; milk is white.

He was black.

No, that would be too simple. And literal. Maybe he was being infantilized for the colour of his skin, like he was a not quite fully formed human being. He had heard of bananas being thrown somewhere. *Go back to Africa, ya great ape!* But baby bottles?

He would look back on that singular event years later and ask with true wonderment, "*Can you imagine?* People throwing baby bottles and yelling at me to get me off the field?"

The thing is that we *can* imagine. It's hard to be surprised anymore by what people are capable of, especially knowing the history of the injustices perpetrated against black people over the last three centuries.

Bernie Custis was still perplexed by such behaviour more than sixty years later. Bernie Custis was a civilized man. He was a schoolteacher, a principal. He coached young football players at the junior, college, and university levels for over thirty years. He won awards, was honoured for those accomplishments. He considered it a vocation, not a career, mentoring the young. And part of that mentoring was teaching students and athletes the nature of respect.

Haddonfield, New Jersey, the site of the bizarre baby-bottle incident, is a borough in Camden County, New Jersey, about a twenty-five-minute drive from Philadelphia on the Interstate across the Delaware River. With a good arm and a hurricane behind you, you could probably fling a baby bottle from Bernie Custis's childhood home in South Philadelphia and have it land at the fifty-yard line in the Haddonfield stadium. For Custis, it might as well have been a thousand miles from the tough but tightly knit mixed-race, working-class neighbourhood where he grew up. Everybody there knew everybody, and for the most part they got along. No one was better or worse off than anyone else. His father had a good job at Westinghouse, and Bernie and his three sisters and brother had a fairly comfortable upbringing.

"My dad was someone who made friends with everyone and he had a lot of friends there, of all races," said Bernie from the comfort of his easy chair in the den of his home at the end of a Burlington, Ontario, cul-de-sac. This was our first meeting. I didn't know it then, but he would become the central figure in the *Gridiron Underground* film. "And I think through him and his experiences, I learned, and so did my brothers and sisters, that you judge everyone by the content of their character and nothing else."

Bernie, who would go on to teach public school for close to forty years in the Hamilton region, learned early the difference a good teacher could make in a young person's life. For Bernie, that was a physical education teacher in his elementary school who recognized not only Bernie's tremendous athletic potential but also his intelligence. High schools, especially in working-class, poor, or black neighbourhoods, were already streaming students into vocational courses to feed the labour force.

"He was concerned that I was involved with a number of the young-sters who were destined to attend vocational schools. And I had shown that I was capable of handling academic programs. And he sort of guided me to go to an academic high school rather than follow my buddies into a vocational school."

That guidance led to John Bartram High School, built in 1939 at the intersection of 67th Street and Elmwood Avenue, a predominantly upper-middle-class white neighbourhood in Southwest Philadelphia. The school, built in the art-deco style of the period, was named after John Bartram, "the father of American botany" and co-founder with Benjamin Franklin of the American Philosophical Society. Small won-der it earned a reputation as one of the top academic high schools in Philadelphia. But the trustees of John Bartram were looking to develop a top-notch athletic program to go with their academic pedigree, and in the States a reputation for excellence begins with a successful foot-ball program.

The second Bernie laid eyes on the school and the athletic facilities, he knew this was the place for him. He didn't care that the neighbour-hood was overwhelmingly white or that he would be one of ten black teenagers in a student body of over three thousand. John Bartram was actively courting top local black athletes. Despite the long daily commute by trolley to get to and from school, Bernie Custis embraced the new opportunity. He would be getting the education he desired and the kind of exposure that could lead to a university athletic scholarship. Even back then, he was looking at the long game.

The day Bernie's high-school football team, the John Bartram High Braves, set out for that game in Haddonfield back in 1946, "Cus," as he was known to his coach and teammates, had no idea what kind of reception lay in wait for him. He had participated in track, basketball, and baseball in and around the Philadelphia area without incident. Signs that this day was going to be different emerged when the bus stopped for a team meal at a roadside diner outside Haddonfield.

"This was probably my first introduction to segregation because I noticed that when the waitress put water down at the table for all the players, she skipped me. And it hit me: 'Uh-oh, I think I'm in a situation where segregation has entered the picture.' I saw the waitresses in a huddle in the corner, and finally one of them came over and said, 'I'm sorry, but we can't serve blacks.' My coach overheard this as well as a number of players, and it caused quite a disturbance."

I remember thinking at the time that Bernie was being old-school, choosing the term "segregation" over the more familiar "racism." Later, I realized that he had accurately defined the difference. If the waitress had simply ignored him or refused to serve him because she didn't like black people, that was racist. But because the restaurant had a policy in place that enforced the separation by race, though still racist policy, it had become, in Bernie's words, "a situation where segregation has entered the picture."

In a scene reminiscent of Jack Nicholson's fit of pique in *Five Easy Pieces*, his coach took his arm and swiped the whole table clean of glasses then announced to the whole restaurant, "Let's get out of here. Because if Cus can't eat somewhere, we're not eating there either!"

It would make for a great scene in a film of Bernie's story, the white coach standing up for the rights of the lone black teenager on his team. Unless you were that black kid. Bernie appreciated that his teammates had rallied around him following their coach's lead, but he burned with humiliation at being thrust centre stage in this roadside-diner drama. He wished there had been a simpler, quieter way of extricating himself from the situation. He was just a kid who happened to be black. Rare is the teenager who wants to be the focus of attention, let alone a target of animosity or, worse, pity, in the outside adult world.

Not to sell his coach short for making a grand gesture against racism, but the situation was also an excellent opportunity for the coach to unite the team around a rallying point. *See, everyone's against us, they don't want us to win — let's win this one for Cus!* As it turned out, the team boarded the bus, drove down the road, and went to another restaurant where everyone was fed without incident. But the table had now been set for the main course: the game against Haddonfield.

When the baby bottles began to fly at the football field, it took Bernie a minute to realize that he was the intended target. *Can you imagine?* He knew it was out of the question to rush into the stands and reprimand a crowd of frenzied football parents for poor sportsmanship, so he decided that excellence on the field might be the best form of revenge. He went out and scored six touchdowns on the day "with a smile on my face." As the teams were leaving the field, bottles were once again launched at Bernie. This time he found himself protected not only by a phalanx of teammates along with his older brother, James, but also by members of the Haddonfield team, who all wanted to shake Bernie's hand — to acknowledge his prolific offensive game and to apologize for their idiotic parents.

That same year, Syracuse came calling with an offer of a full scholarship to play football. The Syracuse football program had fallen on hard times and they were looking to rebuild under Coach Reaves "Ribs" Baysinger. Syracuse was not the only team that approached Bernie about football, but they were the first and that meant something to Bernie. As with John Bartram, it was love at first sight when Bernie visited the Syracuse campus with its aesthetic design combination of beaux arts and Georgian Revival, with wide avenues and green spaces, students lounging and reading or bustling to and fro, books tucked under arms. As a kid from South Philly, he felt that he had been granted admittance to the realm of privilege and academia, and he didn't have to kick down any doors to get there. He just had to carry a football.

When he entered through the hallowed arches of Archbold Stadium, which is built in the style of the Roman Colosseum, and stood on the grass at midfield, his gaze turning to take in the rows of concrete tiers, he could be excused for feeling overwhelmed by its grandeur. But that sense of awe did not last long. Bernie never lacked for confidence and he saw Archbold Stadium as the perfect stage to showcase his future exploits. He would be the gladiator that the fans came to see defeat all challengers. He could not wait to get started.

By 1947, the year Bernie came to Syracuse, the school had more than doubled its pre-war student population. More and more students, including black students, were finding opportunities to attend major universities following the war through the education benefits and initiatives provided by the GI Bill. Universities, particularly in the north, were looking to recruit star athletes regardless of colour to enhance their athletic programs, especially their football teams. College football reigned supreme, as the professional version of the game had yet to achieve the level of idolatry it now enjoys. Archbold Stadium routinely held 30,000-plus fans for a football game, although attendance had tailed off in the last couple of years because the team had fallen on hard times. Even with the recent influx of recruits, Bernie and lineman Horace Morris were the only black players and the first to suit up with the Syracuse Orangemen since Wilmeth Sidat-Singh in the 1930s, the infamous "Hindu" ballplayer.

Sidat-Singh was born Wilmeth Webb to black parents. His father, a pharmacist, died when Wilmeth was only seven. His mother then remarried an Indian doctor, Samuel Sidat-Singh, and Wilmeth Webb assumed his last name. Whether or not Syracuse officials knew that Sidat-Singh was black and not Indian, they certainly encouraged him to act the role of the latter to the extent that they once even suggested he might start wearing a turban around the campus. He didn't do it, but though he never pretended to be anything but African-American, he was tagged with the moniker "Hindu."

"Have you ever been to India?" a reporter would ask.

"No, I've never been to India," Wilmeth would answer truthfully, and someone would write that the Hindu running back had never seen his ancestral homeland.

It was not until a Washington reporter wrote a profile of Sidat-Singh before a big game against the University of Maryland that the truth came out — the star "Hindu" halfback was not Indian at all. The news that he was, in fact, a black man proved shocking. In Maryland, no black player had ever taken the field either *for* the university or *against* them. Presumably, a member of any colour or any race would be welcomed as a combatant on the Maryland gridirons, as long as they weren't a *Negro*. The University of Maryland, in its infinite wisdom, refused to allow its football team to take the field against Syracuse if Sidat-Singh played.

And so Wilmeth Sidat-Singh, the man that famed sportswriter Grantland Rice called the greatest forward passer of his day, did not dress that day. Syracuse had capitulated to Maryland's racist ultimatum.

Bernie, who was an avid reader and enjoyed languages — he had studied Latin and Spanish in high school — enrolled in the school of journalism, which was considered one of the best programs in the country. He aspired to be more than a football player. Football was just a means to an end. Unlike the majority of his teammates, he loved learning, and he harboured dreams of becoming a writer one day. His romance with knowledge did not last long, however. The heads of the athletics program began pressuring Bernie to change courses. The journalism program involved a heavy workload, and the powers-that-be did not want their star quarterback's brain clogged with a bunch of ideas, opinions, and concepts when the rest of his body was required on the field. They wanted Bernie's mind on football and only football.

Bernie, in his laid-back fashion, could see their point. "After all, they were paying my way," he said, "so I decided to switch to a liberal arts program."

In Bernie's first season at Syracuse he won the starting quarterback position with the freshmen team. The following year, 1948, Bernie became the starting quarterback on the varsity team, becoming the first black player to quarterback a major (white) U.S. university's football team. The team, however, was dreadful and won only one game all season. The lone bright spot was the play of Bernie Custis, who, despite the team's 1–8 record, was named All-East quarterback. By the end of the second season, the campus was in open revolt against the head coach. No fewer than three Syracuse University committees undertook investigations into Baysinger's competency as a football coach: the board of trustees, the Varsity Club, and the student body. After three months of fact-finding, opinion-taking, and witch-hunting, all three committees came to the same conclusion. Reaves Baysinger had to go. The man they called "Ribs" and his entire coaching staff were summarily dismissed.

The person brought in to replace Baysinger was Floyd Burdette "Ben" Schwartzwalder, who had transformed the football team at Muhlenberg College in Allentown, Pennsylvania, from a mediocre passel of local boys into one of the nation's powerhouses through a combination of astute recruiting and an innovative offensive system. In 1947, Coach Schwartzwalder had led the Mules to a 9–1 record and a national championship over St. Bonaventure at the Tobacco Bowl in Kentucky. The next season they went 9–1 as well, but this time they declined an offer to play at the Tangerine Bowl in Orlando, Florida.

Where Baysinger had been more of a father figure to his players, Schwartzwalder was distant, a strict disciplinarian who preached a tough-nosed brand of football. He switched the Syracuse offence from its previous "I" formation to a "wing-T," with Bernie under centre playing a more traditional quarterback position with the option of handing off to one of the three backs, keeping the ball himself, or passing. The Orangemen finished that 1949 season with a record of 4–5. It wasn't a huge turnaround in terms of wins and losses, but they were far more competitive in the games they lost. Bernie was a revelation. He had had a strong arm from an early age, working on passing drills with his older brother in vacant lots growing up. But Bernie blossomed under Schwartzwalder's system, earning the nickname "the Arm" from the local Syracuse sportswriters.

Bernie passed for 1,121 yards in 1949, a school record (although nothing spectacular in comparison to today's more pass-oriented game). His breakout season almost single-handedly rejuvenated interest in the football team on campus and throughout the city. The school had to add six thousand seats to Archbold Stadium during the off-season to accommodate the demand for tickets. Syracuse football was once again the only show in town.

There was much expected of the team for the 1950 season and even more expected of Bernie Custis. That season, only three black quarterbacks would play at least one down of football at a major university in the whole country, and two of those went to Syracuse: Bernie and his backup, Avatus Stone. Stone was mainly a defensive safety and punter who might take a few snaps from centre in the midst of a Syracuse blowout to give Bernie a rest. He did play most of one game, a loss, when Bernie was injured and unable to play. As a writer with the *Syracuse Post-Standard* noted, Avatus Stone was no Bernie Custis: "Avatus Stone, brilliant Orange safety man and star punter, filled in well for Custis last week, but he doesn't have Custis' experience or ball-handling abilities, and it is this latter feature that probably spelled doom for [Syracuse]."

"Spelled doom for Syracuse"? There's a sportswriter who didn't shy away from hyperbole. Then again, football was serious business. And because of this serious business of football, black players were under greater scrutiny by their overlords, the board of trustees, than any others. This was where Avatus Stone ran into trouble. He was, in common parlance, a ladies' man. To be more specific, a *white* ladies' man. And in 1950 at Syracuse, as well as every other major university, north and south, that was a no-no. It may very well be that Avatus Stone, as backup quarterback, took the heat from the trustees in place of the starter, Bernie, who played it coy whenever the subject of "the ladies" came up during our conversations. He would only admit to a few "girlfriends." Nothing drastic happened to Stone, who maintained his place on the team, but for years incoming black athletes, including Syracuse greats Jim Brown and Ernie Davis, were warned, "Don't be an Avatus Stone!"

The night Bernie remembered most was the night he came back to his dorm "in the wee wee hours" after an evening out before a big game against Penn State, only to find Coach Schwartzwalder parked in his car outside the building, awaiting Bernie's arrival. Curfew missed; not even close. Bernie's punishment was simple but effective. Instead of being allowed to ride on the team bus with his teammates all the way to Penn State, he would be the lone passenger in Coach Schwartzwalder's car. It was the longest and most excruciating car ride he had ever experienced, 250 miles passed in utter silence except for the vibrating waves of fury emanating from the unspeaking driver.

Bernie laughed in remembering that day. "Wouldn't you know that I had one of my greatest games that day. I set a total offence record, running and passing, and we beat Penn State. [Schwartzwalder] was probably the most shocked individual in the world. And I took it in stride. You know, at that time in my life things were going pretty well and I was a bit cocky, so I just let it pass."

But Schwartzwalder was not about to let Bernie off that easy, especially since the punishment had failed to have the humbling effect intended. So he confiscated Bernie's car keys for a week.

"I deserved it," said Bernie with a smile.

In the last home game of the 1950 season, the Syracuse stadium announcer introduced the senior members of the team, those who would be departing the next year, one by one at halftime. They saved Bernie's name for last and he received a standing ovation from close to 40,000 fans. It was a moment that his sister, Joan, who was nine years Bernie's junior, his parents, Hezekiah (Hezzie) and Nellie, and his brother, James, would never forget. For three years they had driven from Philadelphia to Syracuse for those Saturday afternoon home games, leaving at one or two in the morning after Hezekiah got off his 4–12 night shift at Westinghouse.

As Joan remembers, "At that time there was only one or two other African-American players on the team so with us being there a lot of the fans knew that we were probably related to one of the players. And when they found out we were Bernie's family that was great."

Bernie ended his three-year varsity career at Syracuse with 196 completions and close to 3,000 yards passing, accomplished with a conservative offence that stressed the running game. He set individual records that would last for twenty-five years. The icing on the cake that senior year was the invitation he received to play quarterback in the annual East-West Shrine Game, which pitted the best collegiate football players in the land against one another. The game, an end-of-football-season tradition, would be played at the Cow Palace stadium in San Francisco. Bernie was named starting quarterback for the East squad. He was over the moon. He was being recognized on a national scale for his hard work, determination, and achievements.

And then the Shrine committee asked for a publicity photo of Bernie to help advertise the game. Only then did they discover that their All-Star quarterback attraction was black. Since 1925 when the first East-West Shrine Game was played, there had never been a black quarterback. The organizers immediately called Syracuse to tell them that Bernie Custis would not be the East starting quarterback. He had been disinvited from the big game. No reason was ever given, no explanation, nothing. They left it to Syracuse officials to deliver the bad news to Bernie.

Can you imagine?

Bernie was devastated. The disappointment followed him his whole life, whenever he remembered what it felt like to have such an honour bestowed, a national recognition of personal achievement, and then have it cruelly ripped away. No one had the guts to tell him why. They didn't have to, of course; he knew. Clearly, not everyone lived by Bernie's father's code that you judged a person on the content of his/her character and nothing else. There had never been a black starting quarterback in the East-West Shrine Game and 1950 would be no exception. A history of racial exclusion had been spun as "tradition."

Bernie took a lot of abuse in his playing days at Syracuse. An extra shot given at the end of a tackle. Things said by opposing players at the line of scrimmage. We call it "trash-talking" now, things said by an opponent to get a player off his game, get him thinking about retaliation rather than his immediate task. But today any trash talk that smacks of racism is nipped in the bud, perpetrators dealt with harshly by league officials. Not so back then. A player more or less had to take it and move on. Bernie could deal with that stuff; he just let his game do the talking. But this rescindment on the basis of colour, by a committee whose sole purpose was to bring together the best players in America, was a cheap shot that made all others he had endured pale in comparison.

"I guess there are moments when you are hurt by incidents." He paused, looking for the right word. "Or disappointed." He nods. Yes, that's more what he meant: disappointment in the behaviour of other human beings. "I really felt I deserved to be there. And what are you going to do? At that time it was something that just happened. And if it happened you took it in stride and just carried on."

No one was going to shed any tears for Bernie, least of all Bernie. He was used to being hit hard, bouncing back up from the turf, hiding his pain. And when one door closes, another opens. In Bernie's case a door opened as the Cleveland Browns called his name in the eleventh round of the NFL draft. He showed up at training camp in Toledo, Ohio, expecting to vie for the position of quarterback, even though he knew there was little chance of usurping the starting position from the incumbent, Otto Graham. The Browns had won the NFL Championship the year previously behind Graham, and he was considered one of the greatest quarterbacks in the history of the game. But Bernie had the confidence that he could beat out the other quarterbacks in camp for the backup spot. That, in itself, would be a major accomplishment. So, on the first day of camp, Bernie lined up with the quarterbacks.

An assistant coach came over and asked him what he was doing. He told Bernie that he was going to be a free safety on defence, so he should get his ass on over where the defensive backs were running drills. *Defensive back?* Bernie figured that there had to be some mistake, some screw-up in the paperwork. The coach must have had him confused with somebody else, some actual defensive back who had played that position in college. Why would anyone expect a quarterback to play defensive back? It didn't make sense. He asked to see Paul Brown, the legendary head coach and general manager of the Browns. Coach Brown would figure out the mistake and set this smug assistant straight.

"After practice, Paul met with me, and he said, 'Bernie, I feel that you're capable of playing quarterback and that you're ahead of your time ... *but* there are no black quarterbacks in the NFL at this time. There will eventually be black quarterbacks. But I'd like you to play safety and see how that works out there.' I balked at that. I told him that I feel I can play quarterback if given an opportunity. And he said, 'I will deal with the situation.'"

Paul Brown was, in fact, sympathetic. He had the luxury of having Otto Graham on his team, the best in the game. But even having a black player as backup quarterback was out of the question. Brown was straight with Bernie and Bernie appreciated that. Cleveland and the rest of the NFL teams were not ready to take that next step in the evolution of race equality on the gridirons of America. So Brown looked around for other options on behalf of his player.

"He met me the next day, and he said, 'I know you want the opportunity to compete at quarterback but I'm sorry to say, Bernie, that that opportunity will not present itself here in Cleveland ... *but* there are teams in Canada that have been enquiring about you and if you want to go there you will be given the opportunity to play quarterback.' I said I would prefer to go there." Brown would release Bernie to teams from Canada, but no other team in the NFL could sign Bernie without trading for his rights from the Browns. As Bernie put it, "He traded me to Canada." The next thing Bernie knew he was on a train from Toledo to his new home in Hamilton, Ontario.

Like most Americans, Bernie knew very little about Canada. He knew a list of cities' names: Ottawa, Montreal, Toronto, and, surprisingly, Hamilton, but that was about it. He knew that Hamilton was close to Buffalo and that Buffalo was two hours from Syracuse and that Philadelphia was another six to seven hours (pre-Interstate) from Syracuse. He liked the idea of being as close to the U.S. border as possible. If he got homesick or fed up with Canadian football he wouldn't have far to go to get home.

He arrived in the Hamilton train station at 2:00 a.m. All he had was a suitcase and the address of a boarding house courtesy of the Hamilton front office. He found the boarding house, found his room, and crept in quietly so as not to disturb his roommate … and that's when it hit, the most powerful stench he'd ever encountered: stink-foot so bad it brought tears to his eyes. This is a man who had spent years in gyms, locker rooms, playing fields, and dorm rooms, yet he had never experienced a form of body odour to rival that of his mysterious sleeping roommate. This was poisoned-gas-in-the-trenches stuff. He tried to sleep but the fumes from the other man's feet filled his nasal passages and turned his stomach. Bernie got up, put his clothes back on, and left the boarding house.

He ended up walking the streets of Hamilton, with the lingering stench of those feet in his clothes, until the Tiger-Cats' offices opened later that morning. The first thing he did was announce his arrival and beg for a change of address. He badly needed a decent night's sleep. When he walked onto the field at Civic Stadium (later renamed Ivor Wynne Stadium) to introduce himself to head coach Carl Voyles, he was not exactly welcomed with open arms. Voyles chastised him for being late to camp, a head-scratcher in itself since Bernie had come directly from the Cleveland Browns' training camp. Voyles then provided Bernie with the rattiest uniform imaginable, a sweater with large holes, pants that were too short, shoulder pads with little padding. Bernie was then thrust into a group with six other quarterbacks, wondering what he had gotten himself into. He was puzzled. Hadn't this team been enquiring about his availability to play quarterback? Why was he being treated with such contempt?

The answer lay in Voyles's character. Voyles had been born in Oklahoma and attended Oklahoma A&M where he played varsity football. (The Oklahoma A&M Aggies would achieve infamy in 1951 for "the Johnny Bright Incident" in which Bright, a star black football player, was assaulted during a game on the Oklahoma football field.) Not only did Voyles grow up in the South but he coached football in the South at schools like William and Mary in Virginia and Auburn in Alabama, schools where black football players were not welcome. Even when Bernie played football at Syracuse, there were schools in the South that would not play Syracuse because they allowed black players on their team.

On the second day of practice with the 'Cats, in what some (including Bernie) believe was an opportunity to bring the new kid on the block down a peg, Voyles threw Bernie in as quarterback of a scrubs team — made up of all the second and third stringers and the players on tryouts — against the first string. Before the first play from scrimmage, Bernie, still wearing his raggedy mismatched uniform, gathered his band of misfits in the huddle.

"They want to embarrass us," he told his teammates. "Let's turn the tables on them. Let's embarrass them."

Bernie's brief pep talk worked something of a miracle on the scrubs. In football, it's not a matter of winning the minds of your teammates, it's a matter of winning their hearts. They would have charged across a minefield for a pat on the back from Bernie.

"I was as inspired as I've ever been playing football," Bernie recalled, "and we just ran the so-called 'varsity' team ragged, up and down the field. We just thoroughly beat them. [Voyles] was so angry he just stormed off the field in disgust. If the score had been kept that day I think it would have been something like 40–7."

Voyles had no choice but to install Bernie as his number-one quarterback. He was clearly the best of the bunch in camp, and even a reluctant Voyles would have had a tough time arguing against playing him. Word had gotten around town about the rookie phenom in camp and the press was all over it, declaring Bernie the next great quarterback in Canadian football. According to Bernie, the level of expectation was so great that there would have been a riot in Hamilton — where the fans took (and still take) their football very seriously — if Voyles had not played him. The whole city anxiously awaited Bernie's debut.

Bernie's roommate that first season was Dick Brown, a young black player from Cleveland, Ohio, who followed an unusual path to Canadian football. Brown had come to Canada to enlist in the army in 1942. Brown's father had fought in the American infantry in the First World War and hadn't thought much of the treatment he had received from his own country as a black soldier, both during and after that war. His advice to his son was that rather than risk being drafted into the U.S. Army, he should go to Canada to enlist in the Canadian Army where he would receive better treatment. Together, they drove from Cleveland to Detroit where they crossed the border into Windsor. There, Brown enlisted in the Argyll and Sutherland Highlanders infantry regiment. He remained in Canada and his father returned to Cleveland.

Brown became very close with a fellow enlistee, Walter Kasurak, and spent a great deal of time with Kasurak's family in Windsor. The two friends went overseas together in '44 during the Normandy offensive under the 10th Infantry Brigade, fighting in the northwest Nijmegen Salient of the Netherlands. On January 28, 1945, while fighting against the German fortress island of Kapelsche Veer in the Maas river, Walter Kasurak was hit by enemy fire and died in Brown's arms. Two days later the Germans retreated. (Walter Kasurak is buried in Groesbeek Canadian War Cemetery in Groesbeek, Netherlands, along with 2,338 Canadian soldiers from the Second World War.)

Brown returned from Europe shaken by his experiences. He enrolled at St. Michael's College at the University of Toronto and played football for the college's "Fighting Irish of Bay Street." The university's Varsity Blues soon took notice of the talented freshman running back in their midst and brought him up to play for the varsity team. After Brown enjoyed a particularly explosive offensive game against archrival University of Western Ontario, the headline in the *Globe* read, "Coloured Boy Runs Wild Over Western."

Cringe.

In 1950, Brown joined the Hamilton Tiger-Cats team under Carl Voyles. It was the Tiger-Cats' first year in existence in the precursor to the CFL, the Interprovincial Rugby Football Union (along with Toronto, Ottawa, and Montreal). The team was an amalgamation of two previous Hamilton teams, the Tigers and the Wildcats — thus, the Tiger-Cats. Back in those days, football was not a full-time paying job where players made enough money to see them through the entire year and a carefree retirement. No matter how bright a player's star shone on the gridiron, to make ends meet they needed another job in the off-season. One of the perks of playing in Hamilton was the chance to work for Stelco, the steel plant.

Mark Brown, the son of Dick Brown and a former CFL player himself, although he describes his tenure as having had a cup of coffee in the league, told me his father never liked Carl Voyles — that his father, in fact, "couldn't stand the man." Dick Brown believed, way before Bernie ever showed up in camp, that Voyles was prejudiced toward black players. Voyles's treatment of Bernie only confirmed his belief. But Brown's dislike for the man ran deeper than the issue of colour. It was an issue of integrity.

In this era before agents, players were forced to negotiate contracts and salaries for themselves. After he was named an Eastern All-Star at defensive back, Dick Brown figured he was due for a raise and went to see Voyles in his role as general manager. Voyles listened to Brown's pitch and then calmly told him that he should be content with things as they were. Wasn't he grateful to have a wonderful off-season job at Stelco? Because unless Brown signed a new contract as offered, that job at Stelco would disappear. With a wife and kids to support, Dick Brown had no choice but to sign the contract.

"Coach Voyles had never coached a black player who could play the quarterback position, because at that time there was a stigma that blacks weren't capable of handling a position of responsibility such as quarterback," explained Bernie. "And I think this dictated a lot of his actions until we got into the season and he came to realize that I was just as capable as anyone else, forget colour. And I think … he accepted me that year."

That '51 season, with Bernie as quarterback, the Ticats went 7–5, tied with Toronto and Ottawa but with a total-points differential far greater than either of their rivals. That mattered very little during the playoffs, however, as Ottawa emerged victorious and earned the right to represent the East in the Grey Cup. But Bernie did earn honours as the East's All-Star quarterback in his first year of play.

He had also moved in with Dick Brown and his wife in an apartment on St. Matthews Avenue in Hamilton. Bernie was curious about his new home of Hamilton, not just the geography but the people. He would go on long walks to not only get the lay of the land but also to see if he might come upon other black people in town.

"The first black person I saw in Hamilton was Linc (Lincoln) Alexander," he remembered, "and it was in a park. He was playing with his son Keith. So naturally I went over to him, and I said, 'Hey, Brother, it's nice to see you. Are there any others of us here?' He said, 'Not many.' And I said, 'It's nice to see you and I hope to see you again.'"

(Lincoln Alexander was a lawyer who became Canada's first black member of parliament and first black federal cabinet minister, and who served as the Lieutenant-Governor of Ontario from 1985 to 1991. Bernie and Alexander would have a friendship that lasted sixty-one years, until Alexander's death in 2012.)

Despite having a banner year in Hamilton his first year in the league, Bernie came to training camp in 1952 expecting to improve upon it. He had one year under his belt, knew the offensive system, understood the defences thrown against him, and most of all felt that he could even better exploit the larger playing fields in Canada. That's when Carl Voyles dropped his bomb: he was switching Bernie to halfback.

"Now, I have to ask you a question. Do you know of any All-Star quarterback who had his position taken away from him?" Bernie levelled his gaze at me. The question was rhetorical. "The answer is no. But that happened to me."

Voyles claimed the shift was made for strategic reasons, to diversify the offence. He may have even argued that opposing team defences could no longer focus solely on Bernie. But where was the sense in taking the ball out of your best player's hands?

"I was very disappointed and I think if that situation had arisen today, I would have fought it to the nth degree. If someone performs at a better level than I'm performing, then I will concede that they're better. But that never happened."

The man entrusted with that initial offensive touch was another import quarterback, Bill Mackrides, who had spent five seasons as a backup QB in the NFL with the Philadelphia Eagles. Based on the Ticats' performance that season, in retrospect and based solely on their record, it would be tough to argue that Voyles's changes diminished the overall product in any way. The team went 9–2–1 during the regular season before losing the three-game playoff struggle against eventual Grey Cup winners the Toronto Argonauts featuring Ulysses Curtis. Once again,

Bernie would be named to the Eastern All-Stars, only this time it would be at the halfback position.

Despite his being recognized as an All-Star, Bernie's disappointment and resentment lingered. He had not left the Cleveland Browns camp or his native country to play the halfback position in Canada. He came to play quarterback. And now he felt that he was being unjustly prevented from that by a coach with a certain bias. There were times when he struggled to hide his feelings. But he never let that get in the way of giving his all on the gridiron. So when Mackrides left the team that off-season, Bernie believed that the quarterback position was now his for the taking.

Instead, Voyles went out and got himself another white American quarterback, Edward "Butch" Songin, a player picked 247th in the nineteenth round of the 1950 NFL draft. Butch Songin was an All-American at Boston College; the only problem was that he was named an All-American in hockey, not football. Songin wasn't even Voyles's first choice. He had attempted to sign George Blanda away from the NFL's Chicago Bears, a move that made Bears owner George Halas threaten the Tiger-Cats with a lawsuit for tampering. That was a legal battle the Ticats could not afford. Yet signing George Blanda would at least have made sense: he was a proven NFL quarterback. But Butch Songin? *This* was the player that was going to keep Bernie from the quarterback position he so coveted? At what point does a coach's persistence become an issue of intractability?

The argument can be made that it isn't a coach's responsibility to be popular with his players. His job is to win games. If that means putting his best player in a secondary role where his feelings are hurt or his individual statistics suffer but the team succeeds, that coach is not likely to be second-guessed by the team's owners. Fans may be outraged by their idol's diminished role but if the results are there, so the thinking goes, they will eventually come around to the coach's way of thinking. And any player who is perceived to put his own needs above those of the team is seen as a bad apple, or even worse, a cancer.

Bernie had a point when he argued that Voyles's changes did not greatly improve the team. With Butch Songin at the helm the team attained a mediocre record of eight wins and six losses in 1953. During the playoffs, however, the team steamrolled their way over Montreal to a Grey Cup matchup with the Winnipeg Blue Bombers led by Jack Jacobs at quarterback. The Tiger-Cats emerged victorious in the Grey Cup game, but it took a tremendous defensive play by Lou Kusserow, knocking down a pass intended for Winnipeg great Tom Casey at the goal line with just seconds remaining in the game, to preserve the slim 12–6 victory.

The score flattered the Tiger-Cats. Jacobs completed thirty-one of forty-eight passes that game, a record for passes attempted and completed that stood for twenty-seven years until Danny Barrett of Calgary broke it in the 1991 Grey Cup game against Toronto. The Hamilton cause was aided by two interceptions deep in Hamilton territory. One of those interceptions was made by Dick Brown. And then, of course, there was Kusserow's heroic save as time ran out.

That Grey Cup victory, however, remained the most disappointing day in Bernie Custis's pro football career for what it might have been. Bernie touched the ball six times that day. He was the best offensive weapon the Ticats possessed and he was given the ball a mere six times. On those six carries he managed to gain thirty-six yards, an average of six yards per carry. Why would anyone ignore someone who gained six yards every time he touched the ball?

Butch Songin did not call his own plays. Jack Jacobs did for Winnipeg but he was the exception and had had a number of years in the NFL under his belt before coming to Canada. Plus, he threw for 11,000 yards in his brief career in Canada. The point is that it would not have been Songin's call on how much to use Bernie. That call belonged to Carl Voyles.

"I think it was to prevent me from reaching any kind of stardom that day."

Bernie felt he could have contributed a hell of a lot more to the game *and* to the score had he been given the opportunity. The score did not have to be as close as it was. And that's what tore him apart, the thought of what could have been. He was genuinely happy for his teammates and for the city of Hamilton when they won the game, there was no question about that. But he was stung by his exclusion from any apparent game plan on the biggest football stage this country had to offer.

The thing to understand about Bernie Custis is that it actually pained him to think the worst of people's motivations. He was also reluctant to use a term like "racist," because he felt it obliterated any differentiation between thoughts, words, and deeds, and any scale of offence from minor to major. It was a word with a power that could not be taken back; for someone described or accused as racist it was next to impossible to prove the opposite. And for those reasons he never used the word and would never ascribe it to Carl Voyles. That would be for others to decide.

"It was just something that happened and you move on."

The 1954 season brought changes in Bernie's personal life. He married long-time girlfriend Lorraine Dafoe, who worked for the hydro company in Hamilton. Lorraine died in 2002; they'd been married forty-eight years.

Lorraine Dafoe was white. "When we got married," Bernie said, "her dad told us that we were twenty-five years ahead of our time. But that he was behind us 100 percent."

When I suggested to Bernie that it must have taken a great deal of courage on both their parts to get married, he just shrugged it off.

"We knew it but we loved each other. And we just said, 'This challenge, it isn't anything.'"

Bernie took particular delight in recounting a time when he and Lorraine were walking down King Street, one of the busiest streets in Hamilton. A stranger stared so intently at the couple as they passed that he walked straight into a pole.

"You could hear the ringing of the pole for about a block away. And I was close enough to say, 'You've just been punished.'"

In 1954, Voyles went with the same basic lineup that had won the Grey Cup the year before, with Butch Songin at quarterback and Bernie once again at halfback. Results are the measure of a team's success, and, despite a mediocre season the year before, the team had won a Grey Cup. It was hard to argue that the coach's private agenda was hurting the team so Bernie kept his mouth shut. The Tiger-Cats actually improved on their regular-season record, going 9–5. The Montreal Alouettes, however, behind their All-Star quarterback, Sam "the Rifle" Etcheverry, the son of Basque sheep farmers who had immigrated to New Mexico back in the 1920s, took first place with an 11–3 record and crushed the Ticats in a two-game, total-points format.

Bernie had his best season in the CFL that year, racking up well over a thousand all-purpose yards: 400 yards receiving, 500 yards rushing, and a further 400 yards in kickoff returns. He was the Eastern All-Star halfback and the Tiger-Cats' nominee for Most Outstanding Player in Canadian football. He would lose out in that category to Sam Etcheverry, who threw for 586 yards during *one game* that season, a single-game record that would stand for thirty-nine years. When it comes to awards, an outstanding quarterback on a successful team has a distinct advantage in the eyes of voters over any other outstanding position player. Bernie did not see it as a slight. He was only twenty-six years old and at the top of his game. Nevertheless, it burned that he was not the guy going head-to-head with Etcheverry as a quarterback.

And then came 1955. First, the good news. Butch Songin was gone and the quarterback position was open. This, closely followed by the bad news. Carl Voyles traded for a new quarterback, Nobby Wirkowski, who had led the Argonauts to the Grey Cup in 1952 but had lately fallen on hard times in Toronto. For Bernie, this good news–bad news scenario got even worse. The man Voyles traded to get Wirkowski was none other than All-Star defensive back Dick Brown, Bernie's best friend. Now this really had to be some kind of joke. Nobby was known to be about as mobile as a garden gnome. He could throw but he could not run.

Dick Brown, on the other hand, felt as if he'd hit the jackpot. He was sad to leave Bernie behind but his euphoria at being free of Carl Voyles more than made up for it. It didn't matter to him that the Argos were a bad team only surpassed in futility by the sad-sack Ottawa Rough Riders. It seemed that once again Carl Voyles had gone out of his way to alienate his star halfback. Matters grew more complicated when Bernie sustained a thigh injury that was not healing properly. This was before athletes could just have an MRI to determine the nature and extent of an injury. Voyles insisted that Bernie was capable of playing despite Bernie's insistence that something was seriously wrong. When Bernie refused to play until his thigh healed, Voyles suspended him from the team.

When Bernie didn't show up at the next practice — and why would he since he'd just been suspended? — Voyles called him at home asking him why he wasn't at practice, as if having had a timeout in the corner to think about his misbehaviour, Bernie would have come to his senses. As he had all along, Bernie insisted that he could not play, that he was injured.

That conversation marked the end of Bernie's football career in Hamilton. Voyles sold Bernie, who was basically damaged goods, to Ottawa. Back then, players had few rights or protection, regardless of race, creed, or colour, and no recourse but to accept their fate. (This would change with the formation of the Canadian Football League Players' Association [CFLPA] in 1965.)

"I went to Ottawa and that was probably the worst experience I ever had," he said. "They were in disarray in Ottawa."

To say the least. After three straight seasons out of the playoffs, Ottawa had brought in University of Tennessee assistant coach Chan Caldwell to take the Rough Riders' reins, yet another American coaching prospect who had no familiarity with the Canadian game. He promptly led the Rough Riders to a 3–9 record and a fourth straight year out of the East playoffs. Bernie's transfer to Ottawa did not improve the condition of his leg and he saw limited action in only seven games that season. He was, however, reunited with former Syracuse teammate and backup quarterback Avatus Stone, who had come to Ottawa in 1953. Avatus may have been inspired by Bernie's presence, because he enjoyed his best season in the CFL, winning the Jeff Russell Memorial Trophy as the Most Outstanding Player in the East.

After the season limped to its sad conclusion, Bernie decided that he had had enough of playing football. Lew Hayman, who had integrated the league when he brought Herb Trawick to Montreal back in 1946, was now the general manager with the Toronto Argonauts. He called Bernie to see if he would like to coach the East York Argos, a senior men's team in the old ORFU, which functioned as a farm team for the big club. Lew Hayman also happened to be a Syracuse graduate and had followed Bernie's career with interest throughout his college and professional playing days. Hayman was fishing to see if Bernie would be willing to be both player and coach for East York, but Bernie told him he was flat-out done with playing. He did, however, accept the offer to coach.

"[Playing] wasn't what I wanted to do in life, but I didn't want to walk away from football."

On the drive home from an East York practice one day shortly after taking the position, Bernie pulled his car over to the side of the road. If the moment fell short of a road-to-Damascus-like experience, it was, nonetheless, an epiphanic moment in Bernie's life.

"I asked myself what it was that I did want to do in life, what I wanted to get involved with. Teaching hit me."

He enrolled at Hamilton Teachers' College and spent his days in school while he worked nights at Dofasco (Dominion Foundries and Steel Company). At the end of a year he had earned his teacher's certificate, gotten a job teaching in Hamilton, and begun a career in education that lasted for the next thirty-seven years, with all but two of those years spent as a principal.

"When I look back on that I just say, 'Wow.' Once again, determination entered the picture."

Teaching and coaching would go hand in hand for Bernie over the next four decades. He would become one of the most successful amateur football coaches in the history of Canada. Bernie coached the Oakville Black Knights for four years in the ORFU, winning two championships. He coached the junior Burlington Braves from 1964 to '72, winning three Ontario titles to go with the two Eastern Canadian ones. This was followed by a stint with the Sheridan Bruins, where he won provincial community college championships in six of the eight years he was in charge. From there he went on to coach the McMaster University Marauders for another eight years and was named Ontario University Athletics Association (OUAA) Coach of the Year in both 1982 and 1984 and Canadian Interuniversity Athletic Union (CIAU) Coach of the Year in 1982. His contributions to the field of amateur and university football would lead to his induction into the Canadian Football Hall of Fame in 1994 in the builder category.

"You know, the number of players I've had the pleasure to coach is just unbelievable. They're all over the place. And you know what the rewarding part of that is? I've got a lot of young men coaching high-school teams that played for me. Those are the rewards you get from all this."

Some years after Bernie retired, he received a phone call at his home in Hamilton. The voice on the other end of the line belonged to Carl Voyles, who was visiting friends in Hamilton and heard that Bernie was still living there. Voyles had retired from the CFL after the 1955 season and gone into real estate in Toronto. He had done some scouting for Hamilton during the '60s and '70s. He and his wife had retired to Vero Beach, Florida.

"I had met his wife here during his time coaching and I asked him how his wife was," recalled Bernie. "And he started crying on the phone. He told me that she had passed away. But he said, 'I also called, Bernie, to apologize to you for the way I treated you during your time here when you were playing for me.' I thought that was tremendous. I told him I appreciated the fact but that I also understood that he had not been exposed to a black player in that position and that we all perhaps, in life, have a tendency to do a wrong thing. It's good that one realizes it and is willing to try and make amends. I told him that I don't hold any grudges and I wished him well. And that was my last dealings with Coach Voyles."

It's hard not to think about what Bernie might have accomplished as a quarterback in the CFL. All his life Bernie had opened eyes and changed minds with his determination and ability to accomplish whatever he set out to do. His football career was cut short by an injury he might have avoided had he not been made a halfback where he was required to either block defenders or take hits on virtually every play. The city of Hamilton embraced Bernie Custis from the moment he stepped on the field. The fans did not give a damn about the colour of Bernie's skin. They were excited to have him. He could throw, he could run, he could do it all. He was, in modern parlance, "the man." And Bernie repaid their adoration by becoming the Big Four All-Star quarterback in his first season.

There are many who would choose to give Carl Voyles the benefit of the doubt, saying that just because he was a southerner it did not necessarily make him prejudiced against black people. Their argument would no doubt centre around the fact that the Ticats won a Grey Cup without Bernie at quarterback. True enough. But the question isn't whether Carl Voyles was prejudiced against black people. It's whether he was prejudiced against black quarterbacks. As for winning the Grey Cup, could it not also be true that the Tiger-Cats might have won more than one Grey Cup had Carl Voyles simply allowed the best quarterback on the team be the best quarterback on the team?

"Funny you should ask me that," Bernie Custis said in a 2011 Tiger-Cats halftime interview, projected across Ivor Wynne Stadium on the giant scoreboard. "When I became a citizen, which I am now and have been for thirty or forty years, the judge asked me to speak to the group that day on what it meant to become a Canadian. I told him that there's one word that I can use to set the basis and that's 'freedom.' In defining freedom it meant that I felt I can do most things that I would like to do. And pursue aspects of life without any hindrances. See, I couldn't say that if I was living in the south of the United States."

The occasion for displaying Bernie's ten-metre-high face over the end zone was the celebration of the sixtieth year since he became the first black quarterback in professional football back in 1951. Bernie was escorted to midfield by CFL greats Tony Gabriel (whom Bernie had coached in Brantford and gotten into Syracuse on a scholarship), Chuck Ealey (who won a Grey Cup at quarterback with the Tiger-Cats in his rookie season of '72), and Damon Allen (who retired as professional football's all-time leading passer in yardage).

Introductions were made. The fans gave Bernie a tremendous reception. Very few had left their seats to hit the food concessions. Bernie's initial deer-in-the-headlights look disappeared and a beatific smile lit up his face. Standing at midfield in the midst of a standing ovation, he slipped a small piece of paper from the front pocket of his black warmup pants, a piece of paper he had been folding and unfolding all day to continually reassure himself that the words he had written were still there. He was just beginning to show signs of forgetfulness and uncertainty that within five years would develop into full-blown senile dementia and require full-time care. As the crowd roared their approval, Tony Gabriel patted his back, reminding him, "You the man, Bernie, you the man."

And then Bernie began to speak.

"Sixty years ago I left my homeland and came to a strange city … in a strange country … to play a position I would not be allowed to play in Cleveland or any other city in the National Football League."

Bernie's sister, Joan, had come from Philadelphia for the occasion. As she had all those years ago at Syracuse, she cheered her brother on, mouthing the words of his speech along with him, having committed them to memory from his repetitive readings aloud over breakfast.

"For as great a country as the United States was and remains, it was not yet ready to allow a black man to be a starting professional quarterback.

And it was not ready for Chuck Ealey … Warren Moon … or Damon Allen. I am proud of the city of Hamilton" — here he paused to let the cheers die down — "for opening its arms to a young man from Philadelphia who never believed that the colour of his skin should be the determining factor in the measure of a man. Thank you Hamilton and thank you Canada for agreeing with that young man."

Bernard Eugene Custis died in Burlington on February 23, 2017, in his eighty-eighth year. On September 17, 2018, the Hamilton-Wentworth District School Board announced that a new secondary school being built directly across the street from Tim Hortons Field, home of the Hamilton Tiger-Cats, and scheduled to open its doors in September of 2019 will be called Bernie Custis Secondary School.

Chapter Five

THE JOHNNY BRIGHT INCIDENT

He led the CFL in rushing four times in front of cheering Canadian throngs less encumbered by ignorant hatred that our country has still not entirely purged. Those who know the story well have an obligation to pass it on. Those who don't will be better just for listening.

— Terry Hersom, *Sioux City Journal*

October 20, 1951. The Drake University Bulldogs out of Des Moines, Iowa, were in Stillwater, Oklahoma, for a game against the Aggies of Oklahoma A&M, a game that could amount to the Missouri Conference championship. The Bulldogs had begun the season 5 and 0 behind the offensive talents of Johnny Bright. For three years straight Bright had led the nation in total offence — running, passing, and receiving — and was the odds-on favourite to win the Heisman Trophy, an annual award that goes to the most outstanding college football player in the United States. If he won the Heisman, he would be the first Black American to achieve that honour.

In three seasons, Bright had heard his share of racist taunts and endured the usual cheap shots administered by opposing tacklers when the referees weren't looking. Back in 1934, the head coach with Iowa

State (and a former Drake football coach), Ossie Solem, was quoted after a particularly brutal game against Minnesota, "There's no use kidding anyone — a Negro player, even if his opponents play cleanly, always gets plenty of bumps and particularly when he is a star football carrier." Solem was referring to his black running back, Oze "Ozzie" Simmons, who was knocked out three times during that Minnesota game. "They were blatant with their piling on and kneeing me. It was obvious, but the refs didn't call it," said Simmons, years later. Nicknamed "the Ebony Eel" by a white press given to hanging ludicrous monikers on sports figures, Ozzie would be a victim of his times, one more black athlete who would never get to measure his game against the best in professional football because of the colour of his skin.

The Drake Bulldogs, including Johnny Bright, had actually played against Oklahoma A&M in Stillwater, Oklahoma, two years previously. Bright was the first black player to set foot on the Lewis Field turf, in a game that the Aggies won by a score of 28–0. There had been some concern at the time about how Bright would be received, especially by Drake supporters, but after the game Bright said that A&M was one of the cleanest teams that he had played against. Some of the Aggie players had even shaken his hand after the game. That might have been the influence of the Aggies' head coach at the time, Jim Lookabaugh, who had gone on record as saying that Johnny Bright would be treated with respect by his players. Oklahoma A&M had aspirations of moving beyond the Missouri Valley Conference and becoming part of a larger, more prestigious conference. It would not further their cause to appear like some backwater breeding ground for psychopathic rednecks. So restrained was their conduct that Drake's athletic council chairman, Frank Gardner, wrote a letter to the Oklahoma A&M leaders express-ing his "deep appreciation" for the manner in which Johnny Bright had been treated.

But that was 1949. By 1950, Jim Lookabaugh was gone. Oklahoma A&M brought in a new head coach from Georgia, J.B. Whitworth, whose philosophy was fairly basic: if it moves, hit it hard. He rode his defence relentlessly, especially the end, Wilbanks Smith, whom he accused of being soft. In the run-up to the game against Drake there was talk that Whitworth had made a point with his players about targeting Bright, accusing him of not being a team player, of faking injuries, of being a prima donna, the kind of negative traits associated back then with talented black players. He never told his team to go after Bright because he was black. One of Bright's teammates was told by an A&M student that Whitworth had gone so far as to encourage his players to get Bright out of the game "even if you have to kill him." One player took the coach's advice very much to heart. That player was Wilbanks Smith, defensive end.

There was a different vibe in the air that day of the game. Racial tension had spread from the playing field into the mainstream media. Articles had appeared in both the university and local newspaper warning that Bright was a marked man. The locals had heard rumbles all week that there was a price on Johnny Bright's head and had come to see whether one of their beloved Aggies would collect that bounty. Two photographers, Don Ultang and John Robinson from the *Des Moines Register*, had set up early on the press-box roof.

They had heard the rumours circulating and decided that they would focus their cameras on Bright. That way, if something did happen on the field, they might get a decent shot. But if something was going to happen, it had better happen early; the two photographers had to fly back to Des Moines, and if they were to make the paper's deadline they could not stay for the entire game. They wouldn't have to stay beyond halftime. In just the first few minutes of the game, they would get more than they bargained for. They would get a Pulitzer Prize.

If hearing rumours of his own demise on the gridiron was not worrisome enough, Bright had to contend with the standard issues of segregation in Stillwater and the surrounding region. Bright had been turned away from the hotel where the team had stayed just two years before, so the coach had decided to take the whole team elsewhere. The team found accommodations in the A&M student union hall but, once again, no black people were allowed. Finally, the team was able to arrange for Bright to stay with a local black minister. If Bright was overly concerned about the rumoured threats against him, he did not let on. He was more concerned with matters of the future. Just a few more games left in the season, and if he continued to produce as he had been, he would be a shoo-in for the Heisman. Just two weeks earlier he had rumbled for 265 yards and four touchdowns in the first half of a game (at which point his coach had applied the mercy rule and replaced Bright at halftime). Winning the Heisman Trophy would guarantee him a top spot in the upcoming National Football League draft and a sizable pro contract that would allow him to provide his family with a quality of life he had never known growing up in Fort Wayne, Indiana.

On Drake's first play from scrimmage, Johnny Bright took the snap from centre. He handed the ball off to fullback Gene Macomber. As Macomber burst through the line, defensive tackle Wilbanks Smith made a beeline for the unsuspecting Bright, who stood watching the play unfold. Smith drove his forearm into Bright's jaw, knocking him to the turf. His jaw broken, a dazed Bright picked himself up off the grass and returned to the huddle. On the next play, he launched a pass deep to receiver Jim Pilkington, who snagged the ball and continued into the end zone untouched. A sixty-five-yard completion for a touchdown. But the pain in Bright's jaw was so intense that he barely celebrated.

The Bulldog defence stopped Oklahoma and the Aggies were forced to punt. Drake's offence, led by Bright, once again took the field. On the first play, Bright handed off to his wingback and, as before, Wilbanks Smith ignored the runner and went after Bright. Once again, no penalty was called despite an apparent attempt to injure. Drake's news director, Paul Morrison, watched uneasily.

"I was in the press box at the time and there was no question that this guy Wilbanks Smith was the designated hitter. After two or three plays I said to [*Des Moines Register* sportswriter] Maury White, I said, 'Boy, they're really getting after John.' They just decided that to win the conference championship, they had to get rid of John."

On the next play, Bright ran a sweep and gained seventeen yards. As he lay at the bottom of the pile, absorbing further punishment, he heard the word, a snarling hiss in his ear. *Nigger*. Bright slowly made his way back to the huddle, *the word* reverberating in his helmet. He saw the hateful stares of his opponents, any one of whom could have uttered the vile epithet. But Johnny Bright was not about to back down. On the next play, he handed the ball to Macomber, who went left, then cut back up field. As Bright followed the play, he failed to see Wilbanks Smith approaching, his arm drawn back to launch another forearm into Bright's unprotected jaw. In the stands, Ultang and Robinson were ready. The shutter clicked six times. The two photographers looked at one another and wondered whether anyone else had noticed what they had just witnessed.

Johnny Bright's chance at the coveted Heisman Trophy ended on the grass of Lewis Field that day. After only two sets of downs he was forced to leave the game, his season all but done. His jaw was fractured, his teeth wired shut for weeks. He would lose close to twenty pounds. No coach in his right mind would let him play despite his protestations that he was *fine, just fine.* The risk of further or permanent damage was too great. He had no doubt been concussed but who kept track or even noticed back then? *He had his bell rung. He saw stars.* But a broken jaw was another matter. There was no way to hide the evidence.

The fallout from that single game by far overshadowed the importance of the game itself as it pertained to the standings, or the effect on Bright's collegiate career or even the slipping away of the Heisman Trophy from his grasp and the chance to make history as the first Black American to win it. That day would live on in infamy through the power of the photo sequence taken by the team of Don Ultang and John Robinson, who would win the Pulitzer Prize in photography for their shots. That sequence would become known as "the Johnny Bright Incident." The photographs first appeared in the *Des Moines Register* on October 21, 1951, the day after the game, and would be picked up by every major newspaper in the country.

The pictures show Johnny Bright handing the ball off to the running back, Gene Macomber. Bright then watches as Macomber cuts back against the flow of play to head upfield. As other Aggies give chase, one lineman does not. Wilbanks Smith. He is seen heading straight for Bright, who remains oblivious to the danger approaching. It's like watching a sequence of photographs of a shark fin approaching a swimmer who's casually floating on his back, without a care in the world. As Smith draws closer to the unsuspecting Bright, he pulls his fist back. In the final shot, his right forearm comes into contact with Bright's unprotected face, seeming to crush it almost flat until it disappears inside his helmet. There was clearly no attempt to deviate from his course or limit the damage inflicted on an uninvolved and unsuspecting victim. The evidence was there for the whole world to see. The *Des Moines Tribune* printed a series of opinions from various newspapers the following week.

> Oct 20 should go down in football's record book as "Black Saturday...." Bright's teammates, headed by Capt. Bob Binette, charged that the boy's injury was "deliberately inflicted...." And all who saw the pictures of the "incident" in Monday's *Denver Post* must agree with that charge.
>
> — *Denver Post*

> Some are considerate enough of the offending young man to contend that he was out to "get" Bright not because he was a Negro but because he was a star athlete. Even such a concession is anything but complimentary to both the young man and his coach. But we don't go along with it. To us what happened is reflective of a racial intolerance which is by no means restricted to Oklahoma.
>
> — *Mason City Globe Gazette*

> Certainly the least that should be done is to bar Smith from any further competition. But whether he was instructed to slug Bright at every opportunity or concocted the murky scheme himself, his coach and school should be held responsible.... It's about time steps were taken to make football a game again.
>
> — *Marshalltown Times-Republican*

There was immediate outrage across the country from football fans decrying the horrific acts of violence perpetrated against Johnny Bright. Bright himself was quoted in the *Morning Democrat* in Des Moines: "When he hit me the first time I thought nothing about it. Those things happen in a game. But when he repeatedly struck me, doesn't it seem pretty obvious?"

Warren Gaer, Drake's head football coach, expressed curiosity as to how the opposition would respond. "I'll be very interested in seeing what Coach Whitworth will do about Smith after he sees pictures like this."

But Oklahoma A&M coach Whitworth took a page from the modern political playbook and simply denied the truth that was evident to all.

"I can say right now our boys didn't gang up on anyone," Whitworth said. And in a slippery way, he was telling the truth, for it was hardly a group action but the work of a lone assassin, or, as Paul Morrison called him, a "designated hitter."

Drake University president Henry Harmon petitioned the Missouri Valley Conference council to take action against Wilbanks Smith, but his attempts were blocked by what amounted to a determined resistance on the part of the so-called Southern Bloc of the conference, who had no intention of upholding sanctions against either Smith or Oklahoma A&M. Harmon then met with the presidents of the participant universities, again to no avail. While the general consensus was that Smith may have crossed a line, there was no clear admission of wrongdoing or collective will to do anything about it. With the domination of the Southern Bloc, Harmon discovered the hard facts of Jim Crow attitudes and unspoken laws. For instance, any school that yielded to the temptation to integrate, whether to build a winning football team or just because they thought it was the right thing to do, had lost the right to expect justice on some moral higher ground.

Harmon had a fallback plan. He proposed that Oklahoma A&M issue a public apology for the on-field behaviour of Wilbanks Smith and the Aggies players. Not only would such an apology satisfy Drake officials but it would also go a long way to appeasing Bulldogs fans throughout the state of Iowa. Oklahoma representatives refused. To issue a public apology would be to openly confess that their players were in the wrong or, worse, that they had conspired to target Johnny Bright because a) he was black, or b) he was great, or c) he was both black and great. Harmon was furious. With no punishment for Smith nor any acknowledgement that he had transgressed or even just felt a hint of remorse for his blatant attack on Bright, and with no apology from Oklahoma A&M for the actions of their football team, Harmon threatened to take Drake University right out of the Missouri Valley Conference.

"Our fans and constituency kept hounding at [Drake] to take some action," explained Paul Morrison.

When Oklahoma officials failed to respond to this ultimatum, President Harmon called a meeting of Drake's athletic council and made it clear that his decision would be based on the council's recommendations. He also made it clear that he felt that the university should have nothing to do with a conference that abided the actions of Oklahoma A&M. The council agreed. With the support of the Drake student body and the vast majority of Iowans on his side, President H.G. Harmon announced that Drake University was resigning from the Missouri Valley Conference on November 27, 1951. Bradley University in Peoria, Illinois, also announced that they were leaving the conference in a gesture of solidarity.

"Johnny Bright's broken jaw now has lost the Missouri Valley Conference two of its most influential members," announced Iowa's *Waterloo Daily Courier*, which sounds like a case of blaming the victim. Bright never asked anyone to do anything on his behalf. He certainly never expected the university to pull out of the Missouri Valley Conference in order to make a statement against overt acts of racism (which it wasn't so much as a statement against the stubborn refusal to apologize). Johnny Bright was a black man. He knew the score better than those acting in his so-called best interests. After all, he had been forced to live off-campus because he was black. He recognized that his athletic prowess had earned him a measure of esteem among his student peers but never true acceptance. What did a white administration honestly think could happen to a black man on the playing fields of the South? Only two years before, Drake officials had sent a letter to Oklahoma A&M praising them to the skies for not crippling or maiming Bright on his first visit to Lewis Field. And now suddenly they decided that they could no longer be a part of a conference that condones racist ideology?

Fortunately for Johnny Bright, he would recover fully from his injuries, too late to finish his senior season of college football or attain his dream of winning the Heisman Trophy, but he would partake in both the East-West Shrine Game and the Hula Bowl, two All-Star games featuring the best collegiate players in the country (although he saw limited action because of his injured jaw). At the NFL draft held on January 17, 1952, at the Hotel Statler in New York City, the Philadelphia Eagles chose Bright as the fifth-overall pick. The Eagles naturally assumed that Bright would jump at their offer to play pro ball. He was poor; he was black. They added insult to injustice by offering him much less money than they would have offered a white player of similar capabilities; that is, if they could have found a white player with similar capabilities.

But Johnny Bright was a changed man. His eyes had been opened by the treatment he'd received in Oklahoma. He knew that the NFL was full of white Southern players who, like Wilbanks Smith, would love to take a free shot at a cocky young black star. Did he want to subject himself and, by extension, his family to that sort of treatment? But what else could he do? He knew his options were limited, that it was a rigged game, especially for Black Americans.

And then representatives from two teams in the WIFU, the Edmonton Eskimos and the Calgary Stampeders, came calling. Bright, on the advice of Coach Gaer, let the Eagles know that teams in Canada were interested in signing him. That way, if the Eagles were sincere about him, they would have to increase their offer.

"I would like to see Johnny play the toughest ball because I'm absolutely certain he could play with the best," Gaer told reporters. "However, if this offer [from Canada] is such from a dollars and cents standpoint that Johnny can't turn it down, then I think it would be right by playing in Canada."

The cards were on the table. The Eagles thought he was bluffing. Why would any American football player, regardless of colour, go play football in some rinky-dink league in the Arctic wilderness or wherever the hell they played up there? And then the Stampeders made their offer: $12,000 a season plus a $2,000 signing bonus. It was an offer that blew Philadelphia's out of the water. Still, Bright thought it only proper that he give Philadelphia general manager Vince McNally one last chance to make an offer Bright could not refuse.

"The Eagles' offer will have to be a good one or I'm going to sign with Calgary," Bright told the press.

The story goes that Stampeders president and Calgary oilman C.E. Chesher, perhaps sensing that all Johnny Bright needed was a small display of financial sincerity to get his name on a contract, came to Des Moines, took Johnny Bright to the legendary Blue Willow, a hugely popular local café for Drake students, and laid out twenty $100 bills in a row across the table, the full amount of his bonus offer. He told Bright that he would be more than the face of the Calgary Stampeders — he would become the face of professional football in Canada. It was a nudge in Calgary's direction that Johnny Bright could not resist.

"I have worked four years to get in a position where I could help my mother and dad. I just couldn't let the offer go by," he told reporters.

McNally was outraged when he heard the news. He went to the papers and claimed that Bright had not given the Eagles a final chance, not that it would have changed their position. McNally had made it pretty clear that he had no intention of budging on his initial offer. Bright had gone back on his word, he claimed, having promised to come to Philadelphia for a final contract discussion. McNally painted himself as the deeply wronged party who lost out on Bright by being patient and not wanting to crowd him regarding a decision. According to the *Philadelphia Inquirer*, "McNally added that he hoped Bright knew what he was doing. The circumstances, he said, indicated that the halfback was high-pressured into signing with big promises and a display of large greenbacks." So apparently the story of Chesher's Blue Willow sales pitch, whether truth or whimsy, had reached the Eagles' ears. It's hard not to detect a condescending tone in McNally's comments and his suggestion that Bright might be too naive to understand the big picture, so dazzled was he by the colour of money.

Bright was stunned by McNally's posturing.

"Everything I've said lately seems to have been changed around to insult someone. I don't want hard feelings."

What McNally did not figure into Bright's decision was a quality of life factor. Not even Calgary could guarantee that Bright would never encounter racist attitudes again, but he would not have to face *Southern* racist attitudes in Canada. As Bright admitted years later, he was never sold on the idea of playing for Philadelphia.

"I would have been their first Negro player. There was a tremendous influx of Southern players into the NFL at the time and I didn't know what kind of treatment I could expect."

There was no rejoicing in Canada (except in Calgary) when Johnny Bright signed with the Stampeders, not because of his race but because of the price the Stamps paid to sign him. Even then, throughout Canadian football there were predictions of doom and gloom if salaries escalated, especially when it came to import players. There was a real concern that teams with deeper pockets than others could create a great imbalance in talent. The Johnny Bright signing particularly rankled the western-based teams. Al Anderson, general manager of the Edmonton Eskimos, called it "the beginning of the end for Canadian football," according to the *Winnipeg Free Press*. "That's too much," he went on. "Canadian clubs can't stand it."

Calgary's signing of Johnny Bright also became a matter of some concern with teams in the NFL who feared that other first-round stars might follow Bright's lead and head north. That was really the beginning of what the U.S. press began labelling a "war" with Canada, a war that heated up even more when Heisman Trophy winner Billy Vessels, a white running back from Oklahoma and first-round pick of the Baltimore Colts, signed with Edmonton one year later. Though Baltimore matched Edmonton's offer, Vessels still chose to go to Canada.

"Up in Canada, they also get me a job," said Vessels, when asked what the deciding factor in Edmonton's favour was.

What really angered the Americans was that they no longer had their draft picks over a barrel. They would have to negotiate, something they had never had to do when it was their way or the highway. Now that highway actually led somewhere. It led to Canada.

Rollie Miles, one of the greatest all-purpose backs in the history of Canadian football, did not come to Canada to escape racism in the South. Rollie Miles didn't even come to Canada to play football. He came to play baseball for the Regina Caps of the Southern Saskatchewan Baseball League. Baseball was his game. But at his alma mater, St. Augustine's College, an all-black school in Raleigh, North Carolina, he had been (and still was) one of those natural athletes who played several sports. St. Augustine's is also where he met his wife, Marianne, now a retired psychologist in Edmonton.

"He came with a group of five athletes from Washington, D.C.," said Marianne, "and these five guys were just outstanding in all areas of athletics. So [the administration at St. Augustine's] wanted to do something to improve or upgrade the school. It was small; they called it a liberal arts college.... I was working in the library, it was one of my jobs, and most of the students there were all black. They didn't say black then, they said 'coloured.'"

The library was within walking distance from her grandmother's house where Marianne was living while attending school. It was also the house where she had been born. Her mother had come down from Harlem when she was pregnant with Marianne so that her own mother, who was a midwife, could deliver the baby. Later, Marianne and her mother returned to the family home in Harlem.

St. Augustine's may not have been Marianne's first choice for college but it seemed the most logical. "I knew I could live in the house I was born in, and we didn't have money for tuition." But Marianne, as a northerner and a native New Yorker, found the Jim Crow attitudes and laws of the South demeaning and absurd.

"You could go to Catholic Church, but you sat upstairs in the balcony. If you went to confession you had to wait until all the white people had confessed. Doesn't that sound ridiculous? But we did it. We thought, well, we'll go to hell if we don't go to church."

And so she went to the on-campus church and that's where she met Rollie Miles for the first time, coming out of the church. She had seen him before on campus, walking with his friends, their fashion sense setting them apart from the locals.

"He was wearing what they called dungarees in those days. Rolled up, white bucks, argyle socks, and a red sweater, V-neck, with a T-shirt underneath. And I was, mmm, he's pretty fine, but he's probably got a chick already."

She invited him over to her grandmother's for something to eat and he brought all his friends along. Soon enough, Sundays became a regular meal day at Marianne's grandmother's house for Rollie and his friends. By the next spring, Rollie and Marianne were married.

Rollie and Marianne's son, Brett Miles, an Edmonton-based jazz musician and writer, remembers his father telling him of his barnstorming days during his summers off from St. Augustine's, playing the baseball circuit with and against teams from the Negro leagues, teams that were dependent on the money earned on the road playing exhibitions and tournaments.

"A couple of teams would go to a little town and play games against each other all weekend," he told me. "And then the same two teams would go to another town. And that's how they made their money."

Satchel Paige did this all over the United States and developed such a reputation that people, black and white, flocked to see the famous — some would say "infamous" — Satchel Paige pitch. His fame was almost entirely word-of-mouth. He was a living legend. According to Brett Miles, Rollie once hit a double off "Satch," a little piece of well-deserved glory that he carried with him all his life.

Rollie signed a contract with the Boston Braves and they farmed him out to the Regina Caps in 1951. The Caps had been the first-place club the previous season. Post-war western Canada was a hotbed of baseball, with teams at every level from amateur to semi-pro to major league farm teams carrying players on professional contracts. American Negro-league teams would tour the Prairies, playing local teams or tournaments.

"It is doubtful if any Saskatchewan baseball fans will have a look at old Satchel Paige this summer," read a June 3, 1950, article in the *Saskatoon Star-Phoenix*. "The Satch's terms are a bit too high for the average club operator. All he's asking is a cool $500 per inning."

One team owner complained that he would have to charge fans $3.00 a ticket to pay Satchel the kind of money he demanded, presumably for nine innings' work, which would have set him back $4,500 and required at least 1,500 paid attendees. But if there was any pitcher on the planet who could demand that kind of payday, it was Satchel Paige. If you thought that a black ballplayer like Rollie Miles would be conspicuous on a ball diamond in Regina in 1951, you'd be wrong. There were seven black players on the 1951 edition of the Regina Caps, five position players and two pitchers; eight, if you include the manager, Bob White.

So high was the demand for exceptional professional baseball in the West that in 1950 the mayor of the town of Indian Head, Saskatchewan, population 1,500, travelled to Wichita, Kansas, the home of the National Baseball Congress, an organization representing a number of amateur and semi-pro leagues across the United States, and bought the Jacksonville Eagles, a team that up to that point had been part of the Negro American League. The Jacksonville Eagles, in their entirety, boarded a bus and rode it 2,215 miles (3,565 kilometres) from

Jacksonville, Florida, to their new home in Indian Head, Saskatchewan, where they were re-christened the Indian Head Rockets. In retrospect, "Rockets" would seem an appropriate name. They must have felt as if they'd been hurtling through infinite space in a metal tube for an eternity before landing on an unexplored planet. Who knows what thoughts must have gone through their heads as they stepped down from the bus into the vast, flat, empty prairie that would be their home for the next six or seven months. That season the Rockets played no less than eighty games including tournaments and exhibitions.

Much of the money to be made in these various western leagues lay in tournament play, where ball teams from different provinces would come together with a certain amount of prize money on the line. One such tournament was scheduled for August at Renfrew Park in Edmonton, sponsored by a Saskatchewan oilman to the tune of $7,300. Rollie Miles and the Regina Caps were in town for that tournament, plagued as it was by rains and a muddy infield. In the press box to cover the Caps' first game was Edmonton sportswriter Don Fleming.

"Miles was an outstanding second baseman and a good hitter," said Fleming, quoted in author Brant E. Ducey's *The Rajah of Renfrew*. "After the game, I mentioned him to Regina's owner, Cliff Ehrle. He said, 'Yeah, and he's some kind of football player. Came out of one of those small colleges and nobody knows anything about him.'"

Fleming phoned Annis Stukus, the head coach of the Edmonton Eskimos football team, to tell him of his discovery.

Stukus recounted the story to sportswriter Graham Kelly (in Kelly's *The Grey Cup: A History*). "Stuke," he remembered Fleming saying, "there's a kid here with the Regina Caps who is an All-American football player. He's got a bad ankle, but he's stolen seven bases so far."

Stukus was desperate for running backs, having lost a couple to injuries. He told Fleming to tell Miles to stay over after the tournament and Stukus would fly him back to Regina. With nothing better to do, Rollie went out to the Eskimos' practice. He made an immediate and lasting impression on Stukus.

"I was running a short-side play. I couldn't get a guy who could run to his left and throw a pass," Stukus told Kelly. "I hear a voice behind me. 'Hey, Coach, I can run that.' I turned around and there was Miles in uniform. The way he ran it, you'd think I'd been dreaming of Rollie Miles when I designed that play."

After Rollie played a few games on a tryout basis (with pay), Stukus had seen enough and signed him to a three-year contract to play football for the Edmonton Eskimos.

From the very first moment they arrived in Edmonton, Rollie and Marianne let it be known that they were not the type of people who were afraid to rock the boat on matters of racism and injustice whenever they encountered it.

"When we got here," remembered Marianne, "the first thing I saw, going down Jasper Avenue — they had billboards on top of the buildings — was a little black boy; it was really animated, or what, I don't know what the right word is, but they had overexaggerated the lips. It was really a put-down, or what they used to call 'pickaninnies.' It was advertising black Vicks cough drops."

(Pickaninnies were caricatured depictions of black children with huge bulging eyes, big red lips, and wild kinky hair, given to chowing down on watermelon and fried chicken when they weren't being chased or eaten by alligators. It's hard to imagine more racially offensive depictions.)

"Rollie went down to the company in Edmonton who put it up, and they took it down and apologized."

It makes for a good story, a commentary on the Canadian temperament. *How do you get a hundred Canadians out of a pool on the hottest day of the year? You ask them.* That is, of course, how we like to see ourselves, issuers of apologies, willing to right our wrongs. There are certainly worse national traits to promote. It clearly never occurred to the advertisers of Vicks cough drops that their billboard would be considered offensive among an over-whelmingly white populace. It was exactly that kind of casual, thoughtless racism that Rollie and Marianne Miles were determined to call out whenever they came upon it. People had to be made aware. They had to be educated.

In 1953, Rollie Miles had a career year and considered himself in the running for the Schenley Award in its first year of existence, an award for the Most Outstanding Player in the combined IRFU (the East) and the

WIFU (the West). Prior to the Schenley, there were separate outstanding player awards for East and West: the Jeff Nicklin Memorial Trophy in the West and the Jeff Russell Memorial Trophy in the East. That first year, the Schenley went to Miles's Edmonton teammate Billy Vessels, playing in his first and only year in Canada. Rollie felt that he himself had deserved the award and, although he didn't outright accuse the voters of racism, he could not help but feel that racism had played some small part in the choice of Vessels over him. As Normie Kwong, who had endured his own brand of racism during his playing days, not the least of which was the moniker hung on him by the press, "the China Clipper," later admitted, "Conditions in the country then weren't conducive to a person of colour winning awards."

There was no doubt in Marianne Miles's mind who was the more deserving player.

"That was Rollie's award."

Billy Vessels, however, had the right pedigree. He was the Heisman Trophy winner in 1952 with the Oklahoma Sooners. He was the second-overall NFL draft pick in 1953, chosen by the Baltimore Colts. He was the All-American golden boy who chose Canada over sure stardom in the States. He had the hype, drew attention, created a buzz wherever he went and whenever he played. By any standards of the day, Billy Vessels had an outstanding year. But even Vessels thought Rollie Miles was more deserving of the award.

"Whenever I asked my dad about [the award], he said he didn't care because that was the year he had incentives on his contract," Brett Miles said. "But even Billy Vessels said my dad should have won in his acceptance speech. He said, 'This is Rollie's.'"

Marianne laughed remembering Rollie's reaction to Vessels's embarrassment over winning the Schenley. "Rollie kept saying, 'Then give me the money. Give me the money, Billy, if that's how you feel.'"

Expectations were high in Calgary when Johnny Bright arrived in training camp. The Stampeders' management sold tickets on the slogan "Things will be brighter with Bright," after the team had gone 4–10 the previous season. Quarterback Keith Spaith and receiver Sugarfoot Anderson, both capable players, were still with the team. But early in that first season with Calgary, Johnny Bright injured his shoulder and, though he continued to play, he was never without pain. Nevertheless, Bright managed to rush the ball 144 times for a total of 815 yards and two touchdowns. His rushing yardage led the WIFU that season. He also completed twenty-nine passes from the quarterback position for a further 494 yards and two touchdowns. Behind Bright, the Stamps made it into the playoffs for the first time in three years. In the first game of the two-game, total-points semifinal against arch-enemy Edmonton, Calgary came away with a 31–12 victory. Bright caught passes for two touchdowns and rushed for a third. A nineteen-point lead going into the rematch seemed more than enough to guarantee the Stamps would be moving on. But anyone familiar with the history of Canadian playoff football knows that nothing is ever a sure thing. This time it was Rollie Miles who shone for Edmonton, with two touchdowns, one on a pass and the other rushing. The final score was 30–7. Edmonton would advance on total points, 42–38.

During the off-season, Bright worked on rehabilitating his shoulder but it did not seem to improve. Early in training camp he developed appendicitis, which set him back. The shoulder and a number of other nagging injuries limited Bright to seeing action in only nine games, mostly in a defensive position. He carried the ball only thirty-eight times all season. The first of the grumblings that Bright might be "injury-prone" began to surface and would run over into the next season when Calgary started slow out of the gate, losing their first two games. By that time, Bright was seen as damaged goods, and the Stampeders' management unloaded him to Edmonton, who were only too glad to have him.

It was early on in that 1953 season that Marianne and Rollie Miles and the kids were out for a drive around Edmonton, indulging in one of their favourite pastimes: searching for other black people. They would lay bets on who would spot the first black person on the streets.

"That's how we found Johnny Bright," explained Marianne. Bright was in town with the Stampeders for a game against the Eskimos.

"Stop the car!" shouted Marianne that day. "There's a black man. Stop the car!"

"No, it isn't," Rollie answered, a fierce competitor in any contest, from Scrabble to skiing. He kept driving.

"There he is! Stop the car! I can tell by the way he walks."

Rollie stopped the car and got out. He and Johnny Bright shook hands for the first time. And Marianne won the bet.

Early the next season, Johnny Bright was traded to Edmonton and the friends were reunited. Calgary had already gifted Normie Kwong to the Eskimos a couple of years earlier in a lopsided trade, and this deal represented yet another bone-headed move by Calgary management. There was one more offensive great added to the Edmonton backfield that year — Jackie Parker from Mississippi State, another triple-threat back capable of throwing, catching, and running. Edmonton's coach Pop Ivy saw a different role for Bright coming over. With Bernie Faloney at quarterback and Miles, Kwong, and Parker in the backfield, he decided to install Bright in the linebacker position, a perceived weakness on the team that Bright could fill.

Bright was given few offensive touches that year, which bothered him as far as wanting to be a major part of the team's offensive success, but it did allow his body to avoid the added wear-and-tear of playing both ways constantly. That year the Eskimos went 11–5 and made it all the way to the Grey Cup game in Toronto against the heavily favoured Montreal Alouettes led by Sam "the Rifle" Etcheverry and perennial All-Star Herb Trawick.

The outcome of that game hinged on a now-famous fumble by Chuck Hunsinger, which Parker smoothly recovered and then ran ninety yards for a touchdown. The ensuing controversy surrounding that play — was it a fumble or an incomplete pass? — and a blown whistle negating another fumble recovery and touchdown run by Herb Trawick took some of the sheen off the Edmonton victory. Montreal players and supporters suggested that calls on the field were heavily slanted Edmonton's way and contributed to their fluke victory.

Today we would have had a coach's challenge on the Hunsinger play, watched it repeatedly from a dozen angles in slow motion, and then seen the ruling on the field overturned or upheld. Johnny Bright thought it was a fumble. He was hoping to scoop it up but the ball took a favourable bounce toward Jackie Parker, who picked it up instead and went the distance. Ironically, Chuck Hunsinger had told a teammate on the bus on the way to the game, "The only thing I don't want is to be a goat." Poor Chuck. For every prayer answered there can be an emphatic and crushing denial.

The 1955 season saw Johnny Bright becoming more of a contributor offensively to the "Split T" formation and its multitude of options. Parker moved into the quarterback position when Bernie Faloney returned to the States to fulfill his military obligations, and Bright took Parker's vacant spot in the backfield. Bright had three times the number of touches he had had the previous season and gained 643 yards on the ground. Rollie Miles now found himself with the fewest rushing attempts of all the backs, only one-third the number of times he had handled the ball in his breakout year of 1953.

Once again, Edmonton was matched up with Montreal in the Grey Cup, which would be played at Empire Stadium in Vancouver, the first time the Grey Cup game would be held on Western turf. Montreal was seeking to avenge their previous season's loss to Edmonton, a game they felt that they should have won in a cakewalk. Edmonton players were seeking vengeance as well, but for entirely different reasons. They felt that they had been so disrespected by the Montreal players and their fans for last year's victory that they hoped to shut a few mouths this time around.

The Eskimos lacked the flair of Montreal's offence, built around Etcheverry, who filled the air with beautiful arcing spirals from anywhere, any time. In essence, Montreal thumbed their noses at Edmonton for not playing their style of game and instead relying on a brand of football that simply wore down teams, deceived and confused defences, and won games doing it. As one Toronto Argonaut lineman complained after a game against the Eskimos in 1955, "I made nineteen tackles but not once did I get the guy with the ball."

And that was more or less the story of the 1955 Grey Cup. Before the largest crowd in Grey Cup history until that time, the Alouettes' defence, physically and mentally exhausted from chasing sleight-of-hand illusionists around the gridiron, collapsed from fatigue in the second half. The final score was 34–19, despite Sam Etcheverry's passing for a Grey Cup–record 508 yards. The Esks outscored the Alouettes 16–0 in the second half. Johnny Bright scored one touchdown on a forty-two-yard run from scrimmage. But it was his second rushing touchdown, though it was much shorter, that would prove the most memorable for him.

Throughout the game, a defensive back with the Alouettes, J.C. Caroline, had been trash-talking Bright and painting elaborate mental pictures of the damage he was going to inflict on Bright if he got half a chance. With the ball on the eight-yard line, Parker called for a pitchout to Bright. Here was the opportunity both men had been waiting for.

"I turned the corner on the pitch," said Bright. "I ran over J.C. and knocked him out and scored a touchdown. From there on nobody challenged me very much in that game."

The big question entering the 1956 season was could the Edmonton Eskimos win the Grey Cup for a third time in a row and achieve, in today-speak, a three-peat? Actually the bigger question might have been could anyone stop the Eskimos from winning or should they just hand them the Grey Cup and play the season for the right to be runner-up? At the end of the regular season and the playoffs, the Grey Cup matchup was settled and, once again, Edmonton would be facing their sparring partners from the Big Four, the Montreal Alouettes. For their part, Montreal hoped not to achieve their own three-peat distinction as losers.

Three quarters into the game the score was deadlocked 20–20. Would Montreal finally get revenge over their Western nemesis? Uh, no. From that point on the Eskimos outscored the Alouettes 30–7. The final score was 50–27. Once again the Alouettes' defence had been run ragged. With Miles nursing a prior injury, Bright was given a greater workload. He did not disappoint. He rushed for 169 yards (a Grey Cup record until it was broken in 2013 by Kory Sheets of the Saskatchewan Roughriders). He also recovered a fumble, intercepted a pass, and scored two touchdowns in what many sportswriters considered his best game ever. Looking back years later, Bright felt that he really came into his own in that 1956 Grey Cup.

Quoted in Graham Kelly's lively history, he said, "In 1956 I made more of a contribution to the overall success of the team than at any other time. That was the greatest satisfaction I had."

That game would prove a turning point in Johnny Bright's career. No longer would he be one of a number of options out of the backfield. He became the main man, the go-to offensive weapon. In the next five seasons Bright rushed for 7,359 yards, an average of 1,472 yards a season. In 1956 he had carried the ball ninety-three times. In 1957, he was handed the ball 259 times, nearly three times as many as the previous season. And in

1958, he rushed an astounding 296 times for 1,722 yards! Johnny Bright had become the premier running back in Canada. There was, however, a trade-off. As Bright's own career took off, the team did not take flight with him. In 1957, the Eskimos had a 14–2 record, but in the Western final against the Winnipeg Blue Bombers, a team on the rise, they could not find a way to put points on the board despite outplaying the Blue Bombers by a wide margin. Everything that could go wrong did go wrong: fumbles, penalties, and dropped passes. It was one of those nightmare games a player hopes he will wake up from and be able to say, *Ah, it was just a dream.*

"We tried nine field goals in that game and never got a single point," Bright remembered years later, the sting of that loss still evident.

The Eskimos would not return to the Grey Cup game until 1960, knocking off the heavily favoured Winnipeg Blue Bombers in the Western final, a touch of revenge for their 1957 upset. But the Eskimos were a battered group going into that Grey Cup game against Ottawa. They had just finished a gruelling best-of-three playoff series, against Winnipeg, with all three games played in the space of a week. Johnny Bright was hospitalized with two severe charley horses after the series and doctors had to drain blood from his legs to reduce the swelling enough that he could walk. He walked out of the hospital in Edmonton on Thursday, arrived in Vancouver late that night, briefly worked out with the team on Friday, and Saturday took part in the Grey Cup game.

Bright wasn't the only Eskimo backfield member hurting. Parker, Kwong, and Miles were all hobbled by various injuries. Most professional athletes facing a championship game want to play and will hide their injuries, lie about the extent of their injuries, or do and say whatever it takes to get the go-ahead to play from their coach. That was a lot easier to get away with before there were regulations and procedures and medical interventionists and agents, as there are today, that prevent an individual from risking his future career and maybe his life by playing. But in this case, the entire Edmonton backfield might as well have spent the game in the infirmary. Ottawa won 16–6, not a huge disparity in points, but they also managed to hold the trio of Parker, Kwong, and Bright to a mere twenty-two yards rushing.

That game really marked the last gasp of that once-formidable backfield. Normie Kwong retired after the Grey Cup game that year. Rollie Miles retired following the 1961 season. Jackie Parker was traded to

Toronto in 1963. And Johnny Bright, after a couple of seasons of seeing his workload reduced to near irrelevance, retired in 1964. If you had told any of those four back in 1956 that they had won their last Grey Cup as a unit, they would have never believed it. Sure, a season can fall short of expectations and anything can happen in one game, as it did that day against Winnipeg in 1957, when the Edmonton kicker missed nine field goal attempts and never got so much as a single out of any of them. But 1958 through 1960 with Johnny Bright racking up an average of 1,450 yards per season? In that light, three Grey Cup championships, regardless of their being in a row, could be seen as a disappointment.

When Johnny Bright retired, Maury White of the *Des Moines Register*, the sportswriter who had sat next to Drake news director Paul Morrison for that game in Stillwater, Oklahoma, thirteen years before, wrote in his column of August 26, 1965: "The world's best distance runners can cover eight miles, ninety-nine yards in about thirty-eight minutes. It took Johnny Bright sixteen years to gallop that exact yardage. Of course, people kept knocking Bright down."

What White did not say is that for every time Johnny Bright got knocked down, he got right back up. After his retirement from football, Bright went into teaching full-time, as did his great friend and former teammate Rollie Miles, taking up teaching and coaching in the Edmonton Catholic School Board system immediately upon his retirement in 1961. Today, there's an athletic field with a track, bleachers, and a soccer pitch in Edmonton named in his honour: the Rollie Miles Athletic Field.

On September 15, 2010, the Johnny Bright School opened in Edmonton. Principal Scott Miller addressed the media that day on Bright's legacy as an educator and citizen of Edmonton, accomplishments in his life beyond the confines of the gridiron.

"We are able to go to the heritage that Johnny Bright gives us. The sense of excellence. We speak about three pillars. We speak about excellence in academics, excellence in athletics and activities, and excellence in citizenship."

For his part in the Johnny Bright Incident, Wilbanks Smith always claimed innocence as far as the hit's being racially motivated. To his way of thinking, it was not even an illegal hit. It was just a message. *Look out*, it said, *I'm coming for you.* The NCAA introduced measures the following year to discourage the kind of head-hunting Smith displayed that day. One rule read, "In an effort to discourage rough play and make it more costly, ejection from the game has become mandatory in cases of flagrant personal fouls."

There was a second rule change introduced as a result of the Johnny Bright Incident and that involved players' equipment: face masks and mouth guards are now mandatory in college football. Neither change could guarantee that such an event would not take place again, but at least the game was recognizing the potential dangers to the victims of such blatant attacks. And with the national coverage given this incident courtesy of Ultang and Robinson's photography, on-field officials now understood that they could not afford to turn a blind eye to such egregious actions in case an eye in the stands was watching. The advent of televised games would bring the kind of wilful ignorance displayed by the officials in Stillwater on that October 1951 day to an end.

"There's no way it couldn't have been racially motivated," Johnny Bright said years later in an interview with the *Des Moines Register*. "What I like about the whole deal now, and what I'm smug enough to say, is that getting a broken jaw has somehow made college athletics better. It made the NCAA take a hard look and clean up some things that were bad."

In 2005, fifty-four years after the infamous incident, Oklahoma State University (formerly Oklahoma A&M) president David Schmidly wrote an official apology to Drake's president, David Maxwell. It read, in part: "The incident was an ugly mark on Oklahoma State University and college football and we regret the harm it caused Johnny Bright, your university, and many others...." President H.G. Harmon, who had argued so vehemently for action against either Wilbanks Smith or Oklahoma A&M on Bright's behalf, was not alive to receive the long-awaited apology. Neither was Drake's head coach at the time, Warren Gaer, who had encouraged Bright to follow his heart in signing with Calgary and declared that in all his years of coaching, Johnny Bright was the best he'd ever seen. And then there was the man himself at the centre, Johnny Bright, the man whose injuries had touched off the national debate. He had died in 1983 of a massive heart attack in an Edmonton hospital while undergoing anaesthetic preparation for knee surgery. The only one of the major players in the original gridiron drama still living was Wilbanks Smith, and he felt bitter and betrayed by the apology issued by his alma mater. He was now a man alone.

At Drake University today, all the Bulldogs players learn the story of Johnny Bright, the greatest football player the school has ever seen. It's hard to avoid his name. In 2006, the field at Drake Stadium in Des Moines, Iowa, was renamed Johnny Bright Field. Every time those players step on that field they're reminded of his courage, commitment, and singular talent.

Chapter Six

CHUCK E. AND THE CATS

In Jael Ealey Richardson's memoir *The Stone Thrower*, about her relationship with her famous quarterback father, she conjures up an image of Chuck Ealey as a ten-year-old boy hanging out by the railroad tracks on a daily basis with a handful of stones, waiting for the train dragging coal cars labelled Norfolk and Western "in faded yellow" to appear.

"The train moves faster and the ground rumbles as the train roars towards him. He selects a stone and pulls his arm back as a gust of wind rushes through him, the train passing quickly.... He watches for the light between the cars.... He narrows his eyes to focus. *Wait. Light. Throw.* The stone flies toward the coal train, the cars rocking with the rapid motion of the rails. BANG! The rock lands on the *N* and the boy shakes his fist in triumph."

The story manages to create a mythical origin for a quarterback's golden arm, the pinpoint accuracy that led to an unbeaten record as a starting quarterback in high school and university, while at the same time painting a picture of a time, a place, and a set of economic circumstances where a poor black kid entertained himself by hurling stones at passing freight trains. In Portsmouth, Ohio, where Chuck Ealey grew up, there wasn't an obvious metaphorical barrier like tracks that divided the haves from the have-nots. That barrier was a line defined nearly 350 years earlier when the first slave ship hit port in the New World carrying its human cargo below deck.

"You've got to remember during that time growing up, we weren't in the South," Chuck Ealey told me in his Investors Group Mississauga office; it's not the most visually interesting location for our interview, but Chuck appears to be in his element behind a desk. "We were just right across the river from Kentucky in Ohio on the Ohio River. [But] it was almost a Southern flavour, so there was a lot of segregation things that were going on. I lived in what were the 'projects.' You don't have 'projects' here in Canada, not like we have in the States. That area of town was called the North End. That's where we lived. All the black people lived there."

Chuck Ealey isn't kidding about "Southern flavour." Portsmouth's motto is "Where Southern hospitality begins." That's one way of looking at it. Or you could add a second line to complete the thought: "… and Southern attitudes prevail." Although Black Americans make up only 5 percent of the population of Portsmouth, 95 percent of them live in the city's north end where Chuck grew up.

Portsmouth was founded at the confluence of the Scioto and Ohio Rivers in southern Ohio, which made it perfectly situated as a manufacturing base and shipping centre. The population peaked in 1930 at 40,000 but since then has steadily decreased with the loss of industry, a story too common across America, and has now bottomed out at 20,000 inhabitants. Portsmouth is no longer the thriving industrial town of the last century where work was plentiful and easy to find. These days it is better known for its drug problems, predominantly in prescription drugs and specifically OxyContin or, as it is more euphemistically called, "hillbilly heroin." And anywhere you have drug problems you are bound to find an increase in crime.

Chuck's parents divorced when he was four years old. His father, an alcoholic and an itinerant worker, was around, living a shadowy existence in rumours but not a part of Chuck's life. Chuck was raised by his mother, Earline, who cleaned white homes and worked in the local hospital as a nurse's assistant. He converted to Catholicism at seven years old, went to a Catholic middle school, and then started at Notre Dame High School in 1964.

"Growing up in that period of time, mid-late '50s, early '60s, you kind of grew into something that was a prejudicial environment. You understood it. You knew where you shouldn't go, but going outside of the area wasn't like you crossed the line and now you had to be looking over your shoulder. You understood where the black community was, where the white community was, what type of prejudicial issues you were going to run into, but you weren't always running into them. It wasn't a case where you were fearful to go to the high school, that you were fearful to walk in the area. You could go into an area, and someone could call your name or act foolish, and *you moved on.* So it was just a way of the times. There was a great deal of turmoil in society as a whole, and I was just a product of that turmoil. At any time you could run into something that was not necessarily favourable for you racially."

It was not until his junior year at Notre Dame that he got his chance to start at quarterback. He never looked back. Without a father in the picture, Chuck came to view his football coach, Ed Miller, as something of a father figure.

"I had mentors of older guys in the area playing sports like football and basketball that I wanted to be like. So there were community mentors. But Ed Miller became more like a father figure — teaching things about drive and discipline and direction."

Some of the methods that Coach Miller used to instill "drive and discipline and direction" in his players back in the '60s would most definitely be frowned upon today. These were high-school kids, after all, not Special Forces. Coach Miller would withhold liquids during training, substituting salt tablets instead, to make his team more mentally tough. One of the trainers used to soak a towel in cold water so that players he was tending to could suck water from the fabric under the coach's radar. Whether or not restrictions of this sort actually made the players mentally tougher than their opponents is questionable. But it allowed them to *believe* that they were tougher than the other guys, which was more the point of the whole exercise.

Coach Miller not only made Chuck the starting quarterback, he made him the nonpareil star of the team. Each week, a top star of the game would be announced by the coaching staff and for one week that chosen player would get to drive the team's prize car around town, showing off. But it seemed that no matter what a player did on the field in any game, the star of the week, week after week, was always Chuck

Ealey. This clear favouritism drove everyone on the team crazy, but once again it accomplished the coach's purpose. It made every player work that much harder in each and every game to try to unseat Chuck. The car became secondary, a mere status symbol. What it really meant was *I beat out Chuck Ealey.*

Notre Dame's chief rivals were West Portsmouth, who regularly filled a 20,000-seat stadium for their home games. For a Canadian, attendance numbers like that and facilities capable of holding crowds that size at the high-school level seem unimaginable, but in the States, *Friday Night Lights* is not the exception, it's the rule. A stadium like "the Big House" in Ann Arbor, home to the University of Michigan Wolverines, has a seating capacity in excess of 109,000, a mind-boggling number for the average Canadian. The Western University Mustangs, one of the most success-ful college football teams in Canada, play their home games at the TD Stadium, which was built in 2000 to accommodate their devoted fan base. It has a capacity of 8,000, a spit in the ocean that is the American football industry. If Western was ever to play a home game against Michigan, there would be 101,000 displaced persons roaming the streets of London clamouring for a non-existent ticket.

As a small school, Notre Dame played not only West Portsmouth but also other small schools in rural southern Ohio. Notre Dame did have the distinction — or notoriety — of having the only integrated football team in the region, and that just meant they had Chuck and his friend Al Bass. Those two players could be usually called upon to receive their share of attention from opposing teams as well as their fans. Parents of the Notre Dame players were called upon to escort their sons to the team bus after games against West Portsmouth to protect them from thrown objects and curses. White players were under as much fire as their black teammates for the crime of being associated with a team that contained black athletes.

But perhaps the worst indignity occurred when West Portsmouth supporters — oh, let's call them *vandals* — painted a statue of the Blessed Virgin Mary situated in front of Notre Dame High School with black paint *in honour* of Chuck Ealey and Al Bass. If the plan was to get under the skin of the Notre Dame football team, the perpetrators of this sacrilege failed miserably. Notre Dame went undefeated two straight years with

Chuck Ealey at quarterback. That was the beginning of the legend, the unbeatable quarterback.

Bruce Smith grew up in the shadow of Huntsville Prison, more properly called Texas State Penitentiary at Huntsville or Huntsville Unit. It's commonly known as the Walls Unit, so named for its iconic red brick walls. At one time back in the nineteenth century, the prison was reserved for white Texans. This was segregation with a macabre edge. Only whites were accorded jail time; black people were summarily whipped or hanged, the only two options available. Since 1982 and the reinstatement of the death penalty in Texas, 553 death-row prisoners have been executed there by lethal injection. Before this more "humane" method was introduced, the preferred treatment was a massive jolt in "Old Sparky," the state-owned electric chair introduced in 1924 and retired in 1964, which was used to electrocute 364 inmates. If you happen to be feeling peculiarly nostalgic, you can still visit Old Sparky anytime at the Texas Prison Museum out on Interstate 45 north of Huntsville.

Every day on his way to school, Bruce Smith had to pass those iconic red walls looming over him. This was his peculiar bogeyman, a child's daily experience of dread like the huge growling dog on a neighbour's chain that pulls the beast up just short of the sidewalk, the haunted house covered in vines and inhabited by evil witches, or the bully's house that must be passed alone. The walls erected to keep prisoners inside formed their own prison in the mind of Bruce Smith. *If you don't get out of this town this is where you'll end up.* A fatalism born of racism and poverty. And there was a third option open: death. A chill crept into his voice when he spoke of his memories of that institution.

"Huntsville prison was a real bastion of brutality, man. You walk by this big wall, all you could see was a guy up in the gun tower with his dark glasses on like in *Cool Hand Luke,* and you knew, man, that you didn't want to go there. Not a place I wanted to go. And unfortunately, there were a lot of black people in there. For things like one marijuana stick — life in prison. It was just ridiculous. Over fifty percent of the population there was black."

The highlight of the year in Huntsville was the Texas Prison Rodeo, held on weekends throughout October. People came from out of state for the thrill of watching inmates — black and white — busting broncos, riding bulls, and roping calves. One event you didn't find on a regular rodeo circuit, for the obvious reason that it was far too dangerous, was twenty-five inmates in bright red shirts competing with each other to be the first to pry a bag of tobacco loose from a raging bull's horns without getting maimed, stomped, or gored in the act. So great was the demand for tickets that a 20,000-seat stadium was built to accommodate the crowds. What better attraction than a bunch of performers *with nothing to lose?*

Bruce grew up fatherless. The first time Smith remembered seeing his father, he was eleven years old, when his father had invited Bruce and his brothers and sister to visit him in California.

"I remember him driving up in this big shiny Cadillac," Bruce said, seated at one end of a leather couch in front of a window in the Toronto art gallery where we met. The late-afternoon traffic rushed by outside. "Man, was I excited — until I saw this cute little black Barbie-doll-looking woman sitting where my mama should have been sitting. I made up my mind right then not to like her; this would be war."

That anger built up during his adolescent years, creating deep emotional scars that Smith claimed turned him into a bully and got him into a lot of trouble at school. He wasn't just big for his age, he was big for his size. In today's world he would have been the type of kid targeted by anti-bullying campaigns. Sports became an outlet for much of his anger.

"In high school, we only knew about black football," he said. "We didn't know nothing about white football. Everything was black, my high school was black. I was playing basketball, baseball, and football; it was all black. They wouldn't allow us to play with the white kids. You weren't allowed to ride on the same bus as the white kids, we weren't allowed to eat in the same restaurants. We used to eat at the back. You go into the back door, and sit down and eat. There was a special place for coloured only. As a matter of fact, even in the water fountains, it said coloured boys or coloured girls. Everything was marked. We didn't think anything of it. We felt that's just the way it was. We actually felt — at least I did — that white people were superior."

In 1961, the first Freedom Riders began their campaign to pro-test the non-enforcement in the South of the Supreme Court decision against segregated public transit. The first bus loaded with both black and white civil rights activists was to travel from Washington, D.C., to New Orleans. The bus never got that far. It was met by Ku Klux Klan members in Alabama, who slashed the tires and firebombed the bus with the passengers still aboard. A mob tried to keep the people from getting out. They actually believed that these riders deserved to burn to death for their activism. The riders did manage to escape the flames, only to be beaten half to death by the mob. But their message had taken hold and spread far and wide. Soon there were Freedom Riders coming from as far away as Canada to take part in these rides through the South. One of these buses pulled into Huntsville, Texas, in 1966 and the riders began to spread their message.

"I lived in a little place called 'the Alley,'" said Bruce. "One way in, one way out. It was a narrow little place, shacks on both sides of the alley, hardly enough room for a car to drive down, so at the end of the alley [the Freedom Riders] set up shop. I remember the theme song was called, 'Hey you!' just like in the army, and I was like, that's me, they're talking to me. There's these people from up north, a couple of white folk, saying 'Hey, you don't have to eat in the back of a restaurant anymore! You can ride at the front of the bus!' We said, 'That's crazy; they'd shoot you for that!' So I remember we went to our first meeting. They told us about Rosa Parks, they told us about what was happening in other places in America now. How black people were fighting for their civil rights.… So we started to walk and carry our signs, 'We shall overcome' — that was our song."

Rather than institute full-scale integration in 1966, the state of Texas decided it would phase in integration gradually and in select areas.

"They sent — to an all-black school, my school — they sent us a couple white teachers, some white students, and three white coaches. Three white coaches to an all-black school. We freaked out! I said, no way, no way, absolutely no way, will I ever play for a white coach. And they sent us a nervous little white guy, a little fat guy named Morris Magee. I said, 'Well your time here won't be long.'"

Bruce organized a boycott by a number of the black players on his high-school team. Although he had experienced something of a political awakening through the Freedom Riders, his scope was very narrow. He treated it as something of a lark, an opportunity to cut classes or cause trouble. He would have been the first to tell you he lacked conviction.

"We used to sit up in the stands during practice, and those who went along with the white program we called an Uncle Tom. So we're sitting up there, 'You Uncle Tom! You no-good Uncle Tom!' And we were just making fun of the guys. But after two days of that we got bored and wanted to play."

The question was how to continue to protest against the white coaches and still play football. Bruce gathered his charges together and laid out the plan. They would go back to the team, practise as usual, but when it came game time they would just make no effort to block, no effort to tackle. They would make their statement where it hurt the most, on the field and in front of the coaches and the fans. No one would miss the point. And that's what they did during the next game against a highly rated team. At least half the team didn't block, tackle, or make any discernible effort. At halftime they were down 32–0, and those responsible were having a good laugh about it in the locker room.

"We had this young coach named Skeeter. He was only about nineteen or twenty, probably just graduated from university. This guy was red as a beet. He was so mad! You could see smoke coming out of his ears. And he picks up this helmet and slams it against the wall! Against a locker. BAM! He got our attention, let me tell you. So Skeeter decided he was going to talk to us. 'You know, if I were you, I'd probably be doing the same thing.' He said, 'You know what, if you do this, you're going to make everything white people say true about you. If you're going to make a difference, you go out there, and you play the best you can. You show white people you are every bit as good or better than the white teams.' Let me tell you, the speech worked because we only lost that game by two points. And after that game, we galvanized, and we really felt that these coaches were really for us — and they were."

Under that "nervous little white guy," Morris Magee, Bruce blossomed as a football player in his senior year. He had never worked out in his life, but under Coach Magee he began to train hard and for the first time began to take this game of football seriously. It wasn't long before the Samuel Walker Houston High School football team became the best team in the district and Bruce was named captain and Most Valuable Player. He used that outstanding senior year to attain scholarship offers from a number of black universities, including Texas Southern and Prairie View.

He had yet to make up his mind when one day he heard his name over the school intercom telling him to go to the cafeteria. His first thought was, *What did I do now?* When he walked into the cafeteria he noticed a tall, thin, bald-headed white man wandering about on the periphery of the tables. Once again, Bruce's defensive instincts kicked into paranoid overdrive as his mind shuffled through a mental file of possible misdemeanours. *This guy must be a cop.*

That "cop" turned out to be Eddie Crowder, head coach of the University of Colorado Buffaloes football team. He had been scouting players from larger schools in the Houston area when he'd seen this massive linebacker from Huntsville, #61, running all over the field destroying everyone who dared touch the football. Inquiries were made. And that's how Eddie Crowder happened to be wandering about the Samuel Walker Houston High School cafeteria in search of Bruce Smith.

"How'd you like to go to University of Colorado?"

"Where's that?"

"You ever been to the mountains?"

"Nope."

"How'd you like to fly on an airplane?"

"Not too sure about that one."

"How'd you like to be on national TV? You could be playing for a big-time school and be on television next year."

"Sounds good, man. Let me think about it."

There was, however, a caveat.

"All you have to do is take the SAT test and the ACT test. Pass the tests, and you're in."

"Oh, no problem, no problem," Bruce assured him.

Though Bruce was quick with the cocky response, on the inside he was anything but. *ACT test? That's the same test the white kids have to take,* he thought. *How in the world am I going to pass a test that the white kids take?* The old beliefs and fears resurfaced that maybe white people really were superior and that all the things the Freedom Riders had preached about equality were a lie. So he pretended that he wasn't interested. *Who wants to go live in the mountains anyway? I'd rather stay in Texas.* But Coach Magee wasn't going to make it easy for him.

"What about Colorado, Bruce? You could be doing this town a real justice, son. No one from this town has ever gone to a major university. Black or white. You'd be the first!"

Bruce finally capitulated and took the test to get his coach off his back. In his heart, he knew he had failed. How could he not? He couldn't possibly compete with the white kids off the playing field. He put Colorado out of his mind. Instead he turned his mind toward Alcorn State, an all-black university in Mississippi with one of the best football programs in the country. They offered Bruce a full scholarship with a guarantee that he would be starting as a freshman. The road to the NFL looked like it might run right through Henderson Stadium in Lorman, Mississippi.

Morris Magee would not quit. He believed that Bruce was settling for Alcorn State as opposed to eagerly embracing it. Their daily greetings became a routine Q and A.

"What about Colorado?"

"Not interested."

Bruce held tight to his belief that he had failed on his ACT. Coach Magee went ahead and contacted the head coach at Sam Houston University, a major university right in Huntsville. How ironic that the football coach of a high school named after a former slave should reach out to the head coach of a university named after the former owner of that former slave. Only in America. Coach Magee had his hands full in promoting Bruce. Sam Houston had never had a black player on its football team.

"You need to talk to Bruce Smith. He's one of my kids."

"You talking about that black guy? That Negro player? We don't want any Negroes in our college."

"Well, let me tell you something. You don't have a football player on your team as good as him. I don't care if they're a senior or whatever, you'd be a fool if you don't give this boy a scholarship."

"Okay, we'll give him a look. I'm not promising anything."

Bruce was nervous showing up for camp at the Sam Houston University practice field, seventeen years old and the only black kid among the tryouts and veterans. He had drawn his own black cheering crowd, who were watching him through the fence because they were not allowed inside. One thing about Bruce: he never lacked for confidence on the playing field. Never met an opponent he couldn't beat. It was time to show this all-white team what Bruce Smith could do.

"We had our first practice and I just ate them up. I put a beating on those guys. People outside the fence were screaming and going crazy. The defensive coach really liked me. He said, 'Man, we would really like to have you here. You could start with us right now. Middle linebacker is your position.' The head coach though, the whole time I was there, the man never said one word to me."

Meanwhile, Bruce had gotten his test results from the University of Colorado but had left the envelope unopened for an entire month, so sure was he that he had failed. Finally, he opened it. "Lo and behold, I passed!" He went to his last practice at Sam Houston University, rejuvenated and bursting with pride, but he had still been given no indication by the head coach that there was a place for him on the team. As he left the dressing room that night, he discovered the head coach lurking in the shadows behind the facility where no one could see him. The coach called to him from the darkness, his face hidden.

"Hey Smith, come here. I want to talk to you."

"Okay. What about?"

"How would you like a scholarship to Sam Houston University?"

"You know what? That sounds really good. But you're a little late."

"What do you mean?"

"Have you ever heard of the University of Colorado? You ever hear of that place? Because that's where I'm going!"

There are more than 140 quarterbacks enshrined in the College Football Hall of Fame and Chick-fil-A Fan Experience. The Hall of Fame was located in South Bend, Indiana, until 2012. Attendance figures started going down. That's when the National Football Foundation, which runs the Hall of Fame, decided to move to a different market, a more football-friendly universe (and preferably one that served as headquarters for a chicken franchise).

Not one of those 140–odd quarterbacks in the Hall of Fame ever went 35–0 as a starter in American college football. But that's what Chuck Ealey's record was at the University of Toledo. In three seasons, with Chuck installed as number one (freshmen players were not allowed to play for the varsity squad), the Rockets never lost a game, including three straight Tangerine Bowl victories (now known as the Citrus Bowl) in Orlando, Florida.

Chuck Ealey is not in the College Football Hall of Fame.

Now, to be fair, the Hall of Fame has rules governing who gets in and who does not. It doesn't matter in any way what a player might do in his subsequent professional football career, so there are certainly NFL super-stars without a place of honour in the college hall. Here is the sticking point with Chuck Ealey. In order to qualify for a place in the Hall, a player must receive first-team All-American recognition by a selector on the NCAA's list of recognized sources. Chuck Ealey was recognized as such by the *Football News* in 1971. The problem is that the *Football News* was not on the NCAA's list of preferred sources in 1971. It is now, but it's too late for Chuck's bid.

One of the quarterbacks inducted in 2017 is Matt Leinart, former standout QB with the University of Southern California Trojans. No one questions whether Matt Leinart deserves to be in the College Football Hall of Fame. His credentials are impeccable. Over three seasons, he led the USC Trojans to a 37–2 record and a national championship, and on the personal side, he snagged the Heisman Trophy in his junior year. In his first year as a starter, he lost the fourth game of the season to the University of California in triple overtime. After that game and over the next three seasons, Leinart won thirty-four straight games, going into the 2006 Rose Bowl against Texas with a chance for the second national championship in a row.

But in many circles, the national championship between the top two teams in the country took second place to another storyline. If USC were to win the game and national championship, Matt Leinart would tie the existing record for consecutive victories by a college football starting quarterback — thirty-five games straight. That record had been in existence for thirty-four years and belonged to a little-known quarterback from Toledo University named Chuck Ealey. Overnight Chuck had been propelled from the shadows of obscure football trivia into the American limelight. He was suddenly relevant, three decades after his tenure as Toledo quarterback had ended.

For his part, Chuck was rather philosophical about it and grateful for the attention. Records, after all, are meant to be broken. In any interview, when confronted with questions of whether the fact that so few Americans knew of his record or even acknowledged the greatness of his feat was because of racism, he preferred to take the high road. He chose to say that no, he didn't think it was racism. It was because Toledo was a smaller college without brand recognition and, in the days before a multi-channel universe of football was available, Toledo was hardly the school of choice for a large network's televised game of the week. But as he noted in an ESPN interview in the build-up to the Rose Bowl, "It would be a record he would have that would go along with me. But he would have one loss." In other words, Leinart might tie the consecutive-wins mark but he would never be unbeaten, as Chuck had been.

As it turned out, Matt Leinart would have an excellent day at quarterback, completing twenty-nine of forty passes for 365 yards and one touchdown. But Vince Young, the young black quarterback for Texas, would have an even better day, rushing for three touchdowns himself in a 41–38 victory over the Trojans, including a last-minute touchdown and two-point conversion. The two best teams in college football throughout the season of 2005, both unbeaten, left it all on the field in one of the greatest national championships ever played. Lost in the excitement and post-game adulation poured on Vince Young from Texas was Matt Leinart's failure to match Chuck Ealey's winning streak — lost everywhere except among the Ealey family, the people of Portsmouth, and the fans of the Toledo University Rockets in Ohio. The legend of the unbeatable quarterback lived on.

Over Chuck's three seasons at quarterback, the Rockets outscored their opponents 1,152 to 344, which comes out to an average score of roughly 33–10. That is domination. Toledo's success cannot all be attributed to Chuck Ealey, as the team's defence led the nation all three seasons. The line was anchored by defensive tackle Mel Long, who'd become a decorated Vietnam War veteran before going to Toledo University. Mel Long played three seasons alongside Chuck Ealey. Mel Long is in the College Football Hall of Fame. Chuck is not.

Bruce Smith began that season of 1969, his sophomore year, as the starting defensive tackle. At some point during the season, he lost the starting job, not because of his on-field performance but because of his off-field one. When he first came to Colorado from Huntsville, he was something of a backward hick, and he sensed it and kept his distance from everyone, including many of the other black players. There were not many, only seven in that sophomore year, but when they had first arrived on campus, there had been a hierarchy. The more outstanding black players recruited from bigger-name high schools were given a more royal treatment. Bruce was not included in this group of elite athletes. He became something of a loner, except for a few local guys from Boulder, non-football players, who were bent on showing him the ropes in the big town.

"I remember this one guy named Buddy who grew up in Boulder. Buddy had a little MG and he said, 'How'd you like to go to a party?' So he took me to a party up in the mountains, we got the top down, we're roaring up the mountains in this little MG. Man, I'm thinking, *We're going to die!* So we get to the party and this white girl comes running up to him and gives him a big kiss. 'You have got to be kidding, man!' I said. 'They'd hang you for that where I'm from! I'm serious, man. You got a white girlfriend?!' 'Yeah, so what? I grew up like that.' 'Man, where I come from, you *look* at a white girl, and you're dead.' And that was the truth. And then I said, 'Man, this place is a little strange,' and I kept to myself. To be honest, I was really, *really* afraid, because I grew up in the South. You just didn't do that."

That all changed by his sophomore year. His roommate, who was black, was dating a white girl. And in a predominantly white university, in an overwhelmingly white city like Boulder, there simply wasn't an abundance of black women. Because of his size and strength, Bruce had acquired a Paul Bunyan–like reputation. Plus, he was a star on the football team, and that never hurt anyone's chances of finding a date. Bruce finally overcame his inhibitions about talking to white girls, and one in particular. Soon they were "going steady." And that's when the head coach, Eddie Crowder, called Bruce into his office to explain how things worked where he came from in Oklahoma and how they should work in Boulder, Colorado, especially if you were going to play for his team.

"You know something, Rob Bruce?" Coach Crowder always referred to Bruce as Rob Bruce. "You've got a great future."

"Thank you, Coach."

"But you know, Rob Bruce, where I come from we do things a little different."

"How's that, Coach?"

"Well, one thing, Rob Bruce, the coloureds and the white folk don't mix."

"So, why'd you bring us here?"

"Well, I think you understand what I'm saying."

Bruce understood what the coach was saying. He just chose to ignore it. Shortly after this meeting, Bruce was benched. No explanation, none required, point made. He was relegated to the role of full-time observer.

That benching included the Liberty Bowl victory over Alabama.

Bruce had always carried a large chip on his shoulder, ever since his father had cut out for California, abandoning the family, when Bruce was only four years old. Through the years, that chip continued to grow with each new perceived indignity. By the summer of 1970, that chip had become a beam large enough to support his house of anger. The benching proved to be a tipping point. He formed a gang with three other local black students. They called themselves "the Wild Bunch" after the characters in the Sam Peckinpah film of the same title. They wore long duster coats, straight out of a spaghetti western, and cut-off gloves, and they carried a shotgun and a .38 and went about the university campus starting fights anywhere, even in the middle of a crowded dance floor, inflicting maximum damage on whoever or whatever was unlucky enough to get in their way. Though Bruce never personally took drugs, he wasn't above selling them, especially to white people, a hugely profitable business in Boulder, Colorado.

"I really lost my mind. I really did. It was just a lot of anger, a lot of hatred, and I just felt, *I'm going to show these white people*."

Then one night the Wild Bunch engaged in a full-scale brawl against a bunch of white guys on campus. Somebody called the cops and everyone involved, black and white, was arrested. They were brought before a judge and, just as one of the white combatants was providing his testimony, the judge abruptly called a halt to the proceedings and ordered everyone into his chambers.

"He took the four of us and six or seven white guys into his chambers. Just as the white kids are set to speak, the judge says to them, 'I'd like for you to leave the room.' So they just left us in the room with the judge. He said, 'What's up with you guys? You guys are here; I assume you're on scholarship, otherwise, I don't know why you'd be here.' I was the only one who had a scholarship, by the way. He says, 'I don't know if you know or not, but Colorado has a lot of Ku Klux Klan.' And I'm like, 'What's he telling us this for?' He said, 'If I were you guys, I'd really watch it. I'd really cool it.' I'm like, 'This guy's really trying to frighten us and he's telling the truth.' He said, 'I'll tell you what. I'm going to let you go. I'm not going to charge you, but you've been warned.' And we said, 'Man, that was weird.' But we got rid of the guns and the gang disbanded."

Not long after this incident, Bruce woke up in the middle of the night covered in sweat, his heart beating wildly. He was having a full-blown anxiety attack.

"I thought, *If I don't turn my life around, I'm going back to Huntsville — on death row, picking cotton, or dead.*"

That was all the incentive he needed. Right then and there he experienced his epiphany. It was time to rededicate himself to the game of football, even though his chances of playing under an Eddie Crowder–led team seemed as remote as Tibet.

"I got up, and I started just running. I didn't know what else to do."

And he kept on running, training like he never had before. He managed to keep his scholarship. He continued to practise with the team but he had slid way down the depth chart. It would take an outbreak of crippling injuries to the defensive corps for him to get a chance to move up and out of Crowder's doghouse. Then one practice, they brought the scrubs and the doghouse dwellers in to defend against the starting offence. Bruce was in a particularly nasty mood. On the first play, he nearly tore the head off the starting fullback, Bobby Anderson. Cries of "Somebody block 61!" rose from the sidelines. Somebody tried to block 61 and nearly paid for it with his life. *Crunch.* Another back bit the dust. Bruce was a one-man wrecking crew. A ripple of fear went through the entire coaching staff. *Goddammit, he's going to kill somebody.* "Somebody block 61!" But Bruce was on a mission.

"Haven't you guys figured it out yet?! There ain't nobody here can block me!"

"Get back there, Smith!" shouted Anderson. A challenge. Bruce lined up. Gave him the sign. *Bring it on, baby.*

The fullback took the handoff. A hole opened up in the line. Then it slammed shut. *Crunch.* Anderson was slow to get to his feet.

"They couldn't find anybody to block me. So they said, okay number 61, you get over here, and you block for Bobby. So they put me on offensive. They would do anything to make sure I didn't play."

The hope was that Bruce would just get so frustrated being moved around from position to position, without a hope of getting into a game, that he would quit.

"So I get over to the other side and I'm blocking for Bobby. I got my defensive shoulder pads on and I'm blocking for Bobby. And of course I wipe out anybody who gets in Bobby's way. Nobody touches Bobby."

The next day, the coaches had the bright idea of putting Bruce in at fullback, where he was expected to do nothing but absorb punishment. A moving flesh-and-blood tackling dummy. He changed his number from 61 to 32. Put on running-back shoulder pads (as opposed to defensive tackle pads). Taped up his shoes. Got ready for business. There was only one problem with the coaches' plan: nobody could tackle Bruce. He was a horse in the backfield. Bodies hung from him as he dragged them downfield.

So, they left him in the backfield. Way down the list where he'd never see the gridiron except from the bench.

The Buffaloes' next game was against the University of Kansas Jayhawks, to be played in Memorial Stadium, in Lawrence, Kansas. Bruce was fifth or sixth on the depth chart of running backs, playing behind a back named Ward Walsh (who would go on to play for the Green Bay Packers). Walsh was in a panic knowing he was going to have to block for their star running back, Bobby Anderson, against a real beast, Emery Hicks, a linebacker known as the Tasmanian Devil around the league for his vicious tackling. Hicks stood six foot six and weighed 230 pounds. All muscle.

"Ward couldn't sleep that night," said Bruce, his face lighting up with the memory. "I said, 'Man, I heard this guy eats nails.' I was just messing with his head. I said, 'Man, this is the one game I'm glad I'm not playing. Did you see him the last game? I think he was in on every tackle.' And Ward's eyes are like this." Bruce mimed Ward's state of shock, opening his eyes as wide as possible like he just stepped off a curb in front of a runaway Greyhound bus.

Late in the game, a rash of injuries to key players included Ward Walsh. Coach Crowder sent in Bruce with one specific job: block the Tasmanian Devil. In the huddle they called his number, 32. *There must be some mistake, man*, thought Bruce. *They want me to run the ball?* He took the handoff from the quarterback before 50,000 pairs of eyes all glued to this massive running back crashing through the line. Not even a Tasmanian Devil could bring down this bull. Forty-five yards later, the Jayhawks' tacklers finally brought Bruce to the ground. His teammates were all over him, pounding his pads. Shouts of "Man, I told you this guy could play!" and "He should be starting!" arose from his teammates. Many of them patted him on the back as he left the field. He got in for one more play, shook off a couple of would-be tacklers behind the line of scrimmage, and gained seven yards and a first down.

That was it. He never played another down that season. In his senior year, Bruce managed to get into four games. One of those was against the Air Force Academy Falcons. By his own admission, Bruce had "a monster game." So impressed was the Air Force head coach, Ben Martin, that he referred Bruce to the head coach of the Winnipeg Blue Bombers, Jim Spavital. Bruce was excited at the prospect of playing professional football anywhere after his college career had gone south along with his NFL draft status. But the coaching community is a tightly knit brotherhood, and when Jim Spavital did his due diligence and reached out to Colorado's Crowder for his input, he received a less than glowing report. When Bruce arrived at Winnipeg's camp, the first words out of his new head coach's mouth were, "We've got our eye on you. We don't want any troublemakers here."

Spavital, a native Oklahoman, had played his college football at Oklahoma A&M, the same school that, only three years after Spavital had graduated, would find its football program under fire for its open attack on Johnny Bright. His pre-judgment of Bruce based on Crowder's assessment did nothing to endear him with the prickly tackle. Bruce worked hard to make the team, which he did, only to tell the head coach what he could do with the job.

"I told Spavital I would never play for him if he was the only coach on planet Earth."

He found his way to Philadelphia looking to find a job with the Eagles under their head coach, Jerry Williams. Bruce didn't make the roster but he did make an impression on Williams, who, after being fired by the

Eagles, was hired by the Hamilton Tiger-Cats to guide the club into the 1972 season. Williams brought Bruce in for a tryout.

"I remember coming to Hamilton in June of 1972, wearing an overcoat, stocking cap, and gloves, thinking it would be freezing. It was ninety-five degrees."

Bruce understood that you didn't get a lot of second or especially third chances in professional football. If you were black and had been labelled a "troublemaker," coaches were not inclined to give you the benefit of the doubt in any situation. He decided to let his work ethic and his play on the field do his talking for him. He also had the benefit of a coach who saw the enormous potential in Bruce's game and wasn't troubled by his past. He was reunited on defence that first day with his former fearsome foe, the Tasmanian Devil of Kansas fame, Emery Hicks. Bruce took note of another black rookie in camp, a quarterback from the University of Toledo. Story was he'd never lost a game in high school or college. There were already rumours he had the "magic touch."

But Bruce had more important issues on his mind than the fate of some skinny quarterback trying to make the team.

"I decided when I came to Canada, to Hamilton, there was no way I was leaving. I came here with one goal in mind: to make the team. And I made the team the first day. I went against as many guys as would come at me and I basically made the team as a free agent the first practice."

Soon the rest of the league would see what Jerry Williams saw that day. When Bruce Smith put his mind and his body to a task, he could move mountains.

> The candlepower in the Glass Bowl is so low that at night the place is more suitable for séances or Halloween parties than the home games of the University of Toledo Rockets. But they have this hobgoblin quarterback named Chuck Ealey who flits in and out of the shadows to elude tacklers, then zings the ball right on the button to one of his receivers, all of whom can see in the dark like owls. His teammates have an almost mystical belief in his ability to get them out of any jam.
>
> — Joe Jares, *Sports Illustrated*, October 11, 1971

Joe Jares's article about the Toledo team appeared in *Sports Illustrated* after Chuck Ealey and the Rockets had stretched their winning streak to twenty-seven games in a hard-fought victory over Ohio University (no, not the Buckeyes, the other one). The article was titled "Holy Toledo! Chuck Ealey Nearly Lost One." That put Chuck's personal winning streak at fifty-seven games, including the thirty straight he'd attained playing for Notre Dame High School in Portsmouth.

At what point does someone start to believe that he is truly gifted with some otherworldly protection against defeat? Was there a moment where Chuck Ealey wondered whether he had been dipped in a version of the mythical River Styx by his mother — perhaps at the confluence of the Ohio and Scioto Rivers? The secret of his success, removing the general quality of the team surrounding him from the equation, was a combination of confidence and fearlessness equalling grace under pressure. "Fearlessness" meant being unafraid to lose even as the streak grew in number.

"It's not whether [the opposition is] going to beat us or not, but how bad they are going to get beat," he said after the Ohio game. "That's the way I feel."

Two weeks after narrowly escaping defeat at the hands of the Ohio Bobcats, Chuck Ealey and the Rockets met the Broncos of Western Michigan for a homecoming game at the Glass Bowl in Toledo. By half-time the home team was behind 24–7 and a general gloominess had descended on the crowd. The unbeaten streak looked to be coming to an end. There would be no modern fairy-tale ending with the Rockets players disappearing into a cornfield after victory number thirty-five.

But the second half saw a complete turnaround as Chuck and the offence pounded the hapless Broncos into submission, scoring twenty-one points in the fourth quarter alone while the defence completely shut down the Western Michigan attack. The final score was 35–24. Number twenty-nine was in the bag. The rest of the regular season was a series of routs that saw Toledo demolish Dayton 35–7, Miami (of Ohio) 45–6, Northern Illinois 23–8, Marshall 43–0, and Kent State 41–6. Not one team came within two touchdowns of the Rockets.

"I said to one of my teammates after the last game against Kent State, the thirty-fourth win, I said, 'I don't think we understand what we did here.' And we didn't. Each game we were kind of taking one game at a time. And

I know that sounds like a cliché — but that's the way it really was. I don't think at any point we were afraid to think about losing in the sense that it would break the streak. We were never thinking we had a streak. And to this day, the only reason it's come up is because they put it in the history books."

Only one game remained in Toledo's season. For the third year in a row, the Rockets, winners of the Mid-American Conference, were going to the Tangerine Bowl in Orlando, Florida. Their opponents would be the winners of the Southern Conference, the University of Richmond Spiders. The unbeaten Rockets were heavy favourites over the Spiders, who, despite winning their conference, had a mediocre record of 5–6. The surprising Spiders led at the end of the first quarter by a 3–0 score but by full-time, the planets had realigned and order had been restored in the football universe. Toledo won the game handily, 28–3, completing a third straight unbeaten season.

For six straight seasons as a starting quarterback, first in high school and then at university, Chuck Ealey had never known defeat. Not once did he have to look back on a game and think, *If only I'd done this and not that,* and berate himself for failing his teammates. He had gone 65 and 0 in that time — *65 and 0!* He had received national rec-ognition in the pages of *Sports Illustrated,* and for the very first time a player from the Mid-American Conference was in consideration for the Heisman Trophy. He would finish eighth in the final Heisman voting that year. The Toledo Rockets would finish fourteenth in col-lege football rankings at season's end, which is more indicative of the perceived quality of the competition in the Mid-American Conference among the nation's pollsters.

Although football is a team game, the one position that most assuredly makes a perceptible difference, game in and game out, is the quarterback. He's the one you turn to on the sidelines or in the huddle for a sign. To the defence: *just get me the ball back.* To the receivers: *just get open and I'll find you.* To his blockers: *just give me time to do my job.* A quarterback who can turn his teammates (and even the opposition) into true believers is a rare thing indeed.

All of which only makes the 1972 NFL draft all the more puzzling. Chuck and his agent had sent a letter out to all twenty-six teams notify-ing them that he wanted to be drafted as a quarterback and to be given an opportunity to compete for the quarterback position with the team that drafted him. It had been a common practice to draft black quarterbacks with the expectation that they would make good defensive backs or receivers. Chuck made it known that he was not interested in any other position. It was a bold move for a black quarterback coming out of the college game, but it was one that Chuck felt that he could afford to make.

"Most people think you're going into football to get a scholarship so you can play professional ball. Honestly, all the way through I didn't even think about playing professional football until probably my junior or senior year when some scouts came around and were looking at me. And I'm going, 'whatever.' That's kind of the way I felt about it ... professional football was kind of secondary to what I was looking to do."

Not one of the twenty-six NFL teams in existence in 1972 deigned to draft Chuck Ealey of the University of Toledo Rockets. Fourteen of those twenty-six teams had losing records. Four hundred and forty-two names were called over the course of seventeen rounds and not one of those belonged to Chuck Ealey. The Atlanta Falcons even had the audacity to waste a selection on one John Wayne out of "Fort Apache" State as a joke because their head coach, Norm Van Brocklin, had demanded that the scouts draft more "tough guys." Atlanta had just experienced their first winning record in six years of existence with a mediocre 7–6–1 record and yet they still felt they could afford to throw away a draft pick for the sake of an inside joke. (The commissioner of the league, Pete Rozelle, would overturn the pick.) Twenty quarterbacks were selected; only one of them ranked higher in the Heisman Trophy voting than Chuck Ealey at number eight, and that was the Heisman winner, Pat Sullivan, from Auburn.

Some teams did approach Chuck Ealey after the draft as if he might have had a change of heart and would consider signing a free-agent contract to play defensive back or wide receiver, but Chuck said no, not interested.

"My life didn't depend on sports or football. If I couldn't go into the league as a quarterback, I was going to do something else."

That's when the Hamilton Tiger-Cats reached out. They brought him up to Hamilton where he met with the general manager, Ralph Sazio, who sold him on the idea of playing in Canada.

"I didn't know much about Canada at all. I mean the only thing you study down there is American history; you get a little geography but I wasn't familiar with anything in Canada at all."

He was looking for something spectacular or exotic, something that would announce in no uncertain terms that he had entered the enchanted forest, an utterly foreign world. What he got instead was a whole lot of Highway 401 before entering Hamilton. No Eiffel Tower, no Arc de Triomphe, no Big Ben, and no Tower of London awaited him. Instead, he found a city that reminded him a lot of where he came from: an industrial, working-class town with economic and social demarcations.

"It wasn't anything you could notice right away, because everything *almost* looked the same, so I thought, *Everything's going to be okay.*"

After Ealey signed his contract, Sazio said, "You know, you aren't the first black quarterback to play here."

Not that it mattered to Chuck whether he was or he wasn't. He could only think that he was coming to a new country and a new league that he knew so little about. He was just happy that he was going to play quarterback.

"Oh?"

Sazio was only too happy to enlighten his new signee. "Ever hear of a guy named Bernie Custis?"

> This city of barbarians has an occasional moment of civility.
>
> Last night at Ivor Wynne Stadium, Ottawa Rough Riders engineered a last minute drive to beat the Ticats by a single point … ordinarily an occasion for throwing red hot rivets at the home side.
>
> But in the last few seconds, quarterback candidate Chuck Ealey ran around in frantic futility and earned a hand from the 21,000 souls in the ball park for an exhibition game.
>
> Ealey is the quarterback from the University of Toledo who never lost a game in high school or college football, and who was overlooked in the NFL draft, according to some sources because he is black and NFLers do not have confidence in black quarterbacks.

> For that reason alone, he could be the fans' favourite
> here in Hamilton where everyone is an underdog, but
> more than that, he's an exciting player who runs well
> and seems to have a strong arm and the required cool
> to do the job.
> — Eddie McCabe, *Ottawa Journal,* July 7, 1972

"This city of barbarians …" A tongue-in-cheek slight directed at the heavily working-class nature of Hamilton and its devoted, noisy, hearty football fans. Canadian football has always been a game that allowed fans to unleash the inner beast, behaving more along the line of British "football" (soccer) fans — minus the hooliganism — which is now beginning to inform fan behaviour at every sports venue short of the curling rink (whose day, too, could be coming).

But McCabe touches on something else here: the average Hamilton football fan's acceptance and adoration of the underdog. Oh, like any city's sports fans with a deep attachment to the home team bordering on psychopathy, Hamiltonians are just as capable of turning on their heroes. But it was Hamilton fans who twenty years earlier, according to Bernie Custis, would have rioted had Hamilton's head coach not started Bernie in the season opener after the hoopla surrounding his arrival in Steeltown. Chuck Ealey was the latest underdog to be embraced by the wide arms of Hamilton, and fans waited for his ascendancy to the position of starting quarterback.

"Oh yeah, the first season came and I was a rookie," said Chuck, remembering those first exhibition games. "I was playing, I was having a good exhibition season, good practice. I enjoyed the game because it was a wide-open field. It kind of suited my ability to manoeuvre and move around in the pocket or outside the pocket and throw the ball. So I was having a good time."

Jerry Williams had arrived in town that year as the new head coach. Williams had been a fighter pilot in the Pacific Theatre of the Second World War before attending Washington State University, where he became a football star. He was drafted by the Los Angeles Rams in 1949 and played four seasons there, winning the NFL Championship in 1951. He finished his career as a player/coach with the Philadelphia Eagles and went into coaching full-time, a journey that took him through the university coaching ranks and head-coaching stints at Philadelphia and Calgary, before he landed in Hamilton. The man had serious credentials. He was also new to most of the players. There were a couple of notable exceptions.

"I didn't like Jerry Williams," former All-Star defensive back John "Twiggy" Williams Sr. confessed, though a smile played across his face. We were sitting at his kitchen table in his home in Waterdown, a former municipality amalgamated into the city of Hamilton, Ontario, back in 2001. It had been almost ten years since I'd first interviewed him in this house, for the film. He was more relaxed this time, without a camera in his face. John had gotten his nickname during his playing days, a reference to '60s British model Twiggy, for his skinny legs. "I *hated* Jerry Williams. He cut me twice. In Calgary. And the last time he cut me, you know what he told me? He said, 'You can play in the National Football League. If you want me to I can write you a recommendation letter.' *But he cut me twice.* Unreal."

That was a result of arcane Canadian import rules and numbers games that many Canadian as well as American players have fallen victim to over the years. John Williams Sr. had been balancing on a bubble between making the team in Calgary and being released if another American came in, not necessarily a better American player than John, but one that might add insurance at another position deemed more valuable. But Jerry Williams did pay John Sr. a fee just to hang around in Calgary in case he was needed, a pretty standard practice throughout the league.

Bruce Smith, the other player known to Williams, carried his personal grievances like a Bay Street financier carried his billfold — deep-pocketed, close to his heart. Cross him and you were dead, not literally, but in his eyes you may as well have been. Criticism was hard to take. For him, it was deeply personal. That made coaching him all the more difficult. It could make just knowing him difficult.

"When I was playing I was totally introverted," Smith told me. "I would talk to nobody. I wouldn't talk to the media, I wouldn't talk to anybody. I said, if you wanted to talk to me, I do my talking on the field."

He tried his best to keep his unfocused anger hidden away. He was a professional now and he knew that he couldn't treat his adult teammates as he would have when he was younger and could get away with it because of his size. He was an imposing figure but these weren't boys he was playing with anymore. These were men, and if he wanted to get along as a teammate he had better learn the art of self-discipline and respect for others. His size could be a little frightening in itself.

"I remember when Bruce came in," said former running back Dave Buchanan when I pressed him for information about his old teammates on that 1972 Hamilton team. "Oh my God, this guy when he came in, he looked like Hercules!"

"Bruce had this thing, like a bad attitude," John Williams remembered. "He didn't get along with anybody. So I kind of took him under my wing because he was from Texas, too. I had a brand new corvette and I told Bruce, 'I'm gonna let you have my car tonight.' I let him have my car and he just thought that was the greatest thing in the world. I was the only one that could really handle him when he first came up here."

But Jerry Williams knew Bruce from his tryout with the Philadelphia Eagles. He saw the enormous potential in need of a focus. Early in the season, the Tiger-Cats were out for a meal in Montreal the night before the game. And it was there, during an innocuous team ritual of dining out, that Bruce's inner tension erupted in fury.

"We ordered roast beef, and I ordered an end-cut," said Smith. "I always ordered an end-cut. It was a bigger piece of meat, and it was well done. And I remember they brought this piece of meat to me, and it was raw."

Instead of simply calling over the waiter and explaining that the beef was too rare for his tastes and requesting that they cook it more to his liking, he took it as one more sign of disrespect. Something snapped inside him. He rose from his seat and threw his plate down on the table like a bad poker hand, cutlery flying everywhere. Without a word he stormed out of the dining room, went up to his room in the hotel, and slammed the door shut.

"I was just sitting there, fuming, and I hear this knock on the door. It was Coach Jerry Williams. He asked me, 'Can we talk?' And I said, 'We don't really have much to talk about.' And Jerry Williams came up to me and said, 'You know what, Bruce, I don't know if anybody ever told you this, but you are a very important member of our team.' He says, 'I know what you're going through. I know what you felt, but I have to tell you,

you don't have that problem with me. You are part of my team and you are one of my best players. And I appreciate having you here.'"

I could see that Bruce Smith was deeply moved by the memory of this white coach from Spokane, Washington, who, in a Canadian city a million miles from the poor black neighbourhood in the legalized-killing capital of America, showed compassion, kindness, understanding, and belief in this young man. Not a young *black* man, just a young man in need of guidance. An abandoned son who grew up believing that white people were superior because how would he know? Who was there to tell him different? He had never competed against them on the football field or in the classroom. All he knew was that *you'd better not go near their water fountains if you know what's good for you.* Why? Was the water that flowed through their fountains clearer, tastier, and superior as well? Was he not deserving of the same? And if a white man in authority wanted to see you, there's a good chance he thinks you've done something wrong. *You don't want to wind up in "the Walls," man.* Because that's exactly where he thought fate might lead him.

"I got to tell you, man, it flipped me out," Bruce continued. "I loved that man, and he accepted me, and he really made me feel like a son. And to me, that really meant something.... I think he was really instilling in me that I was more than a football player, I was a human being who had value. And let me tell you, that was probably one of the most touching things that ever happened to me."

The regular season started slowly for the Tiger-Cats.

"At that time Wally Gabler was the starting quarterback," Chuck Ealey remembered. "I think we won our first game maybe against Saskatchewan. Then we went out west on this western swing where it was this crazy thing where you played one game on Saturday and played another one on Tuesday. It was like three days' rest or two days' rest, something crazy."

The first game on that road trip was in Vancouver against the Lions, and Ealey played in the second half of a losing cause. Three days later he got the start in Edmonton and was relieved by Gabler in another losing cause. The team returned to Hamilton for a game against Montreal, which they also lost. Their record stood at 1–3 after four games. But a decision had been made.

"Well, the head coach [Jerry Williams] decided that if we were going to lose we were going to lose with this rookie quarterback," explained

John Williams. "And when he made the change to Chuck it just seemed like everything clicked."

Chuck Ealey would be the starting quarterback for the rest of the season, and Ralph Sazio dispatched Wally Gabler to Toronto to replace the injured Joe Theismann. And then the team went on a roll. They travelled to Montreal for a rematch against the Alouettes. This was the occasion of Bruce Smith's pre-game dinner meltdown. Whether Smith's outbreak had any influence on the team for the next day's game is a matter of conjecture, but the Tiger-Cats went out and beat the Alouettes 25–12 on their home field.

"There was something magic about Chuck Ealey," was how Bruce Smith described the rookie quarterback.

The players had heard of Chuck Ealey's unbeaten record in high school and at the University of Toledo. But in the pros, no one puts too much faith in reputations and records attained playing at a lower level. They respect what someone has accomplished, but it's still very much a "show me" league.

"We heard bits and pieces about Chuck's abilities that led to a perfect record," Tony Gabriel, former receiver with that '72 team, told me. "At the same time a lot of things are different when you become a professional."

His teammates didn't know it at the time but they were about to go on another magical Chuck Ealey–led ride, ten regular-season games in a row, a string that would lead directly to the Grey Cup game of 1972 and a matchup with the Saskatchewan Roughriders.

Dave Buchanan went to John Muir High School, which had switched in 1954 from a junior college to a full four-year high school. The most famous student to ever wander the school halls was none other than Jackie Robinson, who went on from John Muir to attend UCLA. In the years that Buchanan attended John Muir — he graduated in 1967 — the black students drew inspiration from the knowledge that the first Black American to play Major League Baseball graduated from their school.

"We wanted to live up to those expectations that he laid out," Buchanan told me over the phone from his home in Pasadena.

Buchanan, a running back, played college football with the Arizona State Sun Devils and was named the Western Athletic Conference's offensive player of the year in 1969. He went undrafted in the 1971 NFL draft and, instead, he signed as a free agent with the Cincinnati Bengals.

"What happened with the Bengals is I went all the way through to the last cut. And the running back coach came in to see me and said, 'Dave, we're going to put you on waivers. But don't go anywhere. The Hamilton Tiger-Cats have your negotiation rights in the CFL. But don't leave.'"

Buchanan paused in his narrative to admit that this was just the beginning of his problems in professional football, revolving around the business side of the game, which would be a recurring theme in the narrative arc of his professional career. But back to the running back coach and his pitch.

"We're going to put you on waivers so that when we get down to the proper roster level — and a team claims you off waivers — we're going to claim you right back. We're going to dangle you out there and dangle you back, dangle you out there, dangle you back. And then teams will say, 'Well, they're just going to keep doing that. And then we're gonna put you on the practice squad [or taxi squad …]'" and that's when Dave Buchanan had heard enough. "I said, 'I'm a better ballplayer than that' and I told him, 'You know what? I'm going to leave. I'm going to Canada and I'm going to make All-Pro and then I'm going to come back.' But what I didn't realize is once you leave, it's very difficult to come back to the National Football League."

And that's how he found himself in Hamilton, where he saw limited action over the course of nine games, rushing for 213 yards on sixty-two carries and catching eight passes for another fifty-six yards. But with the 1972 arrival of Jerry Williams — a coach that Buchanan called "a genius" — he forged a career year, rushing for 1,163 yards on 263 carries, and a further 275 yards receiving for nearly 1,500 yards in total offence. And there's one man in particular that he credited with the turnaround in his performance.

"Chuck [Ealey] was so dynamic it was like he'd always been our starting quarterback. I mean for a rookie or kid to come in there. Man, with Chuck's ability of being able to get out of difficult situations, he put so much pressure on defences. I will tell you that Chuck was as much responsible for the type of year that I had and all the other guys had as we were as individual players. The guy was so dangerous. When I watch that kid up in Seattle [Russell Wilson], I see him and think, *God, that's Chuck Ealey.* If you don't put a spy on that guy he's going to hurt you. And if you do put a spy on him now you're forcing everybody to cover man-to-man. And that's the way Chuck was."

Tony Gabriel was as close to a hometown boy as you could find on that 1972 Hamilton team, having been born in Burlington, one of eight brothers and four sisters. His father died when he was eleven years old and Tony felt the loss deeply. In the summer between grades twelve and thirteen, a friend convinced him to come and work out with the local junior football team, the Burlington Braves, coached by a former CFL player named Bernie Custis.

In a very short time, Bernie Custis had become more than a football coach for Tony. He had become a mentor and father figure. Bernie also seemed convinced that he could secure a scholarship for Tony at his old alma mater, Syracuse. So, one weekend that winter, Bernie and Tony, along with another Braves player, went down to Syracuse University for a football tryout with Bernie's old head coach at Syracuse, Ben Schwartzwalder. A couple of quarterbacks and some defenders were on hand at the Manley Field House to work out the two Burlington prospects for Coach Schwartzwalder.

Tony ran a pattern and made a quick cut, and the linebacker covering him went down on the slick field. Then he made another cut and the defensive back went down. The quarterback threw the pass. Tony reached out and snagged the ball with one hand and pulled it into his chest. Schwartzwalder turned to Bernie.

"I want that boy," he said.

Tony played four seasons at Syracuse University and earned a degree in chemical engineering. He had a chance to sign with the New York Giants of the NFL but chose Hamilton because, he admitted to me when we met in the boardroom of CIBC Wood-Gundy's offices in Oakville, "I was homesick," a perfectly natural state when you're one of twelve siblings. His rookie season with Hamilton in 1971 was "decent" but when Chuck Ealey arrived in 1972 "it really seemed to click."

"Initially, it took a couple of games to become familiar with his combination of scrambling and ability to throw on the run. Then with the natural talents that he had — and some of the good players we had on the team — we seemed to be able to connect. Chuck got better with each game. And it was obvious we were heading in the right direction."

After starting the season 1–3, Hamilton reeled off ten straight wins to finish with an 11–3 record and first place in the East. A number of Hamilton players had career years, including wide receiver Garney Henley (who would win the Schenley Award as Most Outstanding Player), Dave Buchanan, named CFL All-Star at running back, and Tony Gabriel, who had better years ahead but really kick-started his outstanding career in only his second year and was named to the CFL All-Star team as tight end.

"That year was a terrific year for me," remembered John Williams Sr., who also made the CFL All-Star team at defensive back. "I had something like nine interceptions. Two or three of them I ran back for touchdowns. That was my best year."

Chuck Ealey would be the runaway winner of the Most Outstanding Rookie award, but Jerry Williams would lose out on the Annis Stukus Award for coach of the year to the coach of their rival Ottawa Rough Riders, Jack Gotta, whose team lost all three games they played against Hamilton.

So it came as something of a surprise when Ottawa took the first game of the semifinal, 19–7. Jerry Williams was disappointed in the way his team had performed away from home but remained confident and relaxed leading into the second game on the artificial turf at Ivor Wynne Stadium. He referred to the two-game, total-points format as the "game of eight quarters," an outlook designed to reduce the emphasis on needing to win the next game by at least thirteen points. Instead, he encouraged his team to just think about it as being down thirteen points at the half with four quarters yet to play. Uphill but not insurmountable.

Dave Buchanan had a special incentive leading into the second game after what happened during the first game in Ottawa. One of Ottawa's cornerbacks had gotten right up in Buchanan's face and told him, "You can't run the ball."

"I'll never forget that," said Buchanan, still seething at the insult. "And that whole week I could just hear what that guy said and I had a headache I was so fired up for the game. And when we came out for that final game, I think I had a twenty-yard run but what I did — and I really think I could have broken it for a touchdown — I turned and went right for him. And I ran right over him. So whatever comment he made to me I made right back at him."

Buchanan rushed for over 130 yards in that game as the Tiger-Cats beat the Rough Riders by a score of 23–8, giving Hamilton the edge by an overall score of 30–27. The Tiger-Cats were going to the Grey Cup game against the champs from the West, the Saskatchewan Roughriders.

The Roughriders had experienced a mediocre season, going 8–8, before catching fire in the playoffs and ousting both Edmonton and Winnipeg, two teams with better records than them. But the Roughriders had three future Hall of Fame players: quarterback Ron Lancaster, running back George Reed, and defensive tackle Ed McQuarters, two of whom were black.

George Reed finished his career in 1975, having gained a total of 16,116 yards rushing over his thirteen-year career, a record that would stand for over thirty years until Mike Pringle travelled even farther. He had played his university football at Washington State and came to Regina in 1963. That's when he got his first look at Taylor Field, home of the Saskatchewan Roughriders. Reed experienced that most common of American reactions to the sight of some Canadian facilities — pure anxiety. *What have I got myself into?* As Hugh Campbell, Reed's former teammate at Washington and future coach of the Warren Moon–led Edmonton Eskimos, once said, "When I first saw the stadium in Regina, it looked like a farmer had built it."

Reed managed to play his entire career in Saskatchewan, a major feat in itself, especially since he made it known over the years that he had hardly been greeted with open arms by the citizenry of Regina. He remembers showing up for appointments to rent an apartment only to discover that the one he was looking to rent was suddenly unavailable. He spent most of his first couple of years living in hotels and depending on the kindness of teammates.

"I was debating whether I'd even come back after the second year," he told a reporter with the local CBC station in Regina.

Stardom and winning has a unique way of changing attitudes. The Roughriders made the playoffs every year that Reed played, including winning the Grey Cup in 1966 before losing in '67 and '69. He began working during the off-season for Molson breweries, touring the province, shaking hands, pushing product.

"Either I started warming to people or people started warming to me," he said.

Ed McQuarters was born in Oklahoma and played his college ball at Oklahoma University. He was drafted by the St. Louis Cardinals of the NFL but was released after a single season, an action that caused the black players on the Cardinals to declare the organization racist. In an article in *Sports Illustrated* from July 1968, writer Jack Olsen wrote: "The McQuarters case proves neither that the Cardinals have a quota system nor that Negroes are stacked into certain positions while white players get their jobs automatically, as is so often the case on college football teams. But it is suggestive of both possibilities. As one white Cardinal says, 'The front office has nobody but itself to blame if people run around accusing them of cutting Ed McQuarters for racial reasons.... It's possible the Negroes are only being touchy. But who the hell can blame them for being touchy the way they're treated around here.'"

The Cardinals' loss was the Roughriders' gain. In his first season, McQuarters helped Saskatchewan to its first Grey Cup win over the Eastern Rough Riders. He was a CFL All-Star in '67, '68, and '69, winning the league's Most Outstanding Lineman award in 1967. In 1971, the year before the 1972 Grey Cup against Hamilton, Ed McQuarters lost an eye in a freak accident in his home workshop. Despite this horrific mishap, he was able to return to action during the 1972 season and once again become a valuable part of the team's march to the Grey Cup game.

The sixtieth Grey Cup game — if anyone's counting — was played before a crowd of 33,393 fans, with a decided majority pulling for the hometown Tiger-Cats.

"That year, Hamilton outdrew everyone in the league. I think we averaged thirty-three thousand a game, and the stadium only seated about thirty thousand," laughed John Williams, while I sat wondering about overcrowded conditions and stadium disasters and just where they managed to cram in the other three to four thousand fans. "And they had wheelchairs and everything around the track and it was an exciting time. I remember they had a parade, they had Lorne Greene [a Canadian actor best known for his role as Ben Cartwright on the TV series *Bonanza* in the '60s] and all these kinds of people down on the field just before the game. But the thing is, I never got nervous. Everybody was telling me, 'You're going to be nervous,' and I asked the other guys before the game, 'Hey, when are you supposed to get nervous?'"

Asked whether he was nervous going into the game, Chuck Ealey said, "I think that the nerves you have in a game is pretty consistent with every game you go into. I don't think it was any different with this Grey Cup than any other game other than the fact that we were at home. When people see it from a fan standpoint, they see it as a big game. You see it as a game. There is no more pressure on you in that game, at least not for me, than any other game, because you were trying to win that game. You don't have time to think and say, 'Oh yeah, it's the Grey Cup.'"

"That's the way Chuck was," confirmed Dave Buchanan. "For a rookie, his composure was unbelievable. When we say 'field general,' this guy was a field general. There wasn't an ounce of fear in this guy."

Tony Gabriel agreed with Buchanan's assessment. "Here's a rookie quarterback taking command of the team and it's indicative of his leadership talents and his demeanour, off the field and on the field," he said. "He was very cool under pressure."

"Nineteen seventy-two was interesting, obviously," said Bruce Smith, "because [we were] playing against a legend like Ron Lancaster, and Chuck had been a rookie quarterback and a black quarterback. I don't know what went through Chuck's mind but at that time we were galvanized as a team." He recalled a flare-up he had with teammate Angelo Mosca. "We almost got into blows, but it wasn't a racial thing. It was more like, I'm the new guy, he's the old guy, and the coach was always bragging about the new guys, they're quick, they're fast." That obviously did not go down too well with Mosca, the aging don of the defence. "But we got over that. We were just a team. And people [on the team] accepted Chuck, embraced Chuck. People knew that the guy was a winner."

Hamilton drew first blood, a sixteen-yard touchdown pass from Ealey to Dave Fleming in the end zone. Or, according to the Saskatchewan players, *out* of the end zone, as Fleming's foot appeared to land on the sideline. But at that time, before unlimited camera angles and video replays and coach's challenges, there was no way to overturn the call, and so it stood.

With an Ian Sunter convert the score was 7–0 for Hamilton. Later in the first quarter following a John Williams's recovery of a blocked punt, Sunter, a nineteen-year-old kicker from Burlington, hit for a field goal to make the score 10–0, and it looked like Hamilton might run away with the game. But before the half was finished, Saskatchewan had tied it up at 10–10.

"George Reed and I were like one and two in the CFL in rushing," explained Buchanan. "And they expected us to run and we expected them to run and what ended up happening is we passed."

At one point during the game, John Williams approached the line of scrimmage while Saskatchewan had the ball on offence and shouted at Ron Lancaster, "Hey Ronnie, when are you going to throw the ball over this way, 'cause I need some action. I'm trying to win this here MVP." The Most Valuable Player in the Grey Cup at that time was given a brand new car.

"He just called me a bunch of nasty names," said John Williams, smiling at the memory of "little ol' Ronnie Lancaster," as he referred to the former great, losing his cool. But the fact was, Lancaster deliberately threw away from Williams, who was one of the best cornerbacks in the league.

"Every play, they were throwing to Lewis Porter. They were just using their game plan. They knew something."

"Let me tell you about that guy," said Dave Buchanan about his old friend John Williams. "He was wily. This guy was a genius at the corner. What John did, you can't teach that. He was quiet. But when that guy was on the field, he was like, 'C'mon, put your best guy out here.' He wasn't a talker. He'd just say matter-of-factly, 'Hey come on, put your best guy out here.' And sure enough, they would throw away from him."

Both teams were able to move the ball, but neither team really threatened to score in the second half. The game had settled into something of a full-contact chess match. Late in the fourth quarter, Saskatchewan had a third down and one yard to go deep in their territory, and they opted to go for the necessary yardage rather than kick, a daring gamble that could have had disastrous consequences. But when you had a running back with the brute strength of George Reed on your side, the odds had a way of shifting in your favour. Reed picked up the necessary yardage and Saskatchewan retained possession of the ball. A few plays later the Roughriders found themselves in the same situation, third and one, this time at their own fifty-one-yard line. Instead of turning to George Reed to once again smash through the line for a first down, their head coach, Dave Skrien, inexplicably chose to punt the ball away. The Saskatchewan players were stunned. It made no sense. Why go for it deep in your end and not closer to midfield? Why not try to keep the drive alive and go for the winning points? But Skrien hoped to pin the Tiger-Cats deep in their end and force Hamilton to give the ball back with excellent field position. That decision, in hindsight, was the biggest mistake of the day.

Saskatchewan punted and the Hamilton receiver was downed at the fifteen-yard line. There were just under two minutes left in the game. Two minutes for Chuck Ealey to capture lightning in a bottle one more time. By this time his teammates had come to believe in the magic of their starting quarterback. Hadn't he proven it time after time during their ten-game winning streak? No one questioned the unbeaten reputation that began at Notre Dame High School back in Portsmouth and at the University of Toledo, when he had clearly proven that he could do it in the pros. Ninety-five yards away lay the Saskatchewan goal line. This was the opportunity the Tiger-Cats and their twenty-two-year-old black quarterback had been waiting for, the chance to cement the legend.

Up to that point, Tony Gabriel had had a quiet day.

"Chuck hadn't even looked my way for the whole game. We were on our own fifteen-yard line and Regina had been tough all game."

Part of the Saskatchewan strategy that day had been to keep Gabriel bottled up inside, not let him get off the line of scrimmage. But late-game substitutions were made and defensive schemes were altered in an effort to contain Hamilton and prevent a long completion downfield.

As Tony Gabriel described that final drive for me, it was as if I were watching the action play out on the boardroom table between us, holographic figures in motion, through the standard wide-angle CBC camera placement. (Although that could also have been the result of my having watched the game so many times in preparation for my interviews.)

"On a zone play up the middle," he said, "Chuck found me because they were dropping off defensively just to play it safe. I got in the clear and got the first catch of about three in a row."

That first catch went for twenty-seven yards. The ball was now at the Hamilton forty-two-yard line. But the quarterback and his tight end were not finished yet.

"The second one came on the same flood pattern but I had to hook up because of the coverage. And Chuck found me again right over the middle for a first down."

That play went for another eleven yards. It was first and ten at the Hamilton fifty-three-yard line. Ealey then threw to a wide-open Buchanan. The ball hit the turf in front of him, maybe the first sign of nerves getting the better of Chuck. On second and ten, he looked for Gabriel again.

"I had to come off the left side for a button-hook for a decent twelve- to fifteen-yard gain," continued Gabriel. "So, thank God, I caught three in a row and all of a sudden we were threatening in the Saskatchewan side of the field with time running down."

The play was good for exactly fifteen yards and the ball was now on the Saskatchewan forty-two-yard line with forty-two seconds to play. On the next play, Ealey kept the ball and picked up maybe a yard and a half. Second down and eight and a half to go.

"The next play they blitz from the backside so I couldn't go out in the pattern. I had to block. The play before I'd gotten hit in a particularly sensitive area so I was in no shape to run," Gabriel chuckled, knowing I was bound to feel his pain; right on cue, I winced in empathy. "So thank God I was in the backside to block for Chuck because he hit Garney Henley sliding from his right side, and he caught the ball at about the twenty-seven-yard line."

The next play was a handoff to Buchanan, who was immediately swarmed and lost a yard. There was time for one more play in the game. Onto the field came the teenage kicker to make the most important kick of his young life. A thirty-four-yard field goal for the professional football championship of Canada. Garney Henley, the league's Most Valuable Player that season, was the holder.

"Just keep your head down," he told the kid. Sunter followed his advice and kicked the ball through the uprights. Hamilton won the 1972 Grey Cup in front of their hometown fans on the last play of the game.

John Williams did not win the coveted MVP award, much to his disappointment. He blames Ron Lancaster for that. "Little ol' Ronnie" would not throw the ball his way. No, the MVP went to the man who had successfully guided his team to first place and a Grey Cup victory in his rookie season.

"If you had to have a trophy, it might as well be a car," laughed Chuck Ealey in his office when I told him what John Williams said about his dashed hopes of winning the game MVP and the car that came with it. "And so, I remember that quite well. At the time thinking, this is a great business to be in, to play football as a sport, being paid, winning a car. And just having a great time."

As special as that year was in Hamilton, the future looked even brighter. With a rookie quarterback who could only get better, an All-Star running back, a clutch Canadian receiver, and a solid defensive corps, the Tiger-Cats looked poised to win a number of Grey Cups.

It never happened. Hamilton would not win another Grey Cup for fourteen years. The team's current Grey Cup drought is nineteen years long. Only twice have they carried the Cup off the field in the forty-six years since that December day in 1972 on their home field before their hometown fans.

During an exhibition game against Toronto the following season, John Williams would have his leg broken in an illegal block by a big fullback trying to make the Argos. Even today, John remains outraged by such a show of disrespect.

"I remember the doctor who was taking me to the hospital said, 'John, that boy who clipped you. They're gonna cut that son of a bitch, you watch. Knockin' a player of your calibre out.' Wouldn't you know it, the next day [the Argos] cut him. And he sends me a card telling me that he was sorry. And that same guy was in my apartment three days before. He was on his way to Toronto and stopped by my house and had a beer with me. I was just shocked. I had been on top of my game and that guy broke my leg and I wasn't the same anymore."

He returned for the final two games of the season but he knew something was wrong.

"Any time a guy ran a pass pattern on me that year I was scared to death. And I used to *beg* them to run or pass toward me. But I became scared to death 'cause I knew I couldn't run like I ran before."

The next year, John was traded to Edmonton during the great purge of 1974, which came about when the CFL expanded the Eastern Conference schedule from fourteen games to sixteen to match its Western counterparts. The league, however, had no intention of paying the Eastern players for the increased number of games. A number of Hamilton players held a mini-revolt and demanded that their contracts be adjusted to make allowance for the greater number of games they would now be required to play. This did not go down well with Tiger-Cats president Ralph Sazio, who began shipping out those players who were at the forefront of the rebellion. Bruce Smith was sent to Edmonton. Tony Gabriel was sent to Ottawa following the '74 season. And Chuck Ealey — Chuck Ealey! — was traded to Winnipeg halfway through the season.

"It just wasn't comfortable for me because my mother was a single mom," explained Ealey. "And in the East, I could get back to Ohio fairly quickly. She was having some health issues … and just mentally I wasn't comfortable in the mid-west."

He was at pains to express that he had nothing against Winnipeg — "I love Winnipeg!" he insisted. It was just a matter of geographical location. He was still a very young man, only twenty-four years old, and he was comfortable in Hamilton, one year removed from a Grey Cup victory and the Most Valuable Player award. He was looking to start a family with his wife, Sherri. He must have felt that this move was more than just a trade, that it was a banishment, a form of punishment for daring to argue about money in a league without a lot of it to go around. After an injury-plagued season and a half in Winnipeg, he was traded to the Toronto Argonauts where he played three more seasons before suffering a collapsed lung and deciding, *Okay, that's it, time to hang up the cleats.*

Dave Buchanan suffered perhaps the cruellest fate of all, and through his life he continued to blame it all on his own ignorance and naiveté regarding the business of football. He still harboured the dream of returning to the NFL in triumph and proving to all the naysayers, especially the Cincinnati Bengals, that they were wrong about him.

"What I should have done is said, 'Hey, if [Hamilton] is where my career is, this is where I stay, where people love me and where they respect my game.' And not worry so much about getting back to the National Football League."

He had just finished a season where he was second in the league in rushing yardage and first in the number of carries. He had been an integral part of a Grey Cup–winning team. And when he thought about what he had accomplished that season in Hamilton, he concluded, "Wow, I'm underpaid." And so he took the issue up with Ralph Sazio. And when Ralph didn't agree that he should have a significant upgrade in salary, Buchanan decided to play hardball. He would simply hold out until Sazio came to his senses and signed him to a much larger contract. And that, he admitted to me, looking back on it, was his next big mistake.

"I should have gone out on the field, played out my option, and then gone to another team. I tried to force the issue. And when I heard about the World Football League coming in, this was my chance to get back closer to the NFL."

And so Buchanan decided to sit out the year and wait for the World Football League to open for business in 1974. Buchanan believed he could grab a position in the backfield with the novice Honolulu Hawaiians, and so, with this idea in mind, he moved back to Pasadena, got a job in a local Sears, and worked out like a maniac in his off-hours, preparing to get in the best shape of his life for the following year in the WFL. His efforts paid off. He signed with Honolulu and began the 1974 season playing football in Hawaii.

And then Hamilton management discovered that Dave Buchanan was playing football in Honolulu and said, "Uh-uh, sorry, you're still under contract with us." The Honolulu Hawaiians took a look at the paperwork and said, "Yep, they're right, you have to go back to Canada and play out your contract." But Buchanan didn't want to go back to Hamilton; he had burned too many bridges there. There was, however, one city and one organization where he really wanted to live and play.

"I told Ralph to his face that I wanted to go to Toronto. I remember those classy uniforms; they were so far ahead of the game from a fashion standpoint. I used to look across the field and go, *Gosh, I wish I played for them. They are a class organization.* And I told Ralph I wanted to go to Toronto and I must have said something insulting like, 'I'm going to come back and fix you guys,' because what he did was trade me out west to Winnipeg."

So Dave Buchanan came up with a new plan. He would play out the season and then head further west, right out to the West Coast of Canada and the B.C. Lions. That would bring him closer to his home in California. Unfortunately, Winnipeg and B.C. could not work out a deal for his rights and, in utter frustration, he walked away from football altogether and moved back to Pasadena to begin a life in teaching and coaching.

"It wasn't the game that killed me, it was the business part of the game," he said.

Chuck Ealey played seven seasons in the CFL before retiring at the age of twenty-eight. He could have still played if he'd had the desire. The Argonauts wanted him to come back. But by this time he was the father of two children and had a third one, daughter and future writer Jael, on the way. It was time to get down to the business of the rest of his life. Twenty-eight may seem awfully young for a successful CFL quarterback to hang them up, especially given the quarterbacks who have won Grey Cups in their forties in the last fifteen years, like Damon Allen and Henry Burris. In 2017, quarterback Ricky Ray won a Grey Cup for the Argonauts at the ripe old age of thirty-eight. But even as I was writing this chapter, Ricky Ray was in a hospital in Toronto recovering from a hit that saw him carted off the field strapped to a board, his head immobilized, his wife and two young daughters watching from the stands. For the thousands of fans taking in the game and for the players of both teams who stood in stunned silence for the twenty minutes it took to carry the injured player from the field, it was a haunting reminder of the dangers inherent in this game.

"You find out something when you go through professional football that is very different than amateur football," said Chuck Ealey, as our interview neared its conclusion. "People would lose their job in the middle of the season. Trades and things were going on that were very different than amateur life and could impact you. Because it's no longer a game just for fun. It's a game for business and it's those types of things that can be very distracting for athletes as they get older and their livelihoods depend on a game."

And so Chuck Ealey walked away from the game he loved. He had come to understand that pro football was not an end in itself but a path to his next destination.

He went on to forge a successful career in the investment world and, most importantly, has been there for his wife and his children, now grown adults themselves. And like many successful former players who come from less-privileged backgrounds and even just plain hard times, he now shares his experiences and knowledge, and the basics of making "good decisions," with others as a motivational speaker.

"That border, an imaginary line, becomes very real when you cross it on both sides from either direction," he said. "I mean that in a constructive way, in a positive way. Canada gave me a sense of freedom." He listed some of the more obvious aspects of freedom for a family man, like less crime and a sense of security, and then moved to concepts that affect his children's lives, such as being free in a city environment, a sense of "social responsibilities," and, finally, "acceptance."

"Just coming in and having the chance to play quarterback was something that my own country didn't allow me to do even with the record that I had. While it is one of those quietly kept secrets to a certain degree, it's a reality of what was happening, especially at that time. That sort of filtered itself into everyday life and it was very easy for me to make a decision to stay in Canada, with my kids, and family, and everything else because of all the other opportunities where I didn't have to feel like I was limited because of the colour of my skin."

"I remember my first year after the Grey Cup, I went and bought myself a brand new corvette," Bruce Smith recalled. "I filled it up with all kinds of presents and drove it home [to Huntsville] for Christmas. I was Santa Claus. It was great seeing the look on my mom's face, being able to go back home and have some time to process everything. After sort of having a failure in university and not really looking like I was going to play professional football, to go up there [to Canada], make the team, excel, win the Grey Cup, and really and truly have a great year that year in Hamilton."

Bruce's stepfather had started a trucking business. Bruce bought him a new truck. He was able to buy his mother a new house. These were the things that he had always dreamed of being able to do. Football had been the means to that end. And Bruce Smith never made any bones about it: that's all football had ever meant to him. A means to an end. A way to get out from under the suffocating poverty and racism in his hometown. And a way to get out of himself, at least for the length of time it took to play four quarters.

"I did like playing in the CFL. It was a great league. But for me, I never saw football as who I was. I wasn't Bruce Smith the football player. I was Bruce Smith playing football."

There was a popular song recorded in the 1950s called "Wedding Bells Are Breaking Up That Old Gang of Mine." In the case of the Hamilton Tiger-Cats it wasn't wedding bells, it was contractual demands.

"Ralphy [Sazio] didn't want to give any raises," said Bruce Smith. "I think the raise he offered was to paint the stadium or something like that. And so nobody wanted to play for Ralph."

And not many did for very long, including Bruce, who was shipped out west to the Edmonton Eskimos. He played one season there before coming back east to the Ottawa Rough Riders in 1975, where he hooked up with his old teammate Tony Gabriel. In Ottawa, the two became roommates and, more than that, friends for life.

"I really got to know him as a man," said Gabriel of that year, adding what many consider the ultimate compliment: "You could depend upon his word."

The next year, Tony Gabriel would become famous for what has gone down in Canadian football folklore as simply "the Catch," the touchdown reception against Saskatchewan in the waning moments of the 1976 Grey Cup game that gave Ottawa the title. Unfortunately, Bruce Smith would not be there for that game. He spent that season with the mediocre Toronto

Argonauts, where he was reunited with Chuck Ealey. But no amount of Ealey "magic" could save the Argos from sliding into irrelevance in the four years that Bruce played there, despite a defence that built a reputation as "the Dirty Dozen." Chuck played three of those years before retiring, unable to breathe new life into the franchise, which had been on a downward projection for a few years. For both players it was time to figure out what they were going to do with the rest of their lives. One thing was certain: whatever they were going to do, they were going to do it in Canada.

Bruce eventually became one of the top real estate salesmen in Toronto. But despite the wealth and stardom he had attained in Canada, he still lacked a sense of peace. Anger, insecurity, and even despair lay just beneath the surface.

"I've got a great house, nice cars, lots of money, a very successful business, and a big line of credit. I can pretty much do what I want," he knew. Then it hit him. "I realized I was very worried. My thoughts were focused on 'How can someone come from barely making it to this wealth and success? When is this bubble going to burst?'"

One night, his anxieties became so severe that he suffered a paralyzing panic attack, which he thought was a heart attack. It was only then, in the midst of his own dark night of the soul, that he remembered the Bible he had been given as a member of the Toronto Argonauts back in 1976.

"I had never opened that Bible. For some reason I grabbed it and put it under my pillow. That night I got some sleep."

Not long after that, he started going to church. Within six months, he began feeling guilty about the lifestyle he was leading.

"Then one day I reached out to God and He answered me."

He continued to sell real estate, but he also began a quest to find a ministry. That quest eventually led to a position as chaplain at the King-Bay Chaplaincy, a non-denominational chaplaincy in the heart of downtown Toronto. Though the surrounding office towers housed some of the country's most powerful, influential, and wealthy business elite, not even those power brokers were immune to stress and feelings of emotional and spiritual emptiness.

"The whole downtown area is in screaming need," said Bruce in an earlier interview we did for a documentary project I was hoping to make about his lifelong spiritual journey. "There are marriage problems, money problems, alcohol problems, and people who are afraid they will lose their jobs. There is a lot of pain and suffering. People come to the chaplaincy when they are in distress. They come looking for support, help, direction, prayer, and counselling. People come who have other faiths or no faith at all. It doesn't matter to me who you are, everybody needs hope. When you don't have it, you go looking for it."

Bruce Smith undertook an enormous journey, far beyond the geographical distance that stretched from Huntsville, Texas, to Canada. Anyone could make that journey in a couple of days of hard driving. Bruce's journey cannot be measured in miles or kilometres. He went from schoolyard bully and angry young man, acting out the rage and self-doubt he felt inside, to a man who fully opened up his heart to welcome the people most in need of the big-armed embrace of the man once known as "Grizzly" to his teammates.

"They used to call me a grizzly bear," he said, "but now I'm the panda bear."

Bruce Smith passed away on January 3, 2013, from pancreatic cancer. He was sixty-three years old. He is deeply missed by all whose lives he touched.

Chapter Seven

MOON AND THE ARTFUL DODGER

Warren Moon had a plan. He'd always had this plan. There was only ever one plan. It never wavered.

He was going to be a quarterback in the NFL.

At seven years old, Warren became the "man of the house" when his father died of a heart attack at thirty-eight years old. There were six sisters and his mother in the Moon house in West Los Angeles. Warren's mother did not want to lay such a heavy burden on her son's shoulders, but Warren just naturally took to the task.

His mother worried for her son every time he left the house. The '70s saw the rise of street gangs in Los Angeles. You were either with them or against them; it was impossible to be indifferent. Innocence could not save you. It was hard to be a "good kid" — hard-working, ambitious, and athletic — and stay safe. That's why she enrolled him at Hamilton High School. The two closest schools, Los Angeles High School and Dorsey High School, were, in Moon's words, "just really infested with Crips and Bloods." Warren wanted to go where he could get a good education and play football in a respected program. He wanted to play where the right people would take notice, those that could further the plan, the only plan — to get to the NFL as a quarterback.

"You sometimes had to negotiate yourself through certain neighbourhoods, knowing where you could go, and where you couldn't go,"

Moon told me in his office in Irvine, California, a world apart from more humble and perilous beginnings. Moon is the president of Sports 1 Marketing, a highly successful marketing firm whose goal, according to the company's tagline, is very simple: "Make a Lot of Money, Help a Lot of People, Have a Lot of Fun."

"Maybe if you were going to a certain park, or going to a movie theatre," he continued, "and you had to go through one of these neighbourhoods, you knew exactly when to go, where to go, how to get there. Because you knew you might run into some type of encounter with a gang member. So you were very aware of everything that was going on at that time."

Moon's words eerily echoed those of Chuck Ealey when he spoke about the dangers of wandering too far afield from the friendlier confines of his own neighbourhood, except Chuck was talking about dangers associated with white neighbourhoods. Moon's was the fear of straying into the path of gangbangers, the source of so much black-on-black violence in West L.A.

With his enrolment at Hamilton High, step one in the process had begun. There was, however, a trade-off to be made to escape the gang influence: Hamilton was predominantly white. And until the moment he entered the hallowed halls of Hamilton, Warren Moon had never come up against, or certainly never observed so closely, systemic racism.

"I think it's when I went to high school that I first realized there were going to be difficult times trying to play the position of quarterback. Coming in to the high school that I went to, it was predominately white and Jewish. I was one of the three quarterbacks on the sophomore team. Clearly, [I was] better than the other two.... For some reason, [the coach] did not want to play me as a quarterback, and the only time I did play was when we were either really far ahead, or really far behind."

But the next year, under the school's varsity football coach, he was named the starter. Ordinarily, being the starting quarterback on a high-school team brings with it the perks of being the top dog among the student body far beyond the reach of the gridiron — the admiration, envy, and sycophancy that inflates egos to the bursting point. Warren Moon had a very different experience as a high-school starting quarterback. He faced death threats.

"We were going to play Crenshaw High School one particular night, and it was a big game in our conference. The winning team was probably going to win our division. I was approached by a couple of gang members. If I won the football game, [they said,] I was going to be killed after the game was over. Just kind of giving me something to think about."

He told his mother, his girlfriend, Felicia (who would later become his wife), his coach, and his best friend. His coach told the police, who had the stadium surrounded. Hamilton won the game. His mother gave him a ride home while his best friend drove Warren's car in case the gang members had the car targeted. (Now *that* is a friend.) Later that night he went to a celebratory party with Felicia. Some toughs from Crenshaw showed up. Warren figured it might be in his and Felicia's best interests to leave. As they did, shots rang out. Moon and his girlfriend hit the sidewalk. Realizing that they were not the intended targets, they picked themselves up off the pavement and beat it as fast as they could. Just another typical day in the life of a high-school quarterback.

"But yeah, you played with that type of intimidation sometimes, and things were going to happen to you, whether you took it seriously or not. I did take it seriously. But I wasn't going to let it affect the way I play my football game."

Why would he? Just all part of the plan. Step two in this process involved obtaining a scholarship to a university that a) wanted him to play quarterback and b) wanted him to throw the ball, not run it.

"I got a lot of scholarships from schools wanting me to run the football, or change positions. I had actually committed to go to Arizona State University and thought I was going to get a chance to play quarterback. But [the coach] ended up signing on two of the top quarterbacks of the nation, and they came to me and said they were going to change my position to safety. So I told them no, thank you."

So, Arizona State and a full scholarship were out. They simply didn't fit the plan. And when he didn't get the offer he was looking for from any of the major schools, he decided it was time to devise a backup plan. So he chose West L.A. College, figuring he could spend a season there and prove that he belonged in a passing offence in a major university football program. It also didn't hurt that his high-school football coach was going to West L.A. as the offensive coordinator.

After his season in junior college football, the Division I offers began to pour in. As it met most of the criteria he'd established on his checklist — West Coast school, a chance to start, pass-based offence, and a new coach — he finally settled on the University of Washington, led by first-year coach Don James, who let Warren know that the quarterback's job was there for the taking. Once again, everything was going according to the plan.

Within three weeks of joining the team, Warren Moon was named the starter over a fifth-year senior, Chris Rowland, a Seattle native who was very popular with the hometown crowd, despite having led Washington to an underwhelming 5–6 record the year before. Rowland also happened to be white. The move to Moon was not a popular one with the fan base nor with the resident quarterback, who felt he was being sacrificed for a new coach's long-range goals.

"Not to take anything away from Warren, but I don't think he was ready," Rowland said in an interview with the *Seattle Post-Intelligencer* back in 2003.

Rowland was not the only one to think that Moon was out of his depth. The Washington football fans were practically apoplectic about the benching of their local boy in favour of some black upstart out of West L.A. And after the Huskies got off to a slow start, the fans figured that they had every right to voice their displeasure.

"We had one of the toughest schedules in the nation that year," Moon explained. "We played three of the top ten teams in the nation in our first four games. And we weren't winning. And when you aren't winning, the quarterback is going to take the heat, and the head coach is going to take the heat."

Moon understood that the quarterback was going to be the main recipient of any criticism directed toward the team when they weren't winning. He was also going to be the guy that got the most credit for winning. It was the nature of the job. But there is a huge difference between criticism and persecution. And, as an eighteen-year-old black kid in a city where he didn't know many people outside of his teammates — and there were probably more than a few of those who resented him for taking Rowland's position — it was difficult to absorb the vituperation he received from the hometown crowd.

"That made it tough. It made it tough for my girlfriend in the stands and it was tough for my buddies who sat up there with her, listening to some of the things they had to listen to throughout the game."

There were times he wanted to transfer but his mother told him in no uncertain terms that you did not run from your problems. This was the school he chose over all others. There was a reason for that. Did he suddenly think there was going to be some other major Division I school where such problems didn't exist? Where he would not find himself in the same situation? He decided to stay and prove to the naysayers that they were wrong, that he could lead the Huskies to recognition on a national stage.

"I learned that from my mom. Because that's the way she lived her life, that's the way she taught us. That we could do anything. It wasn't always going to be easy, but you had the ability to do anything if you put your mind to it and worked at it."

In his third and senior year, the Huskies accrued a record of 7–4, including a 6–1 record within their own conference, the Pac-8, and won the right to go to the Rose Bowl in Pasadena on January 2, 1978, against the Big Ten's Michigan Wolverines. Michigan, ranked third in the nation, was the overwhelming favourite against Washington. Moon remembered standing at midfield for the coin toss with his fellow captains and reflecting on the path that had led to this moment, the teams that had passed him over as well as the positive steps he had taken on his own behalf.

"I think it was a vindication [against] my high-school coach that didn't want me to play, a vindication [against] the colleges that didn't want to recruit me as quarterback. It was a proving ground for all the fans that doubted me at the University of Washington. It was just a matter of completing it now, that day. You didn't want to get that far and all of a sudden lose the football game, or go out there and lay an egg as a player."

He did not have to worry about laying an egg that day. Washington knocked off the highly favoured Wolverines 27–20 and Warren was named the Most Valuable Player in the Rose Bowl. He was also named the Pac-8 Player of the Year. And to top his season off and to signal that he had finally made a positive impact on the citizens of Seattle after two seasons of targeted bigotry, he was named the *Seattle Post-Intelligencer*

Sports Star of the Year over some very tough competition, not the least of which included a non-human competitor, Triple Crown winner Seattle Slew. By anyone's standards, the Slew was tough to beat.

All seemed in place for the final step in the Warren Moon long-range plan: the NFL draft. It seemed like a slam-dunk that some team would come calling, interested in his services. And they did ... they just weren't interested in his services as a quarterback. *Rose Bowl MVP? Pac-8 Player of the Year? Sorry, not interested.* No team requested a workout. He wasn't even invited to the NFL combines, a chance for college football players to showcase their athletic abilities in front of NFL general managers, coaches, and scouts.

"That was a clear-cut indicator that people weren't taking me very seriously as being a 'field general,' so to speak," said Moon.

Like Chuck Ealey before him, Warren Moon was *persona non grata* as a quarterback because he had, according to Moon, "the wrong paint job." Teams were quite willing to look at him as a defensive back, the default setting for black college quarterbacks. *You'd make a helluva DB.* Or maybe wide receiver. Neither of these positions appealed to Warren Moon. His goal had not been to reach the NFL any way possible. The goal was to be a starting quarterback in the NFL. Not just play any position or hold a clipboard as one of many backup QBs taken late in the draft and doomed to rot on the vine of NFL dreams.

There was, however, another option, one where he could ply his trade as a starting quarterback in a professional football league and be well-compensated, if not overwhelmingly so, for his efforts.

Hugh Campbell was a sure-handed wide receiver out of Washington State University — and former teammate of George Reed — when he came to Canada to play for the Saskatchewan Roughriders. He played from 1963 to 1969, although he retired for one season in 1968. He had three 1,000-yard seasons as a receiver with the Green Riders (so-called for the colour of their uniforms) and one Grey Cup victory in 1966. After retiring from the CFL, he coached football at Whitworth College in Spokane, Washington, for seven years before getting his first opportunity to coach in the pros by returning to the CFL as head coach with the Edmonton Eskimos. In his first year as head coach, Campbell took the Eskimos to the Grey Cup game against Montreal in the Olympic Stadium, or "Big O," in Montreal. The game earned the reputation as the "Ice Bowl" because of the icy field conditions. The Alouettes came up with a unique solution that allowed them to literally run away with the game, 41–6, over a field of floundering Eskimos: they fired staples into the rubber cleats on their shoes, which allowed them to outgrip and outrun the opposition.

That off-season, Hugh Campbell went looking south of the border for the best quarterback that the Eskimo budget could buy. The Eskimos already had two solid quarterbacks in Tom Wilkinson and Bruce Lemmerman, but "solid" wasn't what Campbell wanted. He was looking for the exceptional, someone who could learn from the veterans even as he gradually usurped their roles in the Edmonton offence. And he found the quarterback he was looking for back in the state of Washington. That quarterback was Warren Moon.

Moon didn't know a lot about the CFL at the time. He knew some of the black quarterbacks who had gone up there, having followed them as players in college — Condredge Holloway and Jimmy Jones and Chuck Ealey. But he didn't follow the league. He knew it was there, that it existed as a viable option for players who went undrafted or who simply chose to go north to play football. He understood why black quarterbacks would go. If they were anything like him they would go for one reason only: to play quarterback. Moon had never thought he would have to worry about that option. He was certain that his future in the NFL was written in the cards. All part of the grand scheme of things, until it wasn't.

"Hugh Campbell came down and introduced himself to me, and we sat down and talked football and watched film one day. He talked to me about his team, and what he was trying to build there in Edmonton, what they had done the year before, and told me what he thought about me and my abilities. And he was just very high on me as a player and as a person and he felt that I had a tremendous potential to come up there and play well. Given the fact that he had such praise for me and had confidence in me at the quarterback position — as well as the money they were offering me to come up there to play — and then you look at the other side of it, the cons of the NFL, that they weren't too serious about me playing quarterback and I just wasn't getting any good vibes from them, I decided to go to Canada."

Like two characters from a Dr. Seuss book, Tom Wilkinson was Quarterback One and Bruce Lemmerman was Quarterback Two. As long as both men were healthy, they both played every game, sharing the quarterback duties. This was not a case of going with the "hot hand." Wilkinson's hand could be ablaze, it didn't matter. Lemmerman would come in regardless. That's the way it had been for years. Campbell liked to keep his team on their toes.

"I'll do the deciding who's in there," Campbell told his players. "You just do the playing when the guy's in there. Make sure each of them looks so good that it's a difficult decision for me who's going to play."

On the other hand, maybe he did it to drive the sportswriters and media types crazy, as they endlessly performed the roles of judge and jury, coach, and general manager over the airwaves and in the newspapers.

"The media very much wants to say, 'Well, who's going to be the starting quarterback?' And the second [QB] goes in and does well and they say, 'He has a big decision to make next week,'" explained Campbell in a 2017 interview on the CFL website.

Tom Wilkinson knew his best days as a quarterback were behind him. He was thirty-five years old when Campbell signed Moon. It did not take a genius to see who his heir apparent would be.

"I watched him play in the Rose Bowl the year before," remembered Wilkinson, perched on a chair inside the Eskimos alumni box overlooking the field at Commonwealth Stadium, where I met with a number of former players for an interview. "And after watching the game, in my mind there was no chance Warren Moon was going to be up here, because he could do everything a quarterback could do. He could throw. He could throw a touch, he could throw long, he could drop back, he could throw on a run, and he could run. I mean, I watched that Rose Bowl and the very last thing I thought was that he would be coming here. He would be in the top five rounds for sure, drafted in the NFL."

Tom Wilkinson was not a tall quarterback, which is a bit of an understatement. He was only five foot nine on a good day, he wasn't particularly mobile, and he had an adequate but not strong arm. He remembers practising with his University of Wyoming Cowboys team one day and as he took the snap from centre and dropped back to pass, he bumped into some guy who had just wandered onto the field. *Excuse me?* It turned out that this guy wasn't just some dazed Cowboys fan with too much draft beer in his system, but a professional scout from the Canadian Football League. He had come onto the field with a purpose. He wanted to measure Wilkinson's actual height against his own. And he asked him whether he'd be interested in playing in the CFL.

"The what?"

"The Canadian Football League."

"Never heard of it."

This was Wyoming, not Timbuktu. The scout represented the Saskatchewan Roughriders. *Never heard of them.*

"My dream was either be in baseball or be in the NFL. So I really wasn't that interested in talking to him because my hope was still to get drafted … but I'm glad that I didn't answer up to him because I would've gone to Saskatchewan. And that's way back when there was only one quarterback, and Ron Lancaster happened to be the quarterback in Saskatchewan."

For sixteen years, from 1963 to 1978, Ron Lancaster was "the man" in Regina. But in 1965 Wilkie didn't know that. He'd never even heard of the place. He got a career break by not seizing an opportunity.

"I wouldn't have made the team. And if I hadn't made the team, I would've gone home and used my teaching degree, because I wasn't going to chase it."

And by "chase it," he means the dream. Tom Wilkinson knew he was not the most gifted quarterback physically. What he did have in abundance was guile and leadership, and he relied on those two qualities to work opposing defences to the point of exhaustion. When the NFL didn't come banging on his door, Leo Cahill, legendary CFL coach, general manager, and character, brought him up from the University of Wyoming to play for the Toronto Rifles of the Continental Football League in 1966. Then Cahill took the head-coaching job with the Toronto Argonauts for the 1967 season.

Cahill brought Wilkinson up with the Argos. From there, Wilkinson was off to B.C. and in 1972 he was picked up by Edmonton. With Edmonton, Wilkinson had gone to the Grey Cup every year between '73 and Warren Moon's arrival in 1978, except for the 1976 season, winning two and losing two, including the Ice Bowl, which still left a bitter taste even years later. Still, the Eskimos carried a huge chip on their shoulders going into 1978, Warren Moon's first year in the Canadian "show." The thought of losing 41–6 to Montreal made them, to a man, cringe. If staples were legal, why not flubber?

"We got together and said, 'Bey, let's just work harder than we've ever worked, and show the media that we're good enough to win that game,'" Wilkinson remembered, his competitive fires relit by the memory of that season.

And no one worked harder to prepare for that season than the two incumbent quarterbacks. The Eskimos only carried two quarterbacks. They would have to be in the best shape of their lives. Even the notoriously pot-bellied Tom Wilkinson chipped twenty pounds off his gut. Out of necessity. Someone would have to go, because a third quarterback was on his way. And they knew the one to leave wouldn't be named Warren Moon.

The first thing you notice when you meet Ed Jones, former defensive back with the Edmonton Eskimos, is his front teeth, like a perfect miniature piano keyboard. If the light hits them at the right time of day, you would be well-advised to wear shades. They are most certainly not homegrown. And if you spend any time with Mr. Jones, as I did, you'll see a lot of those teeth, because he likes to smile. He enjoys a laugh. Get him to tell you a story and you'll soon be flashing your own teeth. He's a funny man with a self-deprecating wit, the kind developed after years of locker room banter. It is not hard to imagine that he usually came out on top. For instance, I asked him if Warren Moon was the greatest quarterback he ever saw.

"Quarterback?" He seemed to mull it over as if perhaps Warren Moon played some other position I might have forgotten. Jones was one of the former Eskimos invited to my interview session in Commonwealth Stadium high above the field. "He was *one* of the best. He wouldn't say I was the *best* defensive back he ever saw. He'd give me the 'one of the bests' so right back at him."

Ed Jones grew up in Atlantic Highlands, New Jersey. His parents separated early but when his mother suffered a stroke at thirty-three years of age, the family moved in with his father in Navesink, New Jersey. Ed did not play organized football until he was in the ninth grade.

"It was one of the biggest schools in New Jersey. And I wanted to be a receiver. Looked like a pretty glamorous position. But they told me I was too short. I was only about five and a half feet tall in ninth grade and so they made me a running back. And I could throw twenty moves inside of two steps. Probably the same guy would have the chance to tackle me three times and miss me three times."

Then he started to grow. By the time he was a senior he was a solid six feet tall and a starting fullback. A number of Ivy League schools were after him.

"I ended up going to Rutgers because it was the closest," he said. "With my mom being an invalid and my dad, having suffered a couple of heart attacks, staying home."

At Rutgers he played three seasons at cornerback, earning All-East honours and finishing his time at Rutgers with a total of fourteen interceptions. He was drafted in the ninth round of the 1975 NFL draft by the Dallas Cowboys.

"I didn't really fit in there. I think I was a little too liberal for the coaching staff, which I believe were all from Alabama and down around there. I learned from Drew Pearson [a Dallas receiver] who was from South River, New Jersey ... and he sort of took me under his wing a little bit and tried to tell me the dos and the don'ts there. And there were a lot of don'ts for African-Americans. Such as who you hang out with. I had a problem with that."

But he didn't have the problem for long. At the end of the pre-season, Tom Landry, the head coach of the Dallas Cowboys from 1960 to 1988, called Jones down to his office. That was bad enough. But when he told Jones to bring his "playbook," that meant Jones's days as a Cowboy were over. A team's playbook was a player's most valuable possession, to be guarded with his life, until he was either released outright or traded. Ed Jones was not traded. He returned to his home in New Jersey to figure out his next step. Then the Buffalo Bills came calling.

"I ended up going there as a free safety ... I was going to be the guy. I was the smallest strong safety in the league because I was really a corner. But I could cover man-to-man, which they really appreciated. But they were really impressed at my aggressiveness and tackling skills. I rarely missed tackles."

What really impressed the coaches at Buffalo was that Jones was the only guy in camp who could tackle their superstar running back, O.J. Simpson, the first running back in football history to rush for over 2,000 yards in a single season.

Jones's secret? "[O.J.] ran how I used to run when I was a running back."

Despite playing through a severe arm injury late in the season that significantly restricted his tackling abilities, Jones nevertheless made the NFL All-Rookie team. Naturally, he expected to be compensated for his breakout season the next year at contract time, but instead he discovered that Simpson's demands for a new million-dollar contract were having a negative impact on other players' salary offers, including his.

"[Simpson] got his million. I didn't get my thirty or forty dollar raise. They let me and about six other starters go to pay O.J. I was labelled as having a bad attitude because I wouldn't sign the contract that was offered to me, which I felt was a slap in the face."

A reputation, especially a bad one, has a way of getting around in NFL circles. No team wants some other team's problem. Stick a label on a player, especially a black player, and it's there for life. *Lazy. Uppity. Troublemaker.* Unless a team is absolutely desperate for talent, they are not going to invest the time or money to discover for themselves whether there is any truth behind an affixed label. That's what Jones found himself up against when he went looking for employment elsewhere. Even after several successful workouts with teams seemingly interested in his services: Pittsburgh, the New York Jets, and Washington.

"They all said I was good enough to play, but 'what happened in Buffalo? People in Buffalo have said this about you.' Even the headlines when I was released — too smart for my britches. At that time, there weren't many guys from Ivy League schools in the league. And so, you know, definitely down in Dallas, that didn't go down too well. Because not many of those guys, it seemed, graduated. Came from a lot of small schools, a lot of Southern schools as well. And they understood, I guess better than I did, how you're supposed to act down there. I just brought my New Jersey attitude with me."

In 1976, a "New Jersey attitude" was best left to white rockers like Bruce Springsteen, unless you were "the Big Man" himself, Clarence Clemons, and carried a sax. And then Jones got a call from Edmonton.

"I don't know where Edmonton is. But we're taught that it's cold up here. This is where the cold weather comes from. And so I said, 'Yeah, I'll come up there.' I hopped on a plane, spent about five, five and a half hours in the air. I got here and there was like nothing. It's brown. And this is like the end of September, I'm in a T-shirt and I'm freezing my butt off here. And I'm thinking, 'Where am I?'"

He was also in for a surprise when he checked out the facilities at Clarke Stadium ("Clarke with an *e*," to Ed's amusement). He was used to new facilities like Texas Stadium in Dallas and Rich Stadium in Buffalo, state-of-the-art modern extravaganzas with saunas and gyms and racquetball courts. Someone could live their whole life in places like that and never want to leave. Not so at Clarke Stadium. The minute he entered he was looking for the exit.

"I walked through that locker room thinking, 'What have I gotten myself into?'"

He was on a five-day tryout. If a player didn't impress the coaching staff within five days, they were usually winging their way south out of there. Soon five days turned into nine and it was getting even colder. Should he invest in warmer clothes or pack his bags? He decided it was time to have a sit-down with the head coach, Ray Jauch.

"I told him, 'I kind of think I'm good enough to play, but you have two Americans at the corners.' I didn't understand this Canadian-American ratio. So many Canadians, so many Americans, moving guys around. You could be a healthy scratch if somebody else goes down and they need to fill that [position] with an American. It was really quite confusing to me. But he said, 'Nah, nah, hang around, we have something in store for you. You're gonna play this next game.'"

His first game took place at Clarke Stadium on Canadian Thanksgiving, 1976. He played at the defensive halfback position, which was similar to the strong safety position he had played in Buffalo. The Eskimos won. Jones played three more regular-season games and continued throughout the playoffs. Edmonton beat Winnipeg in the Western semifinals but lost to Saskatchewan in the finals for the right to go to the Grey Cup.

"And I impressed," said Jones. "So that's why I'm still here."

Don Matthews was the defensive coach in Edmonton that season, his first year in the CFL. Matthews had taken over a winless high-school program in Beaverton, Oregon, three years prior to coming to Edmonton and coached the team to consecutive state championships, going unbeaten in his final year. Don Matthews would eventually win five Grey Cups as a head coach in the CFL, but as training camp approached in 1978, little did he know that he was about to embark on a run of five straight Grey Cups as an assistant coach with the Eskimos.

"I remember being in the Eskimo office," said Jones. "Our coach, Don Matthews, says to me, 'Hey, we got this new quarterback coming up here. He's really good.'"

"Oh yeah?"

"Out of University of Washington."

"Oh yeah?"

"Warren Moon," said Matthews.

"Wow," said Jones. He repeated the name. "Warren Moon." Maybe he thought Matthews was jerking his chain. *Is that name for real? Warren Moon?*

"Who's that?" he finally asked.

But what he remembered all these years later was what Matthews didn't say about Moon. He never said, "Yeah, we got this black quarterback coming up here." And so for a moment in time Warren Moon existed in Ed Jones's mind in a kind of pure state of quarterback being, free of labels and identifiers other than that he was "really good." That first impression stayed in his mind.

"We don't see colour up here!" Ed exclaimed before pausing for a quick rethink. He adjusted his statement somewhat to acknowledge that there might be a few out there who very much see colour and nothing but colour. "Not everyone," he said, bringing things down a notch, "but for the most part a lot of guys don't see colour up here. When Warren went down to the States, you know, it was black quarterback this, black quarterback that.... Up here, it was just 'Warren Moon.'"

Matthews did have another message to deliver to Ed Jones that day in 1978 regarding Warren Moon, and this was perhaps the underlying reason behind their discussion in the first place.

"He said, 'We got this good kid coming up here.' And then he goes, 'And we'd like you to stay away from him a little bit. 'Cause he's a good kid.'" Ed Jones reacted with appropriate shock at the suggestion that he might have been a bad influence on the rookie. "And I'm saying, 'What's that supposed to mean?' At that time, I used to party a lot. In fact, I threw most of the parties for the players. I guess he thought I might be too much of a *good* influence on Warren."

And as I had grown to expect from Ed Jones, he laughed.

"Yeah, the thing I worked on the most is teaching him how to throw a tight spiral. And I taught him how to throw sixty, seventy yards down the field. And I taught him to run fast."

This was Tom Wilkinson's sarcastic response when I asked whether he took the rookie phenom under his wing.

"I mean, there wasn't anything I could teach him, as far as being a quarterback, other than just the way you handle yourself and the things you did, and how you call plays. That was something that you didn't sit down with him and talk about. Because that's what coaches do, and I certainly wasn't a coach."

When Bruce Lemmerman went down with an injury that year, the starting job was Wilkinson's, with Moon acting like a reliever in baseball, brought in late to close the game out.

"Campbell didn't hide the fact that I was our most talented quarterback," Moon wrote in his autobiography, *Never Give Up on Your Dream*, "but he made sure I was put in the best possible position to succeed."

It would be difficult to find two more disparate quarterbacks than Wilkinson and Moon. While Wilkinson worked the short game to perfection, Moon pushed the ball downfield. Where Wilkinson went for eight, Warren went for eighteen. But Moon was quite happy to sit back and watch Wilkinson work his mini-magic up and down the field. Canadian football was a different game than the American one. You had to learn, as a quarterback, how to make those differences work for you — the wider field, the number of downs, the number of players in motion before the snap of the ball. One play that Moon witnessed had him utterly baffled standing on the sidelines. Something that could only happen in a Canadian football game.

"I remember the first pre-season game," he said, "where the punter of the opposing team punted the football into the end zone, and we punted it back out, and they caught it and punted it back in, and I was going, 'What the heck is going on out there?' But this was a big part of the game, getting that one point."

(Ah yes, the beloved "rouge." The single point awarded for a missed field goal or a punt that does not exit the end zone. One of the rules in Canadian football that can turn an intricate, well-played, well-coached game into playground mayhem in an instant.)

Hector Pothier, a former Canadian offensive tackle and now a school principal in Edmonton, was a rookie the same year as Moon. When it was his turn in the hot seat high above the Commonwealth Stadium field, I asked him to describe his first impressions of Moon as an athlete, not just a quarterback. He offered a frank assessment the likes of which might appear in a professional scouting report.

"Warren was always an outstanding athlete. I mean he's as tall as I am. He's six foot three. He's strong. I mean, Warren, as a quarterback, had like a 350-pound bench press. Which is pretty impressive. Plus he can run like a deer, throw off his back foot, had an arm like a bullet. He was an amazing athlete. But he was a fairly humble, quiet guy, too. Fairly reserved, quiet, shy."

In 1978, the Eskimos played their last game in Clarke Stadium and moved into Commonwealth Stadium, which had been built for the Commonwealth Games (and eventually the Eskimos) with seating for 40,000. The stadium was expanded in 1983 to a capacity of 60,000. In his first year with Edmonton, as backup to Wilkinson, Moon threw for 1,112 yards on eighty-nine completions. In the Grey Cup game, played at Exhibition Stadium in Toronto, the Eskimos exacted revenge on Montreal 20–13, with Wilkinson carrying the load. Moon only got into the game for one play, a quarterback sneak on a third-down-and-one-yard-to-go situation. On that one occasion, he got the first down. But his lack of playing time during the latter stages of the season and playoffs bothered him.

"I felt I wasn't contributing to the team and wondered if I'd ever get my chance," he told the *Ottawa Journal*. "But you have to be patient."

In 1979, the workload was more equally divided between Wilkinson and Moon, with Moon throwing 149 completions for 2,382 yards compared to Wilkinson's 120 completions for 2,132 yards. Moon also started four games. The team went 12–2 behind both quarterbacks. In the Western Conference final against the Calgary Stampeders, Wilkinson started but proved ineffective against the Calgary defence, and Coach Campbell made the switch to Moon early in the contest. Moon led the Eskimos to a couple of quick touchdowns and Edmonton hung on for the victory. Once again, Edmonton was heading to Montreal and the unfriendly confines of the Olympic Stadium against the Alouettes for the Grey Cup.

Despite pulling out the victory against the Stampeders the week before, Moon had no illusions over who would get the call to start the game.

"I know Wilkie will start in the Grey Cup and he should," he told an *Ottawa Journal* reporter. "He's the man and he's gotten us this far. There's no reason to change."

Wilkinson did get the start in the Grey Cup game but, unlike the previous season's final, he did not finish the game. Moon came on for the second half and threw his first Grey Cup touchdown pass, a thirty-three-yard pass to receiver Tom Scott. Neither quarterback particularly distinguished himself but the Eskimos came out on top, 17–9, in a defensive struggle. It was the fifth time the two teams had faced each other in the Grey Cup that decade, with the Eskimos coming out on top in the rubber match.

Moon had demonstrated that he was ready to be "the man" in Edmonton. He had completed his apprenticeship under Wilkinson and had been well served by it.

"Well you know, Wilkie had his skill set," Moon said. "He was such a crafty guy. He just knew the game really well. Knew his ability, his strengths and weaknesses, inside out. He knew the things we did best in the offence and those were the type of plays that he called. And that was one of the things about our offence, that you called your own plays. So he called the ones that he felt most comfortable with and he succeeded.... No one could stop him, even if they knew what he was going to do. He just out-executed other teams."

"He was quiet, very quiet. He wanted his actions to do the talking," remembered Wilkinson about his protege. "Not his lips. And he wouldn't say much in meetings. He was trying to take everything in. And every year he got a little better."

Moon had also earned the trust of his coach, Hugh Campbell, not just for his obvious physical talents but for the more cerebral aspects he brought to the game. As Moon wrote in his autobiography, "Campbell also told anyone who would listen that I also won games with my head, not just my arm or my athletic ability.... It seemed as if every black quarterback at one time or another has faced his share of criticism about reading defences poorly or not being prepared — the inference being that black quarterbacks are not mentally up to the task."

As expected, when the 1980 season opened, Moon had ascended to his rightful place as starting quarterback. Everything was indeed going according to the Moon plan. The Eskimos dominated the regular season, going 13–3, with Moon throwing 181 completions for 3,127 yards and twenty-five touchdowns. In the backup role, Wilkinson threw for another 1,060 yards. Ed Jones led the league in interceptions with nine. Nine Eskimos were named to the All-Canadian team. Moon's total yardage passing was second only to Dieter Brock's with Winnipeg. Brock, a white American quarterback from Birmingham, Alabama, by way of Auburn and Jackson State University, would win the Most Outstanding Player award that year. But it was Moon and the Eskimos that were going to the Grey Cup in Toronto against the overmatched Hamilton Tiger-Cats, barely one game over .500 and the best of a mediocre East.

If Edmonton won, it would be their third Grey Cup victory in a row, a streak that would match the highly touted Eskimos team from the '50s led by Johnny Bright, Rollie Miles, and Jackie Parker. That was the Edmonton team that all subsequent Eskimos teams were compared against. If any team could match that great '50s squad, it was Hugh Campbell's team.

"It was a great team," said Hector Pothier. "We just had all the right factors. We had great players. We had a great coach, Hugh Campbell, with a great philosophy that allowed us to be men. Basically, we had one rule. Act like a man. And if you don't know what that means come talk to me."

"You know, you were hearing about the guys from the '50s, the three-in-a-row Grey Cups," said Jones, the mischievous smile as wide as ever. "I met all those guys and I got to know them really well. I'd hang out with them. Rollie I used to call Pop 'Roman Numeral' Two. He was like my dad. He sort of looked after me a bit. I could pop in on him at two in the morning if I was on the west side of the city and maybe had a drink or two and didn't want to drive home. I could pop in there and sleep it off. I was almost treated like one of his kids."

The Grey Cup game itself was an anticlimactic rout. Moon threw for 398 yards passing and three touchdowns in a thorough demolition of poor Hamilton. He also picked up the MVP award for the game. It didn't take long before talk swung from matching the '50s Eskimos to surpassing them.

"And first it was like, 'Well, who's won three in a row?'" Tom Wilkinson remembered. "And it was the group from Edmonton — '54, '55, and '56, Jackie Parker and them.... Then it was, 'Well, who's ever won four?' 'Well, nobody.'"

That was all the incentive they needed.

"I enjoyed these guys. These guys were a lot of fun," said Ed Jones and I believed him. If anyone knew about "fun" and could provide a definition, it was Ed Jones. "The white guys [and] the black guys were all treated very equally here. There was nobody walking around with a side arm calling you, 'Boy, come here!' like I had in Texas. That's probably why I stayed here. Because of the friendships I developed and the relationships I made."

Friendships, relationships, and no side arms. Who wouldn't want to stay? Plus now the team had their sights set on the magic number four. The regular season of 1981 played out like one long coronation. The Eskimos went 14–1–1, their lone blemishes a loss to Winnipeg behind Dieter Brock and a tie with the Hamilton Tiger-Cats. The offence was unstoppable and the defence impenetrable. There was talk throughout the league that this year's team was the best Canadian football team of all time. Tough to argue with that. Their only competition came from the West-based teams, led by Winnipeg who went 11–5, with three of the remaining four teams owning winning records. The East was a complete shambles. Outside of Hamilton, who had an 11–4–1 record, Toronto, Montreal, and Ottawa won only a total of ten games and half of those belonged to Ottawa behind an exciting black rookie quarterback, J.C. Watts.

Moon had a tremendous season by any standards with 237 completions for 3,959 yards and twenty-seven touchdowns, numbers only surpassed by Dieter Brock in Winnipeg. But in Winnipeg, Brock was the show. In Edmonton, Hugh Campbell still found playing time for Tom Wilkinson, who chipped in with 1,293 passing yards and eight touchdowns of his own. The team as a whole set a league record with 576 points scored, an average of thirty-six points per game. Wide receivers Brian Kelly, Waddell Smith, and Tom Scott accounted for almost 4,000 yards receiving the ball.

But there's no question who was at the reins of this offensive juggernaut as it rolled over the opposition on its way to the Grey Cup. One man, Warren Moon. For Tom Wilkinson, one play that season came readily to mind that encapsulated Moon's incredible talent.

"There was one game the last year I was here when we played at Commonwealth Stadium. We were going to the north and [Moon] rolled out to his left into a really strong wind and just flipped the ball to Brian Kelly for about thirty-five yards and a touchdown. I didn't have a bad arm but I didn't have a gun. But I'm not kidding, the way the wind was blowing and to be rolling to your left …" He paused in mid-memory to just shake his head in amazement. "I'd have had to throw it and gone and picked it up and thrown it again to get it where Kelly was. And he just rolled out and flipped it."

Asked by Graham Kelly for his book *The Grey Cup* what went into being a good receiver, Brian Kelly answered, "It helps to have a good quarterback. That is one very important characteristic; a quarterback who can put the ball on the money all the time without putting the receiver at risk. Warren Moon can do that."

Moon "was a leader by performance," said Hector Pothier, as succinct as ever.

That leadership would be put to the test in the Grey Cup game of 1981.

The fact that a lowly five-win team, Ottawa, beat a lowlier three-win team, Montreal, in the Eastern semifinals was nothing to get Canadian football fans excited, not even those in Ottawa. It is difficult to take pride in an undeserving team making the playoffs when the bar has been set limbo-dancer low. But when that same team then goes on to eliminate the top team, Hamilton, in the conference final, well, then the reluctant fan gets to thinking that maybe the regular season was an anomaly, that only now were the Rough Riders rising from the smoking embers of a lost season to transform into a thundering flock of phoenixes.

Right.

Even if a fan was dreamy-eyed enough to think it possible that the Eastern Roughies could beat the Eskimos, the odds-makers were saying something different: that Ottawa did not even belong on the same field as Edmonton. Thus, the Rough Riders became twenty-two-and-a-half-point underdogs to the Eskimos. But Ottawa had a secret weapon in J.C. Watts. Not exactly a "secret weapon" because he had played all season, but he was a rookie quarterback; no one could guess how he would hold up under pressure before and during the game. But Hamilton coach Frank Kush — the same man that once tried to recruit Warren Moon to Arizona State — knew how Watts was capable of turning a flaw in his game into a positive quality.

"I think the greatest asset Watts had going for him was his inconsistency," said Kush after the Tiger-Cats fell to Ottawa. "The reason for that is he got back there, scrambled, and came up with the big plays."

Unpredictability might have been a more generous term than "inconsistency," although throughout his rookie season in the CFL Watts proved more than capable of producing as many spectacular fails as successes. But once the game got under way, it was Moon who provided the model of unpredictability — because it was impossible to predict that he could play so badly.

"The first two plays of the game, I remember, I believe he threw outside, one to Kelly, and one to Scott," remembered Hector Pothier, who was providing protection for Moon. "And both [passes] hit the turf in front of the receiver and that was a foreshadowing of the sort of rough half for Warren."

On his next possession he threw another one into the ground and then the next one into the arms of an Ottawa defender. Of his first six passes, he completed only one, not counting the two he completed to

Ottawa defenders, both interceptions resulting in points on the board for Watts and company.

"I mean Warren struggled … there's no doubt about it," said Pothier. "[On the second interception] I was blocking my guy at tackle — we weren't close to Warren at all — and he threw a pass downfield that hit me in the back of the head, went up in the air about forty yards, and they intercepted and ran it down to about our ten-yard line."

Watts, on the other hand, was doing what he had to do while Edmonton imploded. He turned Eskimo mistakes into points and raced out to a 20–0 lead. In his post-game interviews, Moon was at a loss to explain why he began the game so poorly.

"I don't know what it was. I threw the first two passes into the ground when I had guys open. The third one I tried to force the ball in just to get a completion and a guy intercepted it."

Hugh Campbell had seen enough. Early in the second quarter, he sent in Tom Wilkinson to take Moon's place.

"I want you to go out there and get me some first downs," Campbell told Wilkinson, "so we can show Warren some things at halftime, some simple things that work."

And that's exactly what Wilkinson did. Slowly but surely he worked the team down the field. Ottawa was willing to give Edmonton the short plays in order to prevent the deep threats. But that was precisely Campbell's strategy in putting in Wilkinson. He wanted to remind Moon that he didn't have to make big plays to get back into the game. Work the field and work the clock and there was still an entire half to play. As it turned out, Edmonton had to settle for a single point off a missed field goal, and they went into halftime trailing 20–1.

"I said almost nothing at halftime," Campbell told reporters after the game. "The feeling was that we knew we could score twenty points — undoubtedly — in the half. We knew we could score three touchdowns in three minutes. The important thing was getting the first one."

When the second half started, Moon was back at quarterback. He promptly led the Eskimos down the field for a touchdown. 20–8. J.C. Watts rolled out deep in his zone, was hit by an Edmonton tackler, and fumbled the football, with Edmonton recovering it on the three-yard line. A Moon quarterback sneak, and just like that, the score was 20–15. Ottawa kicked a field goal. 23–15. Later, a one-yard quarterback sneak by Moon and a two-point conversion. Tie game, 23–23. And with three seconds left on the clock, Dave Cutler kicked a field goal for Edmonton to win the game.

It was hardly Moon's best game and, quite frankly, could be rated as one of his worst. He threw another interception in the second half to go with his two in the first. He was matched in that category by Watts, who also threw three interceptions and made a costly fumble deep in his own territory. But it was J.C. Watts who was named the game's offensive MVP for keeping the game interesting and close. Inconsistent — or unpredictable — to the end.

Interestingly enough, the player most credited with leading Edmonton to victory in its fourth Grey Cup in a row was Tom Wilkinson, who played less than a quarter of the game.

"Inspired by 15-year veteran Tom Wilkinson, the heart and soul of the Eskimos," read the *Nanaimo Daily Free Press* on November 23, 1981, "Edmonton answered with a 25-point second half to nose out the victory."

Not to take anything away from Wilkinson, who went 10-for-13 for eighty yards during his stint at quarterback, but what did he accomplish in that playing time? A single point on the board. To credit Wilkinson with turning the game around, as many newspapers did across the country, was to ignore what Moon did in the second half. Wilkinson did what he had always done, moved the ball and ate up time, providing Moon with a breather and allowing him to get his bearings. There had never been any question in Campbell's mind who would start the second half.

Perhaps it was just the press heaping excessive praise on the little overachiever from Wyoming as he rode into the sunset. But no more would Warren Moon have to read or hear about who should be or not be starting any game. The job was all his heading into the 1982 season. And once again, a black quarterback from the East was set to rise up and challenge the reigning champ for supremacy in the CFL.

In Tennessee, they called him "the Artful Dodger." But if you're thinking of the filthy little master pickpocket from Charles Dickens's classic *Oliver Twist*, forget it. Wrong guy. This Artful Dodger was a five-foot-ten black quarterback from Alabama, whose skin colour prevented him from playing quarterback for a major school in his home state. Instead, he went to the University of Tennessee where the head coach told him, "If you can play quarterback, you can play at Tennessee." That was all he needed to hear. Alabama's loss would be Tennessee's gain. He played varsity quarterback for three seasons for the Tennessee Volunteers, electrifying fans every time he touched the ball (which, it so happens, was every offensive play from scrimmage). No one knew what to expect from one play to the next. Not even his coaches.

His name was Condredge Holloway. And he would be the first Black American to ever play quarterback in the Southeastern Conference.

Condredge Holloway could steal an opponent blind. They might think they had him comfortably trapped behind the line of scrimmage but they'd blink and he'd be gone, leaving his opponent grasping at air. There is a story — difficult to absolutely verify in the game film — where it is said that, in a game against Georgia State, every player on the defensive side of the ball got a hand on Holloway and he still scored the touchdown. It is a remarkable thing to watch, that run. He bounced, he pivoted, he turned completely around, regaining balance and direction, not resisting the tackler but allowing himself to be twisted in the direction the tackler took him and using that force to gain momentum, as hands slid helplessly away. And then the next wave, arms stretched, fingers extended, grazing ankles ... then nothing. Teammates clashed against each other like bowling pins, a would-be sandwich missed, toppling over one another like some staged extras in a forgotten gridiron classic of the silver screen. *There he is ... no, there ... no, there!* All that was missing was a Harpo Marx–like honk to rub it in.

As his former Tennessee teammate Lester McLain comments in Kenny Chesney's cinematic ode to Holloway, *The Color Orange*, on Holloway's unbelievable touchdown run, "Only in a cartoon can you get away that way." And maybe that's what makes it so compelling to watch time after time, the cartoonish improbability of it all.

Condredge Holloway was born in Huntsville, Alabama, the grandson of a former slave on his father's side who gained emancipation as a child in 1865. He went to an integrated Catholic school until grade six and then, like all black children in Huntsville, he attended segregated public school. During the '60s, Governor George Wallace was something of a divine ruler in Alabama — if you were white, that is. At his gubernatorial inauguration in 1963, with the rising tide of civil rights threatening to overwhelm the white power structure, he made his famous American apartheid declaration. "I say segregation now, segregation tomorrow, and segregation forever."

In his inaugural year, after the U.S. Supreme Court ruled segregation unconstitutional, Wallace stood blocking the doorway to the enrolment office at the University of Alabama, flanked by state troopers, to prevent black students from enrolling. His personal blockade ended when President John F. Kennedy sent in National Guard troops to force integration. Two months later, Martin Luther King delivered his "I Have a Dream" speech from the steps of the Lincoln Memorial in Washington, D.C., and felt obligated to draw attention to Wallace's rhetoric.

"I have a dream that one day in Alabama with its vicious racists, with its governor having his lips dripping with the words of interposition and nullification, one day right there in Alabama little black boys and black girls will be able to join hands with little white boys and white girls as sisters and brothers."

But Alabama football was suffering under Wallace's apartheid system. Alabama was one of the last teams in the United States to have an entirely white makeup. The once-powerful football team, under Coach Bear Bryant, was falling behind schools that were taking advantage of Alabama's racist policies by recruiting the best black athletes out from under their noses. Bryant saw the writing on the wall and was trying to work to change the system from within. It was not until the famous game between Alabama and USC on September 12, 1970, the first time an integrated football team from outside the state would play on Legion Field in Birmingham, Alabama, that things would change. USC, with an all-black backfield, hammered the Crimson Tide in front of a stunned crowd. Bryant had made his point. Integration on the gridiron was an absolute must if Alabama ever hoped to top the nation again.

Which brings us back to the young Condredge Holloway. In high school, he discovered that friends he had known from Catholic school were now picking sides. He decided that rather than get caught up in peer pressure he would pour his energy into sports, and he was able to do that at an incredible level. He was a three-sport star athlete, receiving university recruitment letters in basketball (from John Wooden at UCLA) and football. The Montreal Expos drafted him fourth overall as shortstop and offered the seventeen-year-old Holloway a handsome contract. Signing the contract would have meant forgoing college, and Condredge's mother would have none of that. Her son was going to get a university degree. And the best bet for that to happen was by means of a football scholarship.

He did get an offer from Bear Bryant to play football at the University of Alabama. There was, however, a caveat. He would not be allowed to play quarterback. Alabama was not ready to have a Black American as the face of its most famous football team.

"I was told by Bear Bryant that it wasn't his problem, it was the governor's problem," said Holloway over the phone from his office at the University of Tennessee where he is now an assistant athletic director. "He was the one who said, 'Segregation now, segregation tomorrow, segregation forever.' Coach Bryant and I had a great relationship. But he told me he can't override the governor of Alabama. That was out of his hands."

So, instead, Holloway accepted an offer from the University of Tennessee.

"Believe it or not, my coach here at Tennessee, Bill Battle, was a former player for Bear Bryant. He was just in a state that didn't have problems like that or believe in that. He asked the governor of Tennessee, 'Can we have a black quarterback?' And he said, 'If he's good enough, yeah.' They had no problem with anything."

It is hard to imagine in Canada that the head of the football program at a major university would have to go to the premier of a province to make a player personnel decision. But in the South of the United States where racial prejudices could reach a fever pitch, under the threat of funding cuts or open fan revolt, especially where older, more staid alumni were concerned, the University of Tennessee football program needed to know if they could have a black quarterback. Did Holloway ever feel an added burden as the first black quarterback in the Southeastern Conference?

"I never worried about that," he said. "I played as hard as I could, I played the best I could. That's just the way I was brought up. My dad and mom always said, 'Always play the best you can play and fix whatever you messed up.' That's just the way we were. I never felt that I was on a platform where I had to play for anybody. Not at all. Ever."

His parents' advice "to fix whatever you messed up" must have been echoing in his ears in his very first game as a starter against Georgia Tech. The Volunteers were on the march for a touchdown when Holloway threw "a quick out" to the sidelines. The pass was tipped at the line of scrimmage and fluttered toward the receiver, giving the defensive back enough time to step in front and intercept the pass at about the Georgia Tech twenty-eight-yard line. In *The Color Orange*, there is wonderful footage of the defensive back sprinting down the sidelines for a certain touchdown. Not showboating or high-stepping, just flat-out sprinting. There is no one else in the shot. He's having his moment in the warm brilliance of the sun. And then, out of nowhere, Condredge Holloway enters the shot, crossing the forty-yard line on an angle toward the interceptor. The thirty, the twenty, ten … Holloway dives and brings down the most surprised human on the planet. *Fix whatever you messed up.* The Volunteers held Georgia Tech to a mere field goal when, moments before, a touchdown had seemed a sure thing. In the film, he calls it the best play he ever made.

"If I don't catch him, I'm probably a defensive back the next week," he says in the film.

Beginning in that rookie season as varsity starting quarterback in 1973, for three seasons Condredge Holloway thrilled the Volunteers fans who flocked to Neyland Stadium and the millions of Tennesseans watching the televised games at home. For his Houdini-like escapes on the field, he was dubbed "the Artful Dodger" by the Volunteers' play-by-play voice, John Ward. He wished he could have been known by a different tag, something that might have proved less stressful on his body.

"I would much rather stand back and throw it like Peyton [Manning] and not have a hip replacement, two knees, and a shoulder," he admits in the film.

As exciting as it is to watch and marvel at his daredevil escapes online, one cannot miss noting that he took a hell of a lot of punishment. By his senior year he was playing injured much of the time and it was affecting his game, although not enough to prevent Tennessee from going to a third bowl game in a row with Condredge at the helm. He was drafted by the

New England Patriots in the twelfth round of the 1975 NFL draft. They made it clear that they were not interested in him as a quarterback. And he wasn't interested in being a defensive back.

Then the Ottawa Rough Riders contacted him. They never told him he'd make a hell of a defensive back; they wanted him to play quarterback. They had another rookie quarterback in camp that year, one with an even higher profile than Holloway's. Tom Clements had been the starting quarterback at Notre Dame from 1972 to '74, leading the Fighting Irish to the national championship in 1973. The following season, his senior year, saw Clements finish fourth in the Heisman Trophy voting. The two quarterbacks would share quarterback duties that first year with Clements getting the lion's share of the playing time, throwing for 2,013 yards as compared to Holloway's 984. That would be the pattern for three straight seasons with roughly the same ratios of playing time and yards passing. When Ottawa went to the Grey Cup game in 1976, both quarterbacks' second year, Clements would play the entire game, despite having a miserable first half. He would, however, redeem himself by throwing the winning touchdown pass to Tony Gabriel with twenty seconds left in the game to beat Saskatchewan 23–20. Clements would win the Grey Cup MVP despite completing just eleven passes in thirty-five attempts for 174 yards.

By their fourth season, 1978, there was no longer a discrepancy in their playing time, and their statistics from that season prove it: Clements threw for 1,990 yards and Holloway for 1,970. One statistic in particular stood out in Holloway's favour: he only threw two interceptions that season while Clements threw twelve. In fact, throughout their whole careers Clements tended to throw a lot of interceptions while Holloway did not. This can probably be explained by Holloway's greater mobility. He didn't have to throw into dangerous situations, because he could tuck the ball away and run. Clements was considered the traditional drop-back passer while Holloway was considered a much greater threat running the ball.

In 1979, that quarterback partnership ended when Tom Clements was traded to Saskatchewan, who flipped him to Hamilton midway through the season after a poor start. Any thought that the job was all Holloway's ended, however, when Ottawa picked up Jimmy Jones from

Montreal. Once again Condredge found himself sharing minutes with another quarterback, although this time he was the starter and Jones was in the backup role.

(Jimmy Jones owned a unique distinction. He had been the first black quarterback to appear on the cover of *Sports Illustrated*, back in 1969. At the time he was the starting quarterback for USC. That season the Trojans went undefeated, 10–0–1, their only blemish a 14–14 tie with Notre Dame. USC beat Michigan in the Rose Bowl, ending the season ranked third in the nation. In the 1972 NFL draft, he went undrafted. He came to Montreal where he was named the Eastern All-Star quarterback in 1974. That same year he led the Alouettes to victory in the Grey Cup over the Edmonton Eskimos.)

Holloway played two more seasons for the Rough Riders before he was traded to the Toronto Argonauts, the league's sad sacks and whipping boys for close to thirty years. Their last Grey Cup had been in 1952, when Ulysses Curtis was their backfield star. In 1980, the Toronto Argonauts had named Willie Wood, former Green Bay Packer defensive back and double Super Bowl winner, as head coach, the first black head coach in CFL history. Thirty-four years after he had signed Herb Trawick to the Montreal Alouettes, Lew Hayman, now president of the Argos, was back breaking boundaries.

"Even if Willie was white I would have hired him," Hayman told the press. "I hired the first black player and now I've hired the first black coach. Whether it's a player or a coach all I'm concerned with is if he can help us, that's the guy I want."

Willie Wood saw something of his own story in Holloway's struggles to find a job coming out of college. Back in 1957, he had been the starting quarterback at USC, the first black quarterback in not only USC's history but in the entire Pac-10 (which is now the Pac-12). In the now all-too-familiar scenario, he went undrafted by the NFL. But Wood sent out letters to all the pro teams and got a hit. Vince Lombardi, head coach of the Green Bay Packers, was interested in giving him a tryout. In this case, however, Wood allowed himself to be turned into a defensive back. That move happened to work in his favour. In twelve seasons, he never missed a game, made All-Pro eight times, and won two Super Bowls.

The 1981 season started poorly for the Argonauts. They lost their first three games by a total of only five points. And then came a disastrous and humiliating blowout in Hamilton. Two weeks later the Argonauts appointed Ralph Sazio president of the club, replacing Hayman. Unless Willie Wood could do the impossible and turn his team's fortunes in the opposite direction, his tenure as a head coach would not last under Sazio, who was known for having an itchy trigger finger. The Argos ran their losing streak to ten games. When Wood confessed to reporters that he had "already tried everything" in his bag of coaching tricks to turn the team around, he as good as signed his walking papers.

But according to Holloway, Wood took far too much of the blame.

"Willie Wood was a great coach and an even better player," Holloway told me, in his former coach's defence. "A lot of stuff gets blamed on the coach when you've got players who can't play. We were two and fourteen because we had two-and-fourteen players. Willie never played a down."

That off-season, Sazio went out and hired Ottawa's assistant coach from 1976 to 1981, Bob O'Billovich. He brought with him offensive coordinator Darrel "Mouse" Davis, who had developed a unique offensive system he'd perfected as head coach of Portland State. The system was known as the "run-and-shoot" offence, and both men believed it perfectly suited Condredge Holloway's gift for improvisation.

The run-and-shoot offence emphasized the passing game, putting multiple receivers in motion parallel to the line of scrimmage, a means for the quarterback and receivers to determine the defensive coverage being used. That, of course, was just the beginning. The system granted the receivers the freedom to adjust their pass routes according to the coverage. The quarterback would also adjust his thought patterns to match the receiver's and throw to open spaces soon to be occupied by the receiver. It was a complex system requiring improvisation within rigid patterns. Asked for a rough explanation of the run-and-shoot system from the quarterback's point of view, Holloway gave a sigh that said, *Oh no, not again. I'm being forced to explain Einstein's theory of relativity to a barnyard chicken.*

"The run-and-shoot is an offensive scheme just like the 'I' formation or split formation," he began. "It enhances a lot of motion. And the reason it works so well in Canada is because you have unlimited motion. In the U.S., you can't run three guys across the field. In Canada you can line up four guys on one side, run three of the four in motion across the formation. If the defence doesn't move, they're in zone coverage. In Canada, you can run two one way and one back the other way. Maybe you can find out if they're in man-to-man and who's covering who, and if they're not they're in zone and you can find out exactly which zone they're in before the ball is even snapped. That's the luxury of motion."

Got that? It was also a system that required a quarterback with brains, guile, mobility, and toughness. But it could take its toll on quarterbacks. They tended to get hit a lot because they were such active members in the flow of motion, often waiting until the last moment before unloading the ball.

Hugh Campbell was familiar with the system and had heard all about Mouse Davis and the offence he was running down at Portland State. No matter how much Campbell may have admired the run-and-shoot, he was not willing to run the same risks with his most valuable commodity, Warren Moon. That may have been the reason that, before the season began, Toronto acquired quarterback Joe Barnes from Saskatchewan. It wouldn't hurt to have two quality quarterbacks drilled in the intricacies of an innovative offensive scheme in case one of them goes down. This is not a system where teams could airlift in an emergency replacement and hope to teach him on the fly.

Once again, the season started slow for the Argonauts as the players acclimatized themselves to the new playbook. They also needed to build up confidence in their ability to close out games. The year before they had come to believe that at the end of the day, they would always lose. It was O'Billovich's job to change that mindset. To make them believe that they would win. And just as much as he had to sell that change to the players, it was important to change the minds of the fans, those who resorted to the derisive drone of "Arrrgggggos" as the team staggered toward each inevitable loss.

"One thing when I came to Toronto from Ottawa," Holloway said, "everyone just wanted to talk about the history and all that stuff and how [the Argos] were so bad. I didn't engage in that. Of course, I was part of it [that first year] but Obie was adamant about 'We gotta change the culture.' One thing about changing the culture is you have to forget about the past and not dwell on it. But I can see how people who had been there a long time were used to it and kind of expected it. You're never going to change *everybody's* mind, but if you play well, sometimes they come around."

And gradually, the team began to make believers out of the players and the fans. Late in the season, the Argos lost back-to-backs against Winnipeg to drop to 7–6–1 before bouncing back to win their final two games against Saskatchewan and Ottawa, closing out the regular season with a 9–6–1 record. What a difference a year makes, from 2–14 in 1981 to first place in the East in 1982. Condredge Holloway had his greatest season in the CFL, throwing the ball over 500 times, connecting on 299 of those passes for a 59 percent success rate and 4,661 yards, almost twice as much yardage as he had thrown the year before. Thirty-one of those completions went for touchdowns. Holloway's trio of favourite receivers — Terry Greer, Paul Pearson, and running back Cedric Minter — accounted for 208 of those completions and 3,266 yards. As well, Holloway ran for another 448 yards, an average of 7.2 yards every time he took off on his own either by design or for purposes of survival. That brought his total yardage over 5,000 for the season.

A good year. Good enough to win the Schenley Award as the CFL's Most Outstanding Player. Condredge Holloway has never been one to revel in his accomplishments. Make no mistake, he is very proud of what he has accomplished, but he's not one to dwell on the past, except when fans and interviewers come calling. When the subject of his Schenley arises, Holloway, humbly and matter-of-factly, tells it as he sees it.

"Should have been Warren Moon. But sometimes you get lucky. He had a heck of a year. Go back and look if you have a chance. I'm not blowing smoke. Warren had a hell of a year that year."

He's right. Warren Moon did have a "hell of a year." But when I reminded him that his own season wasn't exactly chopped liver, Holloway was willing to concede … slightly.

"Well, it wasn't a runaway, let's put it that way."

The Edmonton Eskimos had been so good for so long, maybe to sports-writers across the nation it was difficult to pick one man out of the many CFL All-Stars on those teams and declare Moon the most valuable. The Esks had won with Tom Wilkinson. Tom had even won a Schenley as the Most Outstanding Player back in 1974. Back then the Eskimos were really just coming into their own as the closest thing to a dynasty the league would see over the next decade. And besides, it was Tom Wilkinson, not the most gifted of athletes, a blue-collar white guy from Wyoming. Most CFL fans could identify with him. He had that gut. No abs, no six-pack. A gut. Just like your average Joe. It was never an aesthetic experience watching Wilkinson work the field, but he was not being paid to make the gridiron his canvas. He was being paid to win.

Warren Moon had inherited the pre-eminent quarterback position in the land. The presumption was that he would use the mighty Eskimo machine to roll over the opposition. There were expectations for him not just to win but to win magnificently, to eschew the more conservative approach of a Tom Wilkinson–led offence in favour of an exciting, deep-threat aerial game. And if he did not match their expectations, as was the case in the 1981 Grey Cup game, then he heard his share of boos. But that was all right with Warren Moon, because as far as he was concerned, the fans had every right to express their displeasure over a poor performance.

"It was so much easier for me to play [in Canada]," Moon conceded. "Not going out with the burden of wondering what the crowd reaction was going to be. Not walking out of the tunnel before the game started, and kind of tightening your shoulders wondering what you're going to hear from some fan right outside the tunnel. Because that's what you were exposed to sometimes in the United States. Going out there in Canada, you just knew if you were on the road you got booed along with the rest of the team. If I didn't play well on the road, I got booed for it. If I didn't play well at home, I got booed for it — fortunately that didn't happen often. You were cheered and booed for the *right reasons.*"

In fact, Moon might have heard a few hometown boos early in the 1982 season as the Eskimos started off 3–5. And then one day it was as if the team awoke from some collective somnambulism, took a look around, and decided *enough of this nonsense* — and rattled off eight straight wins to finish the season. If the fans were looking for an exciting air show that year, they were not disappointed. Moon threw 562 passes, completing 333 of them for 5,000 yards. While Holloway had his top trio of receivers, Moon had what seemed an unlimited supply of targets: Brian Kelly, Waddell Smith, Tom Scott, Brian Fryer, the water boy, the mascot, and anyone that could run a route and hang onto the football. It was a Schenley Award year by anyone's standards. But Moon did not have to carry a team with two wins the previous season on his back to first place in the East. Moon merely took a 14–1–1 first-place-in-the-West team to an 11–5 first-place team. And that worked in Holloway's favour with the Schenley voters.

In the Eastern final that year, the Argonauts had an easy time polishing off the 5–11 Ottawa Rough Riders. The final score was an unflattering 44–7 in favour of Toronto. Edmonton, on the other hand, barely squeaked by the Winnipeg Blue Bombers in the Western final, and the media pundits began calling it the beginning of the end for the Edmonton dynasty. No one was quite ready to crown the Argos before the game, remembering that only a year before they had been a 2–14 team, but they had managed to beat the Eskimos once during the season, so anything was possible. With the game being played at Exhibition Stadium in Toronto, the Argos could only benefit from a hometown crowd cheering them on.

The Eskimos opened the scoring early in the first quarter, with Moon moving the offence into field-goal range for Dave Cutler. 3–0. Toronto responded shortly after that when Holloway tossed a screen pass to Emanuel Tolbert, who raced eighty-nine yards to the end zone. 7–3. Moon then moved the Eskimos eighty-two yards in eight plays, finishing off the drive with a pass to Brian Kelly for the touchdown. Just like that, 10–7. The game was quickly becoming a case of "anything you can do I can do better" as Holloway proceeded to march the Argonauts down the field, mostly by means of his own scrambling, before launching a touchdown pass into the end zone to Terry Greer. Holloway got crushed as he let the pass go, his helmet ripped from his head. He bounced right up. 14–10. The 54,741 fans in the stands were going crazy, despite the freezing temperatures and cold southwesterly winds. How did Warren Moon respond? He once again marched the Eskimos down the field before calmly rolling out and throwing a forty-one-yard touchdown toss to Kelly.

17–14. Cutler added another field goal before the half to make it 20–14 in Edmonton's favour before the rain and snow and colder temperatures blew in and ended the Argonauts' hopes for an upset on the artificial turf of Exhibition Stadium. Final score, 32–16. Edmonton had their fifth Grey Cup victory in a row.

When I suggested that perhaps the Argos were beaten as much by the weather as they were by the Eskimos, Holloway scoffed.

"I think we could have scored against the weather but Edmonton was hitting us in the mouth and that's one of the reasons we had a really hard time."

Warren Moon rushed for ninety-one yards that day and threw for another 319, winning the game's Most Valuable Player award. If his victory over Michigan in the Rose Bowl had been a vindication for the years of verbal abuse and criticism he had received from the Washington supporters and media, so too was the '82 Grey Cup game.

"What makes this one so good is that I did it on my own," he told reporters after the game. "Up until this year they kept saying that Tom Wilkinson had been holding my hand all this time."

It probably irked him that Wilkinson had been given so much credit in the media for supposedly showing Moon how to get the job done during the Grey Cup game the previous year when it was Moon who'd led the second-half comeback. And it bothered him that his regular-season performance was once again overlooked by the Schenley voters. Moon had nothing personal against Condredge Holloway. After all, quarterbacks don't play against quarterbacks. That's just part of the media hype-machine, which heightens conflicts and invents personal battles, always ready to pounce on a morsel of controversy. (A hockey goalie is commonly said to "outduel" the opposing goalie even though neither one takes shots on the other.)

"I played against the defence of Edmonton," said Condredge. "The only guy I was going head-to-head against was Dan Kepley [Edmonton's middle linebacker]. That's the guy I had to worry about. Warren was on the sideline when I was playing. I was on the sideline when he was playing. Now, for the press, we were going head-to-head."

True enough. Still, one can only imagine the hype that would have surrounded this particular contest if it had been played south of the forty-ninth parallel. It would be six years before a black quarterback even made an appearance in the Super Bowl. In 1988, Doug Williams led the Washington Redskins to victory over the Denver Broncos, copping the MVP award in the process. Twenty-five years would pass before a black quarterback won another one, Russell Wilson in 2013. In the seventy-two years since the NFL integrated, only six black quarterbacks have played in the championship game. And never have two black QBs ever faced each other in an NFL Championship or Super Bowl. Did the significance of two black quarterbacks vying for the national championship of Canada two years in a row enter into Warren Moon's thoughts before, during, or after the game?

"It did and it didn't," he told me, "only because of where I was. If this was something happening in the United States, it would have been a huge deal. Because it was Canada and we played against each other all the time, race was just not a big deal. And that was what was so refreshing about playing up there. It really didn't matter where you were from or what the colour of your skin was. You were just a quarterback, and you were playing a position."

Change was in the air in Edmonton after that fifth Grey Cup victory. For one thing, Hugh Campbell was leaving to take a head-coaching position with the Los Angeles Express of the fledgling United States Football League (USFL), which was meant to be a rival league to the NFL, although it would play a spring and summer schedule that would not put it in direct competition with the NFL for the football audience. There were also rumours in the air that Warren Moon was set to jump to either the USFL or the NFL, neither of which was true at the time.

"I signed a ten-year contract at one time with an 'out clause,' but I felt that I was going to play my whole career in Canada. That's how much I was enjoying it. I was just enjoying playing football. I was being paid pretty well. My family was enjoying it."

The biggest negative, if one considers it a negative, was going back and forth between Southern California and Edmonton, living in two places. His kids were reaching an age where he and his wife would have to make decisions concerning their future. Were they going to commit fully to living in Canada year-round or keep moving back and forth every six months? And, lest we forget, there was the Plan. Always in the back of his mind there existed the thought of returning triumphantly to the States and proving to all those professional NFL teams that they were wrong to overlook him because of the colour of his skin.

The Eskimos of 1983 were, if not exactly in turmoil, certainly trending downward, no longer the great invincible Edmonton machine. Hugh Campbell's replacement as head coach was himself replaced halfway through the season by former Eskimo star Jackie Parker. But even "Ol' Spaghetti Legs" could not lift Edmonton out of its mediocrity as the Eskimos finished the season 8–8, good for third place in the West. That mediocrity, however, did not extend as far as Warren Moon's play. Moon had, from a purely statistical standpoint, a career year. He threw an unprecedented 664 passes, connecting on 380 of those for 5,648 yards and thirty-one touchdowns. It took a mediocre season by Edmonton for the Schenley voters to finally recognize Moon's true value and achievements. He might have been speaking in the "royal we" when he said, after winning the Grey Cup and game MVP the year before, "I have given up thinking that we will get the recognition we deserve."

Meanwhile in the East, Toronto had sailed along to a 12–4 record, including two wins over Edmonton, partial repayment for the Grey Cup loss. Though Condredge Holloway had established himself as the number-one starter, Joe Barnes, back from injury, was much more than a backup quarterback. This was another Warren Moon/Tom Wilkinson two-man quarterback show, with Holloway throwing for 3,184 yards and Barnes for 2,274. But the real star performance on that 1983 team belonged to Terry Greer, who caught 113 passes for an astounding 2,003 yards.

Toronto brushed aside the Hamilton Tiger-Cats, another five-win team from the East, in the Eastern final. By the time they had done that, however, they already knew that they would not be facing a rematch with the Eskimos, as Edmonton had been blown out by Winnipeg in the semifinals of the West. Winnipeg, in turn, were beaten by the first-place B.C. Lions. For the third season in a row, the Grey Cup game would be contested by two teams fronted by black quarterbacks, Holloway and Roy Dewalt of the B.C. Lions.

The 1983 Grey Cup would be the first Canadian football championship contested indoors under an inflatable roof at BC Place. For the first time since the Grey Cup's inception in 1909, the Grey Cup competitors would not be at the mercy of the fickle Canadian weather in November. No mud wrestling. No need to fire staples into shoes to promote traction. No fog, rain, sleet, snow, freezing cold, or wind to affect the handling of the ball or the ability to run with it. There did, however, remain one distraction that could have affected the outcome of the game. The NOISE. And with a hometown crowd well-versed in the art of maximizing noise levels indoors, especially when the opposition had the ball, they could make it very difficult for visiting teams to hear the quarterback.

From the beginning, it was clear that Holloway did not bring his A game to the big event. He had only thrown five interceptions all year in 372 passing attempts and yet, on the second play from scrimmage, he threw a pass directly into the arms of a B.C. defensive back. The Argos' offence never really got on track, Holloway in perpetual scramble mode, missing opportunities. Down 17–7 at the half, O'Billovich did not wait to see whether Holloway could turn his game, as well as the team's fortunes, around. Instead, he inserted Joe Barnes into the game. The Argos came from behind and won the game with a couple of minutes left when Barnes hit Cedric Minter with a three-yard touchdown pass. The final score was 18–17.

"Condredge was having trouble running the football team. He was not sharp," explained Obie in his post-game comments. He mentioned a hamstring, the flu. He had no desire to throw his starting quarterback under the bus. What was the whole purpose of having two quarterbacks capable of being starters if not for moments like this? Condredge Holloway is not the kind of man to fall back on excuses.

"Didn't play well," he said, looking back on his performance that day. "That's the way it was. To win a Grey Cup, to win any championship, you've got to be a little bit lucky and you've got to play well, that day, at that moment. If you win, you win as a team and if you lose …" He left the rest unsaid. "Sometimes you just don't get things done you should."

Holloway was the consummate professional and team player. Could he have delivered in the second half if Obie had left him in? After all, Barnes hardly blew the doors off the game, putting up only eleven points in his half, with seven of those coming in the last two minutes of the game. But to wonder "what if" is to miss the point. Holloway and Barnes had each other's backs all season long. There was nothing personal in Obie's move, no lack of respect for his starter. Just an awareness that it was time for a change.

"All egos are gone when you get into the Grey Cup and when you are so far into your career," acknowledged Holloway.

Once Hugh Campbell left Edmonton for the USFL, a stepping stone in his own plan to reach an NFL coaching position, the writing was on the wall for Warren Moon, writ large in ten-foot graffiti letters for the world to see. What else was there left to accomplish?

"I got to a point in Canada where I had done everything I could possibly do as a player. I won multiple championships, I won MVP awards of the game, I won the MVP award of the country. Our team was getting older, guys were starting to retire. I knew our run had pretty much ended. I didn't want to go through a rebuilding process."

And in the back of his mind was the question, "How good a quarterback am I really?" Over six seasons he had proven that he was the best quarterback in the Canadian Football League. There was nothing left to prove.

"I think the only way you can measure yourself on how good you are is to play against the very best. The very, very best to me were still in the National Football League. So that was the curiosity I had inside of me. And the challenge inside of me. I wanted to see exactly how good I was."

The Plan had always been there. He had waited for the right moment. And now multiple NFL teams were banging at his door. He didn't have to ask, "What position?" He knew. The time had come for Warren Moon. And to possibly sweeten their pitch for Moon's services, the Houston Oilers hired Hugh Campbell, the man who knew Warren Moon's capabilities better than anyone, as their new head coach. And so Warren Moon signed with Houston for $5.5 million over five years, the largest contract in NFL history at the time. The black player the NFL wouldn't draft because he refused to play any other position than quarterback now stood atop the game.

I just had one last question for the most successful quarterback the Canadian game has ever seen.

"What would you have done if the Canadian Football League hadn't existed?"

"That is a really good question," he began, and I gave myself a mental pat on the back despite knowing he has probably made hundreds of interviewers feel brilliant by beginning his answer with those words. "What would I have done if the Canadian Football League was not there? Again I was a very stubborn, very confident guy that I could play quarterback and that was the only position I wanted to play. It wasn't that I didn't love football. I loved the game of football because of the position of quarterback. So if it wasn't there I don't know. I might've quit and gone to law school or something like that.... But I'm glad I wasn't given that option because I'm glad the Canadian Football League option was there ... it saved my career and made me the player I became. The opportunity of going to Canada did it."

Maybe dreams are for those who can only imagine. But plans, such as those hatched in the Moon house in West L.A., are for those who can see dreams through to their natural conclusion.

Chapter Eight

A FAMILY AFFAIR

John "Twiggy" Williams and John Williams Jr. hold a unique distinction in the Canadian Football League. They are the only black father and son combination to have their names engraved on the Grey Cup, John Sr. with Hamilton in 1972 and John Jr. with the Toronto Argonauts in 2004. John Jr. was born in Burlington, Ontario, back in 1977. But his real place of birth could be found in some mythical atlas located somewhere between Denton, Texas, and a planet called "Football."

The Denton part is easy to pick out. He has a lazy Texan drawl inherited from his father, John Williams Sr., former All-Star cornerback with the Hamilton Tiger-Cats of the 1970s. John Senior was born in Denton. Grew up in Denton. Couldn't wait to get out of Denton and Texas altogether. Not much to do in Denton when you're poor and black and it's the 1950s. You could pick cotton, which John Sr. started doing when he was ten years old. The farmer would drive up in his pickup truck and John, with other boys and some men, would jump aboard and off they went to the cotton fields. They'd pick cotton all day in a dry summer heat that frequently reached 100 degrees Fahrenheit (38 degrees Celsius). There were no city swimming pools to cool off in — well, not for the black kids. Swimming was a luxury reserved for white people.

So it was small wonder that John Sr. wanted to leave Denton, Texas, in the rear-view mirror as soon as he could. And football was his passport. It took him all the way to Burlington, Ontario, and a career in the Canadian Football League mostly spent with the Hamilton Tiger-Cats. He won that 1972 Grey Cup with the Cats. It was the only Grey Cup he would win during his eight-year career. But that's all right; most players never get to win a championship. The vast majority — 98.4 percent — of college football players in the U.S. with aspirations to play professional football never get that opportunity. John Sr. could have played in the States. He was asked many times. But once he'd come to Canada, he never wanted to go back. He thought about it, sure; who wouldn't when someone of the status of Al Davis, legendary lone-wolf owner of the Oakland Raiders, offered you a job?

"You heard of Willie Brown. Played for the Raiders?" John Sr. asked me in his Waterdown kitchen.

"Sure. I heard of him," I responded, though I wasn't as sure as I pretended to be. There was always the internet. (Willie Brown, I later learned, played fourteen seasons in the NFL, eleven of them with the Oakland Raiders. Eight time All-Pro [AFL and NFL]. He won three Super Bowls with Oakland.)

"He used to beg me to come down there and play with him. He said, 'John, you can play that other corner from me.' He said, 'I know Al Davis would bring you in.' I said, 'Okay, Willie, I'll go visit. And see what they say.'"

And so he flew down to Oakland and was met by head coach John Madden, who, at the time he became head coach in 1969, was the young-est head coach ever in the history of the NFL, at thirty-two years of age. He also had a reputation as a player's coach who believed that the fewer rules you put in place, the fewer rules your players could break. He was also a huge man with a huge appetite.

"First thing he said to me: 'Want to get something to eat?'" John laughed at the memory. "Nah, I don't want nothing to eat." Not the most auspicious beginning. Madden managed to contain his disappointment at missing a feed and they went directly to the stadium for a workout. The coaching staff liked what they saw but there was one small problem. John Sr. was still under contract to the Hamilton Tiger-Cats. So someone from the front office told John not to worry, that they knew a guy who knew a guy who knew a guy who could get him out of his contract with Hamilton. But that last guy, whoever he was in the chain, had never dealt with Ralph Sazio, the Ticats' general manager.

Sazio was not the type of guy to let a player just get up and leave when a better opportunity presented itself. In that regard, he was no different from any other general manager who has ownership looking over his shoulder. He must always be looking for leverage in any situation. John Sr. understood the scenario. He had become wise to the ways of football. Something of a Zen master. He had been cut from the Calgary Stampeders ten games into the season back in 1967 after some player that the then head coach, Jerry Williams, knew on a personal basis became available. The team kept him around though. Paid him $200 a week not to play. Just to be available. (The game can break your heart.)

And so John Sr. returned to Hamilton, went to camp as usual, and did his job to the best of his abilities with an absolute lack of resentment. He had a good thing in Hamilton. Why rock the boat?

"When I hear people talking about playing in the NFL versus the CFL thing, it doesn't bother me because I know I could have played down there. This is home for me. I've lived in Canada longer than I lived in the U.S. And I'm very happy with my life."

He met his second wife, Meryle, in 1970 while he was playing for Hamilton.

"I left practice one day, me and three or four other players in a car, and they pulled up beside us, her and a couple of friends. They were going to nursing school and they yelled at us and we yelled back, 'Follow us!'"

And they did. John had previously been married to his high-school sweetheart. She had grown tired of the itinerant lifestyle of a journeyman ballplayer and he had not. He and his second wife married in 1976 and had three kids. The first son was christened John Williams Jr. His godfather was Bruce Smith, defensive tackle with that 1972 Grey Cup–winning Tiger-Cats team. His sister's godfather was Bernie Custis. Bernie and John Sr. had become friends when John Sr. came to the Tiger-Cats in 1969. A teammate on the Cats told him, "You have to meet this guy, Bernie Custis." Bernie was a scout for the Tiger-Cats and something of a coaching guru by that time, not with the Cats, but with the Burlington Braves, a local junior football team in Burlington. He was also a school principal. Bernie and John got to playing pickup basketball at a school gym and over the years formed a tight friendship, so much so that John Sr.'s kids called Bernie "Uncle Bernie."

John Jr. grew up surrounded by former football players and talk about football on both sides of the border, CFL and NFL. College ball, too; again, Canadian and American. His father was a scout for the Detroit Lions for a few years so Bernie, John Sr., and John Jr. made frequent trips to Detroit to see the Lions play or to just attend training camps. Or they would all go to Syracuse, Bernie's alma mater, to watch Orangemen home games. Bernie had never lost contact with his university, and he scouted the local talent through his coaching contacts for potential Syracuse recruits. For American football players, regardless of race, the university where they played fills a special place in their hearts and minds; in a sense, it defines them, in a way that a pro team never will. Once you are in the pros, the love of the game becomes tied up in the politics of numbers, whether they be zeros on a salary, the players ahead of you on the depth chart, or the years you can expect to play before injuries and age relegate you to the scrap heap of former players. It's all about the numbers.

John Jr. never felt that football was pushed on him as a kid. It was just always there. And when you're a kid it's only natural to want to find a key to the adult world, the jokes and stories and put-downs and laughter that flow easily in the company of ex-jocks. And how inclusive, not dismissive, these football friends were of him, the young John. John Sr. never wanted to put pressure on John Jr. to follow in his footsteps. Those original footsteps had begun as a path out of the cotton fields of the South, out from a world of poverty and segregation, a world his son need never experience. After all, isn't this what coming to Canada had provided for John Sr. and his family? An economic, social, and educational freedom that did not necessitate a single-minded devotion to a single goal in order to escape? So it came as some surprise to John Sr. when his wife signed John Jr. up for Little League Football.

John Jr. remembers his first day well. On the occasion of this interview, there were four of us in his car: John, who was driving; my cameraman, Terry Zazulak, scrunched down in the front seat beside him; and soundman Jason Hoeffner and me in the back. Ostensibly, we were there to shoot B-roll for the film (extra footage used as cutaway material from a static interview shot). While we were at it, I thought I'd try to get some off-the-cuff interview material.

"They asked me, 'What position do you want to play?' And I said, 'Quarterback. I want to be a quarterback.' So I get home and my dad says, 'How did it go?' And I said, 'Oh, it went good. They asked me what position I wanted to play and I said quarterback.' And he was like, 'No. You're going to be a running back.' And I was like, 'Running back?' And he said, 'I always wanted to be a running back. So you're going to be a running back.'"

In Canada, hockey reigns supreme. Over the years hockey parents have received a lot of flak for being too heavily involved in their children's success or failure. We know there is an investment, not just a financial one, but one of time. Young players have multiple games and practices each week and, depending on their level, destinations get farther and farther afield, requiring more hours at the wheel, not to mention tournaments that seem to pop up with greater and greater frequency. And if a family has more than one child involved, the parents' personal lives can become as separate as two ships passing in the night. Blow the horn, flash the lights, exchange greetings.

A football dad is harder for the Canadian mind to conjure up, unless your father happens to be a high-school physical education teacher and football coach. Not so in the States. No one down there would blink an eye at the degree to which John Sr. now poured his efforts into his son's development and education as a football player. This was an area where he had attained a level of expertise, after all. Why entrust others with John Jr.'s pursuit of excellence?

John and I returned to the subject of his humble football beginnings more recently in a phone conversation for this book.

"I must have been eight or nine years old the first time I put equipment on, the helmet and everything. And the one thing I always remember about putting the equipment on for the first time was putting in the mouth guard. 'Cause you've got to boil it and let it sit for a few seconds before you put it in your mouth. I used to love biting into a new mouth guard."

When the family moved to Waterdown when John Jr. was still in elementary school, John Sr. took over his son's coaching reins. The family has videotapes of John Jr. running drills in full uniform for his father, taking handoffs, hitting a tackling dummy, veering off on a sharp angle and then cutting back. When John Jr. entered high school, his father got even more involved, becoming part of the coaching staff.

"When we got to Waterdown District High School the football was in a pretty sad state," recalled John Jr. "My dad is one of the people really credited with turning that program around. We had a lot of success and were ranked as high as the top ten of all the schools in Canada at the time."

During those years as well, John Jr. was attending football camps in the summer months including three years straight at Michigan State where he was twice named the top running back in camp. But the camp that sticks out the most in his mind is the first one he ever attended, Jim Kelly's camp at St. Bonaventure University in Western New York.

"I still remember because that was the time when the Bills were going to all those Super Bowls [four in a row; all losses]. I remember being coached by all these guys he'd bring in … Thurman Thomas … and then he'd bring in these other quarterbacks … Warren Moon … he brought in Boomer Esiason. I still remember Boomer Esiason telling us that only 1 percent of people make it to play professional football. He said 'You guys probably have aspirations to play pro football at some level, right? But you need to understand that only 1 percent make it. Right?' It's a daunting number but I don't even think that I thought about it."

Daunting numbers were for someone who was not going to make it to the pros. That wasn't John Jr. He knew he was going to be part of that elite 1 percent. How could he not? He had his dad on his side. Long before John Jr. graduated from high school, his father had begun the process of finding a university in the States willing to offer John Jr. a full football scholarship. Universities in Canada have regulations that limit the amount of athletic-scholarship money available to an individual. In Ontario, the top amount available for any athlete interested in pursuing higher education, as of this writing, is $4,500 per year. With annual tuition costs in the States, at least in NCAA schools, in the area of $25,000, a full athletic ride, covering all expenses, can be worth $50,000 per year. You don't have to be a low-income family living on the edge of poverty to recognize the value in a paid-for education. But the competition is stiff.

"I remember my dad making VHS tapes of me, sending out maybe fifty to a hundred to schools all over the U.S. Just mailing them off every single week. Back then it was a real process. You had to go out and get the envelopes, you had to get the cassettes, you had to put together the tape, you had to get two VCRs together and edit it that way. Then you stamped your name on it, your height, your weight, you put it in the package, and then you took it to the post office and mailed it off. And you hoped that you'd hear back from a coach. By mail. In a digital age, you can just go online and email a coach and send him your film and it pops up right on his computer."

These are the kinds of revelations that make the average parent wonder if they were some kind of slacker, even if they did ferry their kids around the city to soccer, hockey, and baseball practices and games, or music and dance recitals, or whatever and wherever, with no complaints (okay, maybe the occasional grumble). But *fifty to a hundred schools?* And it wasn't just John Sr. doing all the work. It became something of a family vocation, the Williams family acting as talent agents for John Jr. But John Jr. never thought about the financial benefits that a full scholarship could bring, especially to his family. He just wanted to get to the next step in his journey to the pros.

"When you're a kid you don't really realize how much your parents are doing for you," he said in that sheepish way adults have of looking back at their younger selves, not with regret but with informed irony.

And then letters began to arrive in the Williamses' mailbox from universities across the United States. At first a trickle, then a deluge. Ohio. Michigan. These were the big, sexy schools. John Jr. wanted to play in the Big Ten, which has since expanded to a total of fourteen schools (without changing the conference name, as if no one in America could bother to count). If you grew up in southwestern Ontario, this was really the college football conference of choice, with the Michigan Wolverines at the top of the heap. These were not solid offers but queries. Acknowledgements that he at least was on their radar. Keep in touch, keep us up to date. He still had another year of high school ahead of him.

There was, however, one intriguing reply from the head coach at Weber State in Utah, Dave Arslanian, who had coached John Jr.'s half-brother, Charles, at Snow College in Utah. Arslanian was coming to Toronto for recruiting purposes and John Jr. went down to meet him. The coach was accompanied by Rob Hitchcock, who, at the time, was playing linebacker for the Hamilton Tiger-Cats. Not only was Hitchcock a former Weber State Wildcat but he was also a local boy from Hamilton. To say John Jr. was impressed would be to understate the case.

"I'm thinking, man, a real pro."

This in itself is funny. Hadn't he been coached most of his life by "a real pro," who also happened to be his father? When John Sr. coached at Waterdown he used to bring in Bernie Custis to talk to the team. Bernie wasn't just a former player, he was *living history*. Bruce Smith would drop by practice and add his two cents and more. And there were other current and former Tiger-Cats dropping by to check out the team. Some Waterdown players may have been awed by the presence of pros taking an active interest in their football lives, but John Jr. was not one of them. He was used to these guys. They had dinners and barbecues at his house. They were family.

The outcome of this initial meeting with Coach Arslanian was an invitation to visit the Weber State campus. Ogden, Utah, home of Weber State University, lies at the foot of the Wasatch Mountains about forty miles (sixty-four kilometres) north of Salt Lake City. Ogden was once a major railway junction, especially for passenger rail, leading to the town's boastful motto: "You can't get anywhere without coming to Ogden." Times change, mottoes not so much, leaving them empty of relevance but loaded with irony.

There was no literal red carpet awaiting John Jr.'s arrival but what did await was all a bit overwhelming for a teenager from Waterdown. He had never in his life encountered such a combination of flattery, salesmanship, and pressure, so subtle yet relentless. (Of course, he had never been invited on a time-share weekend in the Laurentians either.)

"Man, they tell you everything you want to hear and take you around the facility and talk about strength and conditioning and putting on weight and taking you to a basketball game. There are players that usually tour you around and take you out to dinner. It's really a courting thing. If you're lucky, they'll propose to you at the end of it."

Like being a contestant on *The Bachelorette*. John was one of the lucky ones. The school offered him a full scholarship, which they actually put right into his hands so he could see first-hand that it was more than an abstract offer. This was his future in a purple folder with letterhead, Weber State University. Here is where the pressure could have become overwhelming for a teenager from Canada on his own. He hadn't finished high school yet and he was being offered the keys to the kingdom. All he had to do was sign the papers. It was never said but the implication was certainly there that if he didn't sign right then and there that the school could hardly be held accountable for what the future might hold.

But John Jr. wasn't so naive as to sign anything without running it past Team Williams, especially its CEO, John Sr. He called his father back in Waterdown to tell him the news and ask his advice. John Sr.'s advice was straight and to the point. "Don't sign anything," he said. "Come on home and we'll talk about it."

Back in Waterdown, after much discussion, it was decided that John Jr. would not rush any decision, and so the scholarship offer from Weber State went unsigned. No one was comfortable with the distance between Waterdown and Ogden, Utah, least of all John Jr. So he went back to Waterdown High for his final year of football with the Warriors, a year that would culminate with the team winning another high-school football championship. Once again the recruitment letters were flowing in.

One in particular stood out from the others, this time a query from the University of Indiana. John had always been a movie buff and was "obsessed" — his word — with the film *Hoosiers*, the story of a small-town high-school basketball team that goes on to become state high-school champions. But John's fantasy script for the next four years of his life found the wastebasket when the entire Indiana football staff was fired, their interest in the young Canadian back disappearing with their jobs.

"I guess I won't be going to Indiana," he told himself.

Around this same time, Illinois got into the act. They were very interested in John Williams Jr. This was during a very turbulent time for the Williams family. John's mother had recently been diagnosed with breast cancer; John was still playing football, keeping his studies up, working through the various recruitment letters; and John Sr. was having difficulty coping emotionally with his wife's illness. John Jr. had never in his life seen his father so vulnerable. He had always been the man with a plan. It was a difficult time for the immediate and extended family. One night an assistant coach with Illinois, who called John at home regularly throughout the season just "to check in," detected a downbeat mood in the young potential recruit and asked if there was anything troubling him. John Jr. opened up, told him everything that had been going on — the fear, the uncertainty, the feeling of being adrift.

They talked for ages. The coach was very sympathetic. He told John there was no need to assume the worst outcome. His own mother had gone through the exact same thing. She had undergone chemotherapy and had now been cancer-free for ten years.

John got off the phone feeling hopeful, relieved, and much calmer. He decided then and there that he was going to Illinois. He could hardly wait for the year to end. And then, out of the blue, something inconceivable happened — inconceivable, at least, to a young man of eighteen about to embark on the great adventure. The entire football coaching staff at Illinois got sacked, including his telephone confidant.

"Well, I guess I won't be going to Illinois," he said.

There was no point in getting discouraged, his father told him. Something will come along. John Sr. had been out of high school two years, living and working in Denver, Colorado, to support his first wife and kids, when he got his big break. His older brother, who was in the armed forces, was stationed in Albuquerque at the time. He represented his base at track meets, and one day he was running an event at a meet on the campus of New Mexico Highlands University in Las Vegas, New Mexico. The school football coach came up to him and said, "Why don't you get out of the service and come play football for me? You'd be great."

And his brother replied in that same Denton, Texas, drawl as John Sr., "Nah, I can't do that. But I've got a brother up in Colorado who's pretty good and I know he'd be willing to come down here and play for you."

As fate would have it, the New Mexico Highlands basketball team came up to Denver for a game and the football coach came up with the team. John Sr. had been told by his brother that he should meet this guy and so he went to watch the basketball game and waited for his opportunity.

"I cornered the coach after and we started talking and he said, 'Yeah, you come down to Highlands and I'll give you a scholarship.' So we talked a long time and then he invited me down to visit the school that spring."

That seemed simple enough. John Sr. went down to the New Mexico Highlands University that following spring, worked out, toured the campus, and liked what he saw. The coach told him, "You want to come, I'll give you that scholarship." John replied, "Yeah, I wanna come." That was it. He flew home to Denver and gave his wife the good news.

"We're going to move to New Mexico. And go to school down there. Now you've got to get a good job."

She responded, "Well, I can go to school; they've got this IBM course."

And that's what she did. When John told the coach in New Mexico what his wife was doing, the coach told him, "If she gets that IBM certificate, I'll get her a job here on campus." He was a man of his word. He found her a job on campus making $300 a month.

"That was a lot of money back in those days. Yeah, man, a lot of money. So they gave us a two-bedroom apartment, everything on campus, and that's where it all started for me."

John Jr. had previously attended a "combines" camp run by Ron Dias, who ran similar camps throughout Canada to attract high-school athletes seeking U.S. football scholarships. For a fee, Dias would put the athletes through a series of gruelling physical challenges just like what they would have been put through in similar camps in the States. This gave American coaches a yardstick by which to measure the physical capabilities of the Canadian kids. Dias had started his camps back in 1987 and by John's time had a client list of over sixty American schools who would pay for the results. Ron Dias had John Jr. listed in the top five running backs in Canada.

This ranking got the attention of former quarterback Terry Lynch, who was the offensive coordinator at University of Rhode Island (URI). He had been to some of Dias's camps and seen the level of talent on display. And so the wooing began. Lynch would call John Jr. at home and send cards with head coach Floyd Keith's signature stating the school's belief that they were meant for each other. *John Williams, we want you here. We think it's a place for you. We think you could make a real difference.*

Once again, John Williams Jr. was on the road. This time his destination was the town of Kingston, Rhode Island. He was given a whirlwind tour of Newport, no doubt meant to boggle the brains of impressionable young men from Nowheresville, USA, and (on rare occasions) Canada. They took him to see, in order, Newport proper, historic Newport, the Breakers (the former Cornelius Vanderbilt II mansion), more mansions, the Tennis Hall of Fame, and St. Mary's

Catholic Church, where Jacqueline and John F. Kennedy had tied the knot back in 1953. (On return visits to St. Mary's, the Kennedys liked to reserve pew #10 for personal worship.) It was a first-class excursion through the architectural elegance and aristocratic immodesty of a wealthy, and white, America.

John Jr. was torn by indecision. Part of him still wanted to hold out for a Big Ten school or somewhere closer to home. He talked matters over with his father, who gave him a piece of solid advice. "You've got to go where you're wanted." There was little doubt that Rhode Island seemed genuinely desperate to have him. And so he signed the letter of intent. John Williams was about to become a Rhode Island Ram.

John Jr. spent three unsatisfying years at the URI as a non-starting running back. He never doubted his abilities, which made it all the more frustrating. He felt that the coaches had misled him going into his first season. They had talked about him stepping right into the lineup, but he soon discovered that as a freshman, he was way down in the pecking order. You had to earn your wings through performance, attitude, devotion, and seniority, the latter being the crucial element preventing John from playing more. There were running backs who had been there four years and had earned a degree of loyalty from the coaching staff. You had to be exceptional, a real game-breaker, to jump the queue. John would have to wait his turn.

His parents came down that first year. Toured the campus, watched the team practise, spent some quality (not quantity) time with their son. John Sr. could not believe the change in his son's physique. He seemed to have become massive overnight. It wasn't the result of steroids, just the demands of the game to bulk up, increase strength, and get into top condition. Even though his son wasn't starting, John Sr. got to see the team in game action. He gave his wife a frank assessment of their son's chances to crack the starting lineup down the road based on his years of experience, coaching, and knowledge, not bias.

"Shit, he can play down here," he told her.

John Jr. did get an opportunity that freshman year to show what he was capable of doing in a real game, when a series of injuries depleted the running-back corps, including the starter, a transfer student from Clemson University built like a beast of a linebacker. John was "red-shirted" at the time, which meant that he only played in practices but never in games. He remained in uniform, however, in case of emergency, and this was one of those times.

"I go in the game and I'm playing well, ripping off ten or fifteen yards, and I get hit in the side. And I can tell something's not right 'cause I can't breathe. So I stay in the game. I score and then when I come out it was like someone was standing on my chest."

He had suffered a pneumothorax, a collapsed lung, and the team doctors rushed him to the hospital. A pneumothorax can occur when the lung is punctured, leaking air into the space between the lung and the chest wall, which then applies pressure on the injured lung causing it to collapse. At the hospital they inserted a tube between his ribs to remove the excess air in the cavity. His lung was then able to inflate. The doctors stitched him up and told him that they would like to see him back at the hospital the next day to check his condition. They might as well have saved their breath. John was nineteen years old and invincible. This was just a minor setback, a mere dent in the armour. He left the hospital and didn't look back.

Until it happened again shortly after. Once more, the lung collapsed and this time the doctors put John in the hospital for two weeks, which, of course, meant *no football.* Injuries are nightmares of anxiety for team athletes, who fear that they'll lose their places in the pecking order. John's girlfriend, Lindsey, back in Waterdown — she is now his wife — was planning to visit in two weeks. John told her nothing of his condition and figured that he could pick her up at the airport on the night he was released from the hospital; such is the hubris of youth.

Two weeks later, fresh out of the hospital, John picked her up at the airport, took her back to his place, and told her the news of his lung issues. She became very upset. *Why didn't you tell me?* And he fell back on the well-worn manly excuse: *I didn't want you to worry.* And, naturally, before he could send her on her way back to Waterdown, reassured that his troubles were all in the past, boom! His lung collapsed again. The timing couldn't have been better. He was able to drop her off at the airport, a nervous wreck, before driving himself back to the hospital for another two-week stay. Meanwhile John could feel his freshman year of football leaking away like the air from his poor, damaged lung. His mother called the hospital, in a state.

"I'm coming down!"

"Nah, Mom," said John with a mix of hubris and wisdom filtered through pain medication. "This is all part of growing up."

At the end of his third year, the school fired the entire football coaching staff. With John on the brink of his senior year, the incoming coaching staff introduced a whole new offensive scheme, which involved playing him out of position. The frustration that had been building up over the past three years, as he saw other running backs move ahead of him on the depth charts, was coming to a head. He understood that coaches were not there to be his friends. They were coaching for the right to continue coaching. If they didn't produce a winning program, they were gone and the next group was brought in to turn things around. But when you give your all day after day on the practice field and you follow the rules and bide your time, and still your time never arrives for reasons that are never made clear to you, then you're bound to start believing that it's all been a waste of time.

"When you play Division I football, it's very regimented. It's almost like being in the military where someone tells you where to go, when to eat, what you can do, what you can't do, what class you can take. From the time you wake up to the time you go to sleep, you're being controlled by them. You really live inside of a bubble where you have no social contact with anything that exists outside of that bubble."

John's sister, Adaan, who was on an athletic scholarship for basketball, had recently switched universities to go to Edinboro University in Erie County, Pennsylvania. This region was once known as Conneauttee to the original inhabitants, the Eriez, Cornplanter, and Iroquois nations, which translates to "land of the living snowflake." In naming the region, located in the Erie/Pennsylvania snowbelt, the local First Nations may have inadvertently issued the first travel advisory. Expect snow. Lots of it.

When John began exploring the possibility of switching schools, he was pleasantly surprised to discover that the coach from Illinois who had helped him through the difficult time when his mother developed cancer was now coaching at Edinboro and was eager to have John come and play for the Fighting Scots. For John, it meant dropping to a Division II football program, which, for someone with aspirations to play professional, meant less exposure. But during his three-year tenure at Rhode Island in backup roles, John had never been in danger of being caught in the glare of the spotlight. Maybe this move would prove beneficial in the long run, making him that big fish in a small pond and giving him the playing time needed to take his game to the next level.

The switch turned out to be a good move. With less emphasis on football as the all-consuming Division I program, John was able to feel a part of regular campus life for the first time in four years. He also managed to resurrect his college football career and attract the attention of the B.C. Lions, who drafted him in the fourth round of the 2002 CFL draft.

"I remember leaving for the airport," he recalled, "and my dad telling me that if I don't make it when I go out there, well, that was all right. And that's all he said. And I don't think that I had ever failed in football at any point in my life so it put a little bit of doubt in my mind."

John Williams Jr. was about to recognize his lifelong dream of playing in the Canadian Football League. He would soon discover that getting a foot in the door of that exclusive membership was a battle only half won. Sticking as a Canadian running back in a league where that position was the usual domain of American imports would prove the true test of his mettle. But John Jr. had someone on his side that most players in his situation never have, someone who had experienced life as the poorest of the poor; someone who could say in this day and age that he actually picked cotton as a child; someone who came to a new country to pursue a career in football and had seen it all, experienced it all, from the depths of defeat and rejection to the heights of redemption and championship rings. Someone who had been in his corner since he was born and who had taught him how to play a game that was about to provide him with a possible livelihood if he could stick it out. That someone, of course, was his father.

If John Williams Sr. had introduced an element of doubt into his son's mind, it was only out of concern. Canadian football isn't just a hard-knock life, it's a hard-luck life as well. Find yourself in the wrong time, wrong place, and you can have the turf pulled out from under your cleats. John Sr. spent four years at New Mexico Highlands as a quarterback. He went undrafted by the NFL, and as he did with his son thirty-five years later, he began a letter campaign. But instead of writing to universities seeking scholarship opportunities, he was just looking for a chance to play. He got a hit from the Calgary Stampeders, who sent him an invitation to tryout camp. John Sr. was under no illusion about his chances.

"I know they just brought me in as a warm body, because back in those days they'd bring in like ninety-five or a hundred kids and that was 1967."

While most North Americans his age — most *white* North Americans — were experiencing the so-called Summer of Love, John Sr. was embarking on an anxiety-riddled mission two thousand miles north of his home. He had gone to camp in great shape. He was a good athlete but not a standout quarterback. He knew his chances of making a professional team as a black quarterback in the United States were limited, to say the least. He assumed it was a similar situation in Canada. He'd been working out during the off-seasons with a group of guys in Denver, Colorado, many of whom were playing in the NFL or the CFL.

One of those players was Ernie Pitts, who starred with the Winnipeg Blue Bombers during the '50s and '60s. Pitts had played the first seven years of his career with the Blue Bombers as one of the top wide receivers in the CFL. In 1964, he made the switch to defensive back and became one of the best in the CFL at that position. And it was Ernie Pitts who drilled John Sr. on the intricacies of the defensive back position in preparation for camp.

John Sr. followed a basic strategy for gaining the attention of his coaches: "I hit everything that moved." There is nothing that warms a football coach's heart more than a player who leaves it all on the playing field. Still, he had his doubts. There were just so many guys in camp. How could he be sure that others weren't making an equal or even better impression?

Pete Liske had come to Calgary the previous season as the starting quarterback. Liske had starred at Penn State before playing a season for the New York Jets of the American Football League in 1964. He played for the Argos in 1965 before being traded to Calgary in 1966. One day he came to camp to see how the tryouts were progressing.

"I remember him coming up to the school where we were staying, Mount Royal College, and he was talking about the guys making it. And I said, 'Boy, I sure hope I make it.' And Pete said, 'Oh shit, you know you made it.'

'Well, nobody told me.'

'Well, they haven't phoned you have they?'

'No.'

'Well, in that case then, you go to practice.'"

He continued to go to practice and sure enough he made the team. He played the first ten games that season at the cornerback position. He was the only black player on the defence. There were two other black players on the team, both on offence. One was Ben Woodson, who'd been a star halfback in college with the Utah Utes, and the other was Bob Paremore, who had gone to an all-black school, Florida A&M University (FAMU,) the same school as sprinter Bob Hayes, one-time fastest man on the planet and later a Dallas Cowboy. After ten games, Williams was suddenly cut by head coach Jerry Williams.

He had not seen it coming and it was a real blow, eased only slightly by the $200 a week he received from the Stamps to hang around town until the end of the season in case of emergency.

When the season in Calgary ended, John Sr. went back to Denver and again worked out at a local high-school field with the usual group of pros, including Ernie Pitts, who once again drilled John on the basics of defensive coverage. John was more determined than ever to make himself indispensable at defensive back. But when he returned to Calgary at the beginning of the 1968 season, he found himself on Jerry Williams's list of expendables. That was the end with Calgary. Too late to catch on with another team in Canada, he landed a spot with the Indianapolis Capitols of the Continental Football League for the rest of that season.

Despite the small-potatoes stature of the Continental Football League, a successful season in Indianapolis did manage to put John Sr. back on pro football's radar. One team that came calling that next off-season was the Chicago Bears, who offered John a $500 signing bonus if he signed with them. That seemed like a lot of money to John, who was not exactly flush, so he signed the contract and sent it back. Lo and behold, shortly thereafter, a cheque for $500 arrived in the mail. John thought, "You know, that seemed easy enough. Maybe I can do it again." He was looking for protection in case he was cut right out of camp, too late to catch on with another team. He got in his car and drove to Toronto, where he went to see Leo Cahill, general manager of the Toronto Argonauts, to offer his services as a defensive back.

"I can't offer you much money to sign with me, John," said Cahill. "I just don't have the budget for it."

"Well, what can you give me?" asked John.

"I can give two hundred and fifty dollars, that's all."

"I'll take it," said John, and he signed. He drove back to Denver to await the start of the football camps. Then he got to thinking. *Man, what have I done? I've signed two contracts!* He decided that he would go and play for Chicago and returned the bonus to Toronto. He showed up at the Bears' camp and played really well. One day at camp, he picked off a couple of passes and the head coach, Jim Dooley, who had inherited the head-coaching position from legendary Bears owner and head coach George Halas, ran the length of the field shouting, "Goddammit, John Williams, you're gonna play in the NFL!" Talk about pumping your tires. That made John feel great, that he was a shoo-in to make the team. Almost as an afterthought, the coach added, "If you don't play for us, you're going to play for somebody!"

Well, now that was a little harder to read. On the one hand it was a great compliment, leaving no doubt about John's ability to perform at an elite level. On the other hand, it was not exactly a guarantee that he would be plying his trade in a Chicago uniform. He started two exhibition games against Washington and Miami, and yet he had this feeling gnawing away at him that something wasn't right. And then it dawned on him what was wrong. He wasn't enjoying himself in Chicago.

"I thought to myself, *I like it up in Canada. I don't want to stay out here.*"

He called Ralph Sazio, then general manager of the Hamilton Tiger-Cats, figuring it was best not to go back to Leo Cahill. Sazio had retired as head coach of the Cats after the 1967 season, following Hamilton's 24–1 demolition of the Saskatchewan Roughriders in the Grey Cup, to take on the general manager's role. Sazio had played his college football at the College of William and Mary under Carl Voyles, who would later bring Sazio up to play for Hamilton when Voyles became head coach in 1950. Sazio had been a teammate of Bernie Custis when he played in Hamilton. As a general manager, he had developed a reputation as a cheapskate. If you wanted to argue salary with Sazio you had to be prepared for the long haul, as Dave Buchanan would discover following his breakout season in 1972. Leo Cahill once commented regarding Sazio's infamous tightness, "Sazio throws nickels around like manhole covers."

On this occasion, Sazio told John, "Hell, you can come up here now and step right into the lineup."

"But how do I get out of my contract with Chicago?"

"Don't go to practice."

"What?"

"Don't go."

John followed his advice and did not go to Chicago's practice that day. The general manager called him.

"How come you weren't at practice?"

"I'm not happy."

"What's the matter?"

"I want to go back to Canada."

"Come see me tomorrow. We'll talk."

The next day John skipped practice again and went to see the general manager.

"You know what? I'm going to let you go."

There was, however, a stipulation. John would be allowed to play for Hamilton, but only Hamilton. The general manager didn't want to set a dangerous precedent where players could start coming to him looking to be freed of their contract obligations to seek better opportunities elsewhere, perhaps with the opposition. He was willing to lose a player of John's talent as long as no one else but Hamilton gained from his team's loss.

"You try to play anywhere else and I'm going to stop you," he told John.

John said thanks and left the office feeling like a schoolboy who had just escaped the principal's wrath. The next day he walked out of the Bears' facilities and there were a bunch of rookie players who had been cut adrift, waiting for the first bus out of town. John was a rarity amid this forlorn group, a player with a guaranteed position waiting for him with another professional football team on the other side of the border.

Just then a limousine pulled up and a back window rolled down. It was the old man himself, George Halas. *Uh-oh, here it comes*, thought John. This was the true principal's visit.

"Come on, son, get in the car. I'll take you to the airport," George said.

John climbed in the back seat next to the legend. Halas talked all the way to the airport. The state of the Bears, Canadian football, the weather, everything under the sun that crossed his mind. Finally, he turned to John to tell him what he'd been waiting all the way to the airport to tell him.

"If anything ever happens up in Canada, don't you hesitate to call me personally."

The legend may not have been head coach anymore, but nothing to do with the franchise he'd built and maintained ever escaped his eyes and ears. This was his way of letting John know that though the team would not stand in his way if his heart was settled on playing in Canada, as in the parable of the prodigal son, he would be welcomed with open arms should he choose to return. That was enough for John, just knowing that he could play in the NFL. The legend had given John his blessing and, in so doing, freed him from the need to prove something to himself or to the gods and kingmakers of professional football in his homeland. He was free to follow his heart and the highways of Illinois, Michigan, and Ontario to Ivor Wynne Stadium in Hamilton, Ontario. As John Williams Sr. is prone to repeat several times throughout an interview — as if there could be nothing more an interviewer would want to know about a blue-collar defensive back from Denton, Texas — "and the rest is history."

In B.C.'s camp, John Jr. discovered he was third in line as far as Canadian running backs were concerned. And being a Canadian running back, as John soon discovered, meant his days as a tailback were over. There was only one position for a Canadian running back and that was fullback. He remembered another player coming up to him early in camp and letting him know the way of the world.

"You're a Canadian back? Well you're a fullback now."

The incumbent fullback was veteran Sean Millington, who had been in the league since 1991, most of those years spent with B.C. Millington was a Black Canadian and hometown boy who played his college football for Simon Fraser. He had been a number-one pick by Edmonton in the

CFL draft of Canadian college players back in 1990. The other Canadian running back in camp was the third-overall pick from the year before, Lyle Green, also black, who was born in Kitchener and went to the University of Toledo, Chuck Ealey's alma mater. Green would have his best season in the CFL in 2002 with 343 yards rushing and three touchdowns. He would never get that many touches again. As Mike Beamish wrote in the *Vancouver Sun* in a 2008 tongue-in-cheek profile, "You've got to hand it to Lyle Green because, quite frankly, the B.C. Lions don't. At least not very often. Practically never."

John had little time to get up to speed as a fullback as well as learn how to play on the special teams, receiving and kicking, which he had never done in university.

"I had to quickly get adjusted to doing a lot of blocking as well as playing special teams, so we got to the second game in training camp right before they were about to make the cuts. I got put in at the end of the game and we went down and I scored. So I thought I had a pretty good opportunity to make the team."

Starting the 2002 season, B.C. went with the three Canadian backs, with Millington as fullback, Green as tailback, and John Jr. as backup to both. But John had not given up on his dream that teams would see his value to the team at the tailback position. In his final exhibition game against Winnipeg, Williams rushed for thirty-five yards on only seven carries, a decent five-yards-per-carry average. The team was impressed enough to release two import backs in favour of the three Black Canadians.

Once the season started, John's opportunities to run with the ball never materialized. He played almost exclusively on the special teams, converting from blocker to tackler on the same play. He rushed the ball from scrimmage only once all year and gained three yards. He did not receive a single pass. He returned one punt and three kickoffs for a total of fifty-six yards. The head coach was fired, and Adam Rita, the general manager, took over the reins for the rest of the season. Two import backs were brought in with neither player putting up numbers that John Williams Jr. felt that he could not duplicate or better if given the chance.

"That was one thing I didn't like about the CFL," he told me, "the way they didn't give Canadians the opportunities to play certain positions.

I got all my training going to the States, I went to camps down there, I went to university down there. I've been playing the American game for as long as I can remember. So that was something that kind of irked me when I look back at my time in the CFL. I wish I could have had more of an opportunity to play the tailback position."

Following that first season with B.C., John went home and began intensive workouts along with a diet intended to increase mass. He was going to go into camp bigger and faster than ever before, ready to take on more responsibilities than just those of a blocking fullback. He wanted the ball in his hands. He wanted to be the one to bust through a hole in the defensive wall and break off a long gainer. He even allowed himself to daydream of spending the next ten years with the Lions, achieving that rare distinction in the CFL of being a lifer, someone who spends his entire career with the same team.

The B.C. Lions had also undergone a change in the off-season. The team brought in Wally Buono as head coach. Buono had won three Grey Cups with the Calgary Stampeders, the last one coming just two years earlier in 2001. He immediately set about rebuilding the Lions' offence in his likeness, bringing in former Calgary players familiar with his systems.

"It was the last week of practice and I'm going down in the elevator and one of the front office people tells me to go and see Wally and bring my playbook. Well, I knew it was done for me in B.C."

John Jr. returned home feeling lost.

"It was the first time I had ever failed at football in my life," he said.

He had dealt with disappointments during his college football days but nothing with this cold finality of rejection. John Sr. could hardly believe that his son had been cut. He knew his son's game, inside and out. How could others not see what he did? It was a depressing time in the Williams household. John Jr.'s depression was so palpable, his parents could not help but feel it. No one wants to feel that the dream is over at twenty-five. His father understood his son's gloom. He had been there himself back in 1968 when Jerry Williams had cut him for a second time. Had he not done everything required of him and still fallen victim to the numbers game? He came back, though, and enjoyed an All-Star career. Maybe his son could do the same.

Two months into the season, Edmonton defensive coordinator Greg Marshall called, after John Sr. had reached out to various teams on his son's behalf. Marshall informed John Sr. that the Eskimos were going to be in Hamilton the next week and suggested he bring John Jr. down to Ivor Wynne Stadium and get in a workout and see where it went.

"So I went down to Ivor Wynne and Jason Maas was there, the quarterback, the backup to Ricky Ray, and I worked out with Jason for thirty minutes or so. Went back home, sat by the phone. A couple of weeks went by and I got a call that they wanted me to come in on the practice roster. That was about early August, end of summer. So I flew to Edmonton, got on the practice roster there. Didn't get to play in any of the games, just stood on the sidelines."

Prior to 2013, teams were allowed a practice roster of seven additional players who practised with the team but did not suit up for games. Of those seven players, one of them at least had to be a non-import, and that's where John Jr. was slotted in for Edmonton. As a practice-roster player, John Jr. did not sign a standard CFL contract but instead a practice-roster agreement, paying him roughly $750 a week, or $15,000 for a full season. He enjoyed the company, and it was a learning experience in its own way — but he was after more than learning experiences. He wanted to play and that wasn't happening out in Edmonton.

"I wanted to get back closer to home. I wanted to sign with Toronto. I wanted to sign with Hamilton."

He went to see Tom Higgins, who was both general manager and head coach with Edmonton that year, and told him that he wanted to try to catch on with a team in Ontario, closer to home. It was a tough decision for John Jr. to walk away because Edmonton was having a fine year and would go on to win the Grey Cup that season. John remembers sitting at home watching the Grey Cup and thinking, *Well, I probably blew any chance I'll ever have to be a part of a Grey Cup team.*

He had gotten a job with a local furniture store to pay the bills and worked out every day after work in preparation for the next season. He reached out to Hamilton but they could not give him a definite answer one way or the other. He reached out to Toronto. Same thing. Then Eric Tillman, general manager with the Ottawa Renegades (as they were known then, post–Rough Riders, pre-Redblacks) called and offered him a contract for training camp for the upcoming season of 2004. John's off-season training went into immediate overdrive. By the time training camp came, he was ready. He never wanted to have to say that he should have trained harder.

Joe Paopao was Ottawa's head coach. Known as "the Throwin' Samoan" during his eleven years as a quarterback in the CFL, Paopao had taken the head-coaching job with the Renegades in 2002 and, over two seasons, had put together a record of eleven wins and twenty-five losses. Ordinarily a record like that would get you fired, but not in Ottawa, where mediocrity and uncertainty (regarding the team's survival) went hand in hand year after year. According to Williams, he had a good camp, excelling on the special teams. The final decision came down to a choice between John Jr. and recent Canadian draft choice Mike Vilimek, a 238-pound fullback out of Simon Fraser University.

In a late pre-season game against Montreal, John Jr. broke off a long run from scrimmage so he was feeling good about his chances. But again, players like John Williams Jr. trying desperately to catch on with a team, balancing precariously on the bubble of uncertainty, are never privy to the conversations and logistics that go into a team's decision. That dreaded choice of who is saved and who is allowed to drift away from the raft seems rooted in that indefinable sweeping category known as "politics."

John Jr. got a call from the Renegades' head office.

"Sure as hell it's Paopao saying, 'We're going to let you go.' So at that point I really didn't know if I wanted to play football anymore. Maybe this was it for me."

Once again, John Jr. went home to give his father, John Sr., the bad news. At what point does a father tell his son that maybe it's not worth getting kicked around anymore? He may believe wholeheartedly in his son's gifts but it hurts to keep sending him back to the mill to get ground down again. John Sr. was fortunate. He never had to make that decision. Within twenty-four hours of John Jr.'s returning home, the phone rang. It was Adam Rita, now general manager of the Toronto Argonauts, calling to tell John to get down to Toronto *right away*. Adam Rita was familiar with John; he had drafted John in the first place in B.C.

"So, I was driving down to Mississauga, and the whole way I was thinking about everything I'd gone through since I came to the CFL: being drafted by B.C., getting cut by them, then Edmonton, and leaving there, going to Ottawa, getting cut … and I said, 'I'm going to give it one more chance and see what happens.' So I go down there, practise, and at the end of the practice, Pinball [Michael Clemons] comes up to me and says, 'We're going to put you on the roster this week. We have confidence in you that you're going to do your job and make your blocks.' And from there, it was like we got on a roll."

That roll would lead straight to the 2004 Grey Cup *in Ottawa* against the *B.C. Lions*. If you fail to see the significance in the venue and in the opponent, you have not been paying attention. As John Williams Sr. might have been tempted to remark, "The rest, as they say, is history."

Chapter Nine

A CUP FOR PINBALL

What was the greatest day in your life? Maybe it was your wedding day, a child's birth, standing on a mountain overlooking a scene of such grandeur that you felt a certain peace that has never been rivalled but at least you found it for a moment and the memory can never be taken away.

Here is Chuck Winters's "greatest day": the day his stepfather went to jail. He came home from school and his mother told him the news and he would later describe his feeling as "exhilaration." For seven long years this "stepdad" had put the family through hell, a torment of physical, verbal, and psychological abuse.

Some greatest day.

Years later, as a senior at the University of Michigan, Chuck would return to his mother's home for a visit to find his now-divorced, recently released from jail ex-stepfather threatening his mother with a crowbar. Chuck grabbed a baseball bat and swung for the fences. That ended the threat, but Chuck was taken into police custody and spent the night in jail. He was released in the morning and no charges were laid. The police had gotten it right this time. Nevertheless, word had gotten around to NFL teams that this Chuck Winters was a violent sort, raised as he was in the projects of Herman Gardens, Detroit. His father had been shot to death breaking into someone's home.

Oh, forgot to mention that. Chuck was two years old. His father burgled for a meagre living. And then he went to the wrong place at the wrong time and was greeted with a shotgun blast. The sins of the father, right? *Watch out for that kid.* Chuck is convinced that that hurt his draft status back in 1996.

"When I think about where I came from," he said on camera a few years back, in our first interview, resting on a bench after a workout in the weight room of the Argos' former practice facilities on the University of Toronto Mississauga (UTM) campus, "I don't want people to have to experience what I experienced. To see your mom abused, to see drug abuse ... I'm actually bewildered. Man, I became this person I am after seeing so much negativity? I could've easily gone the other way. I could've easily been an abuser because that's all I saw. I could've easily been an alcoholic because that's all I saw. I could've easily picked up a needle and used drugs, smoked a crack pipe because I saw that *every day*. For me it was never something that ever attracted me. It was something that I never even looked to. It never crossed my mind as an option."

The young Chuck Winters poured all his energies into sports. He had no long-term goal in mind, no dreams of getting out of the projects and becoming a superstar in the NFL. Sports was an outlet for him. His mother worked all day. When he got home from school, there would be a lot of family members around, many of whom he admits were "alcoholics or drug addicts." Sports was not a means to an end, it was a temporary respite from an embattled home front. A refuge.

"I didn't dream when I was younger," confessed Winters, in what has to be one of the saddest admissions regarding childhood and adolescence. "I think you can have an individual grow up in the circumstances that I did but [be] able to see themselves outside of that situation. For me, not until I was outside of the situation was I able to see myself outside of it. All I saw was my environment."

One day his high-school football coach at St. Martin de Porres, in hindsight a very wise man, held out a football in front of his young star athlete.

"This ball," he said, "can take you all over the world."

Chuck didn't get it at first. He was focused on the ball. *Okay, that ball can take me all over the world.* He wasn't putting himself in the picture as actually travelling *with* or *because of* the ball. And then it sank in. *Oh man, this ball. I get it.* The ball was his passport to the world beyond Herman Gardens. His first stop on the new passport was the University of Michigan, in 1992. That same year, he was drafted by the Kansas City Royals in the tenth round of the Major League Baseball draft. An opportunity to sign a professional contract, as a teenager — how incredibly tempting. But his mother wanted Chuck to get an education. Sports was temporary but an education lasted a lifetime. The University of Michigan was also willing to let him play both football and baseball. So he chose university. Of the two balls, he thought, football would probably take him farthest. And, for a young football player from Detroit, playing at "the Big House" (Michigan Stadium), the largest stadium in the United States, with an official capacity listed as 107,601, is a dream come true in itself. Whether he made it to the pros or not, he would never in his life experience the thrill of playing for that many cheering fans again.

In his four years at Michigan, '92 to '96, Chuck starred in both sports. Unfortunately for him, he went undrafted by any team in the NFL following his final year in university. He was a defensive back in football, a position for which there were always plenty of players available, not to mention the standout offensive players who could be transitioned to defence. Chuck is convinced that his past factored into every NFL team's reluctance to call his name from the draft floor. Why take a chance on a kid with a record of violence, regardless of the circumstances? Teams already had enough trouble keeping their players' names out of the papers for one violation or another. Once again, Kansas City picked him in that year's MLB draft, this time in the twentieth round. It seemed his value was rapidly diminishing. He never did sign with Kansas City. He did not feel like investing the years it would take to work through a pro-baseball team's multi-levelled minor-league system. At loose ends, he chose to play for an independent minor-league team for a season while he figured out his next step.

During his years at Michigan, Chuck had created his own clothing line as a sideline. After a season of independent baseball, he headed to New York to try to get this fashion business off the ground. And then one night his mother called. The date and time are implanted in his brain forever: September 18, 1997, 12:20 a.m. It was a phone call he had been dreading. He remembers the first words out of his mother's mouth.

"You know I've always talked to you about choices?"

"Yeah?"

"Your brother made a wrong choice."

Since he was a young boy his mother had always drummed into his head, "The choices you make today will mould you for the future." In the Herman Gardens projects, this was an attempt at street-proofing her kids for the present and the future. Your actions now, she said, no matter how inconsequential they may seem, can have an impact down the road.

This particular night, Chuck's only sibling, a younger brother named Malik, had slipped out of his mother's apartment as soon as she went off to work her midnight shift.

"My brother loved to hang out on the streets, loved to hang out with his boys late at night. Sports was something he tried to get into at a younger age but wasn't really successful. He was decent, you know. He saw the success I was obtaining and he wanted to get to that point. But he had started at a later age than I did, so for him, it was like, 'Nah, I'm not really liking this football stuff or this baseball stuff. It isn't for me.' So he began to hang out, write poetry, stuff like that. But the hanging out part really took precedence."

Malik went out the back window and jumped into a car with a few friends. No purpose, no destination in mind. Just cruising. Their car came to a red light and stopped. Another car pulled up next to them. Words were exchanged. Chuck never did learn the nature of the exchange. Trash talk. The light turned green and Malik's car pulled away. Once again, they hit a red light and stopped. This time when the other car pulled up alongside, whoever was inside fired six or seven shots into the car Malik was in. He was the only one hit, sitting in the backseat. With his dying breath, he held up two fingers. It was his signature gesture and word. "Peace."

"He always used to say 'peace.' That was something that I would never forget. He always did. A couple of his guys told me it was like, 'Tell my mom and brother, peace.'"

Chuck Winters moved back to Detroit to be near his mother. He soon discovered that in a depressed city economy, a degree didn't function as well as a football did when it came to passports. He moved back to Ann Arbor where he still had friends, finished his degree, and got certified as a teacher. Back in Detroit he took on some jobs, nothing remotely approaching a career, just paying the bills. And then one day in 2000, he went for an open tryout with the Detroit Fury of the Arena Football League, a league where football was played indoors in basketball and hockey arenas converted for football. The Fury were new to the league and were looking for a few local diamonds in the rough for the 2001 season. Chuck found himself in a room with four hundred would-be Fury players. It was all he could do to not say, *Forget it, this is ridiculous, what chance have I got?* Instead a calm came over him. Maybe it was everything that he had been through in life or maybe it was just the fact that he was older and wiser now, with a greater understanding of what life had to offer.

"By this time I had built up my morale, done all the motivational talks I could give myself. 'This is the obstacle. I need to face it head on and then go through it.' I went through it and came to find that I was the only guy out of the four hundred to get chosen for the team."

While Chuck was playing for the Fury, the team's defensive coordinator, Rich Stubler, who doubled as a defensive consultant with the Toronto Argonauts of the CFL when the AFL finished up its season, asked him, "Do you want to come up to Toronto and play in the CFL?"

"I'm like, 'Yeah, cool.' Just another step up from arena football, larger scale, more money, bigger platform. Not knowing where it was going to take me. Just thinking, yeah, another opportunity for me. I was young at the time — well, younger, twenty-eight, so I was thinking *I can do this.* It would give me an opportunity to still get to the NFL."

And then he thought about it a minute, as Chuck Winters is apt to do. He is, at heart, a very thoughtful man, as I have discovered over the years in a number of interview situations. He realized that he had gotten caught up in setting unrealistic goals for himself. He was twenty-eight, not seventeen. Football is a young man's game — not necessarily on the field, as players are capable of playing well into their thirties if they take care of themselves and manage not to sustain a career-ending injury or series of debilitating ones, but the setting of goals, the mental and physical preparation required in fulfilling a lifelong dream carried to the highest level, *that's* the young man's game. That is the young man's dream. This is what Chuck had to decide for himself. Should he remove the NFL from his field of vision, let it fade away, and just see what fate might have in store for him in the Canadian Football League?

"And that's what I decided. Let me just take this ride wherever it takes me."

His passport, issued by a high-school coach in Herman Gardens, was about to take him across the Ambassador bridge to Windsor and a four-hour drive on Highway 401 to the home of the Toronto Argonauts and the beginning of a brand new dream.

Few players have ever been more deserving than Michael "Pinball" Clemons of being included in the Canadian Football Hall of Fame. He was not a power runner like a Johnny Bright or a George Reed. As the passing game rose to dominance in the CFL game (and the NFL brand), all-purpose backs like Clemons became more and more valuable, players who could rush for close to a thousand yards per year and catch sixty to seventy passes coming out of the backfield, as well as field kickoffs and punts. In 1990, he won the Schenley Award as the Most Outstanding Player in the league, having accumulated 3,370 all-purpose yards, a single-season record at the time. In 1997, playing with one of the greatest quarterbacks in CFL history, Doug Flutie, and on one of the greatest teams ever, Pinball surpassed his record for all-purpose yards with an astounding 3,840 yards.

He played his entire career in Toronto, twelve seasons. His number, 31, is one of only four jersey numbers retired by the Argonauts. He won three Grey Cups as a player. In a sports market dominated by hockey, baseball, and basketball, Michael Clemons is probably the most beloved sports figure Toronto has ever known. In 2000, his final year as a player, he took over the head-coaching reins on an interim basis when the Argos' management fired a woefully inadequate John Huard after the team got off to a 1–6–1 start. It was a difficult situation for someone who felt the way he did about his teammates. They were brothers; they were family. He knew that as a coach his loyalties and his friendships would be tested as he suddenly had to decide what was best for the team instead of what was best for the individual.

Despite never having coached before, Clemons managed to lead the Argos to a respectable 6–4 record in the remaining ten games of the season. At the end of the season, he was named president of the Toronto Argonauts, a move unprecedented for a black man in the annals of CFL history. That presidency lasted a year and a half until, once again, Clemons was pressed into service as interim head coach after the Argonauts got off to a 4–8 start under head coach Gary Etcheverry, who'd been hired the year before when Pinball was named president.

"I'm not at all thrilled and that's honest," he told the media during a conference after Etcheverry was let go. "I wanted Coach Etcheverry as our coach and I wanted to be where I was, building this organization."

Clemons managed to lead the team to a 4–2 record the rest of the way and a playoff date against the Saskatchewan Roughriders, who were coached by former CFL quarterback Danny Barrett. That playoff game, won by the Argonauts, made history. It was the first time two black head coaches had faced each other during the CFL playoffs. The Argonauts lost to the eventual Grey Cup champions, the Montreal Alouettes, in the Eastern Conference final. Following the 2002 season, Michael Clemons relinquished his presidency and became the full-time head coach of the Toronto Argonauts. In a way, he felt that he owed a debt to the organization that had brought him to Canada, his beloved new home. He would repay that debt to ownership and the city he loved within two years in the most Canadian of ways.

He would coach his team to a Grey Cup victory.

Chuck Winters remembers sitting on the hill overlooking the Argonauts' UTM practice field with a number of players back in 2003, his first season with the Argos, and discussing Clemons's head-coaching abilities. Was he the type of coach who could mould a team capable of winning the Grey Cup? Did he have what it took to manage the team? He didn't yell. He didn't scream. He wasn't a "dictator." He didn't call his players out in front of others.

"He was a players' coach but he was more," Chuck recalled. "He made us accountable. 'What you put in is what you get out of it.'"

But on that hillside in Mississauga, there were still questions. Was Pinball too lax? Not enough of a disciplinarian?

Rich Stubler had brought a number of former Detroit Fury players with him to Toronto when he assumed the mantle of full-time defensive coordinator with the Argos. These players were used to hard-ass American coaches in the college and professional ranks. Winning was the only determinant in judging whether a football program was a success or a failure, unless a coach was selling the powers-that-be on a blueprint for rebuilding a losing franchise. But even then, losing carried an expiry date.

But this man known as "Pinball," or "Pinner," or even "Pin," was an unknown entity. He was not a tactician. He was not an Xs and Os kind of coach. He left the details to his assistant coaches. He was the motivator, encouraging his audience to believe. He did not sell his Christianity and faith as a motivational tool, though there were a number of players, including Chuck Winters, who recognized a kindred spirit in the head coach. He included lessons and messages in his coaching that could just as often be applied to everyday living as they could to the gridiron. He talked about family. He talked about belief. He talked about commitment. He talked about sacrifice. He did not say, "This is how you win." Instead, he said, "This is how you become better." As players? As people? Or were they one and the same?

The Argonauts finished that season with a 9–9 record. They defeated the B.C. Lions in the Eastern semifinal — B.C. was relegated to the East in a crossover playoff system designed to prevent Eastern bottom feeders like Ottawa and Hamilton from tarnishing the concept of "playoffs" — before once again losing to the Montreal Alouettes in the Eastern final. But the seeds of belief had been planted. Coach Clemons had taken the team within one game of the Grey Cup. Now if they could only find a way past the most consistent team in the East, if not the entire league, then they might be willing to admit that this guy could work miracles.

In Damon Allen's twenty-three-year career in the CFL, he played on six different teams, winning Grey Cups on four. When he retired, he was the all-time leader in passing yardage in professional football in North America. (He's since been surpassed by Anthony Calvillo.) But here's the kicker. He also retired as the third leading rusher in total yards in CFL history behind only Mike Pringle and George Reed and just ahead of the one and only Johnny Bright. Think about that one for a minute. The third leading rusher in CFL history *is a quarterback*.

In a 2006 *New York Times* article, when Damon Allen was closing in on Warren Moon's career passing-yardage mark, Allen addressed the issue of being a running quarterback with writer Jason Diamos: "That was what they kind of labelled a lot of African-American quarterbacks as being. Those were some of the excuses they used to keep us out of the league. White quarterbacks like Fran Tarkenton and Roger Staubach used to scramble around all the time, and they were fine with that. It was just part of the excuses that we had to go through as black quarterbacks to get into the league."

Of course, "the league" he is referring to is the National Football League. When Damon Allen came into the CFL, Condredge Holloway was only two years removed from winning a Grey Cup as the ultimate scrambling quarterback. As for racking up career passing-yardage marks, it didn't hurt Allen's chances that he played twenty-three years in the league. But consider this: in his twenty-first year, at the age of forty-two, he won the Schenley Award as the league's Most Outstanding Player.

"I think why we were most successful that year in 2004 with the Toronto Argonauts," said John Williams Jr. when we spoke, himself some-thing of a reclamation project, "[is that] there was a bunch of guys that had just been cut from other places and had a chip on their shoulders and had something to prove. Like Damon [Allen] had been released from B.C. because they got Dave Dickenson."

Damon Allen was actually traded to Toronto for a couple of draft picks but still, it had to sting. Vancouver had been his home for eight years. The Lions had just signed Dave Dickenson as a free agent after he'd spent a couple of years kicking about the NFL for a variety of teams. Dickenson was a former Grey Cup and Schenley winner when he played for Calgary. He was also thirty years old and considered in his prime, while Allen was thirty-nine and perceived to be close to the end of the line. If Damon Allen had a chip on his shoulder, then good for him. It's as good as any reason to seek both redemption and revenge. And on November 21, 2004, the stars would align for a great sweeping of Argonaut shoulder chips into the dustbins of gridiron history.

As anyone who comes from a large family can tell you, families do not always get along. Alliances are formed, resentments build up, favouritism is suspected, discussions turn argumentative, holiday dinners turn into war zones.

It's no wonder that Pinball preached the message of family and belief in one another. Because the Toronto Argonauts of 2004 didn't always behave that way.

There are essentially three separate factions on a football team: defence, offence, and special teams. John Williams Jr. spoke with great affection for his teammates on the special teams that year, bonded by — what else? — their need to prove themselves.

"It was all these guys that had been somewhere else and had something to prove. And I think that was one of the best special teams units that has ever been. These guys could run like a bat out of hell. Special teams units are consistently relied upon for one or two big plays. But every time we touched the ball or went down to make the tackle, we were making plays."

The defence was the envy of the offence. They looked like they were having fun even at practice. There was a reason for that, according to Chuck Winters. The defence, more than any other unit on the team, had bought into Pinball's message. *Who are we? Family!*

"We all stayed here. And during the off-season we worked out together," Chuck told me by phone. "We were always hanging out, our families were hanging out, and that created a bond between all of us that we really wanted to play for each other. Because you knew about the individual as a person and not just as some football guy collecting a cheque. 'I know your family, I know your kids, I know your wife, I know where you stand, I've been over to your house.' We *liked* being together."

And the offence was having all sorts of trouble moving the ball with any consistency and, even worse, was struggling to put points on the board.

"There was a real distinct sense of separation between offence and defence," said John Williams Jr. "The defence were a really, really tight unit and played really free.... They would have these soccer-baseball games every day before they went to walk-through. We'd be over there with Kent Austin, [who's saying] 'I want you to go seven and a half yards and do this and that,' and these guys are over there throwing a Frisbee around. The defence was just a stronger unit. And we depended on the defence and special teams to win games."

The Argos started the season 5–2, second in the East to the Alouettes going into a game at Olympic Stadium in Montreal. They had not been overwhelming teams on the offensive side of the ball, scoring an average of only fourteen points in four of those games, two of which they actually managed to win in a league known for its high scoring. Over those first seven games, the defence allowed an average of only fourteen points a game. It was obvious that the defence was the team's strong suit.

"With Damon, he was either hot or cold, there was nothing in between," John Williams Jr. said. "It was hard to play consistently on offence the first half of the year. Other times it seemed that the defence was constantly getting us out of hot water. Either them or the special teams."

In that game against Montreal, however, the offence took a major blow when Damon Allen suffered a fractured tibia. He would be lost for much of the rest of the season. Backup Michael Bishop, out of Kansas State, took over the role of starter. The Argos lost that game and by the time they played the Blue Bombers at Canad Inns Stadium in Winnipeg, they carried a record of 6–4–1.

"I tell people if there was one turning point in that season," remembered John Williams Jr., "it was when we played Winnipeg and we were beating them and then we lost in the last couple minutes of the game [44–34]. We got in the locker room and then it all came to a head between the offence and the defence — something was said, and all hell broke loose. Guys were being thrown across the locker room. Then after that, it was weird, because sometimes conflict like that will tear a team apart or take it to a new level. And that's what it did for us: it took us to a new level."

With the cathartic locker room explosion behind them, the Argos went on a bit of a roll, and their starting quarterback returned in time for the playoffs. In the Eastern semifinals, played at the SkyDome before 37,835 fans, the Argonauts knocked off the Tiger-Cats behind Damon Allen. The stage was set for a major tussle against the Argos' nemesis, the Montreal Alouettes, to be played at "the Big O" in Montreal. The Alouettes had the best record in football and the nation's leading passer in Anthony Calvillo. The Als were also the first team in the history of the CFL to have four receivers surpass the 1,000-yard mark. They were a team with a lot of weapons.

The game was close in the first half with the Argos taking a slim one-point lead, 8–7, into the locker room at halftime. But only a minute or so into the second half, the game took a distinct Argo bounce when #95, Eric England, journeyman deluxe, rode Anthony Calvillo into the unforgiving artificial turf, ending Calvillo's day at the office. Forced to play their seldom-used backup quarterback, the Als went down in defeat, 26–18. The mighty beast of the East, the Montreal Alouettes, had been vanquished.

"Grandpa's Going to Grey Cup" shouted the headlines in Montreal's *Gazette* in the aftermath of the game, referring to Damon Allen, who could not resist an opportunity to take a shot at the B.C. Lions, who'd sent him packing the year before.

"I think B.C. thought I was finished, but I thought I had a few more years left," he told reporters.

Allen would have an opportunity to exact the ultimate revenge on the Lions in one week's time, as B.C. defeated Saskatchewan in overtime to set up a Grey Cup meeting with the Argos at Frank Clair Stadium in Ottawa. But he had been around long enough, already having experienced Grey Cup victories with three other teams, to know that the game of football, not just the Grey Cup, was bigger than one man's desire for vengeance or vindication.

"He had multiple rings but he understood that in that locker room we had something special," said Chuck Winters about his former quarterback. "And he'd tell us, 'Man, this is special here and you might not see this come around again. Take advantage of the opportunity.' So he'd always talk to us about cherishing the moment. And you knew that he'd been there and done it."

John Williams Jr. did not need any extra motivation for the Grey Cup. He had more than enough, thank you. He was going to be playing the B.C.

Lions, the first team that cut him, in the home of the Ottawa Renegades, who had also cut him.

"I wanted to beat them so bad 'cause all my boys were on the other side. All the guys I had come into the league with."

He remembered telling the long snapper, Randy Srochenski, "Randy, if we lose this game I will never be able to get over it. I'll never be able to be this close to winning something so big. I don't think I'll ever be able to get over it."

As it turned out, John Williams Jr. would not have to spend years getting over it.

Final score: Toronto 27, B.C. Lions 19.

When Michael Clemons was questioned following the game about what it meant to become the first black coach to win a Grey Cup, he seemed uninterested in directing the subject toward that aspect of the game's importance.

"Maybe I don't appreciate it as much because I live here year-round now and we're more of a colour-blind nation."

Clemons was less interested in making history and more interested in seeing his team, his "family," achieve success. And, like a proud Papa, he told *Maclean's* in December of that year that "as a player you win once but when you win as a coach, you win the Grey Cup forty times."

Clemons' laissez-faire methods of coaching would always be debated, even after winning a Grey Cup. But critics like to see their coaches coaching, their managers managing, talking constantly into headsets while pacing the sidelines, consulting charts, covering their mouths when they speak in case the opposition has extraterrestrial lip-readers in their employ. If they don't see sparks flying from a coach's head, they are apt to wonder, *What is it exactly that he does?* Clemons was once criticized by a fan for smiling too much on the sidelines, as if it were a crime to enjoy what he was doing in life.

If you want to know the magic behind the Michael "Pinball" Clemons method of coaching, talk to Chuck Winters. Pinball was yet another mentor for Chuck, who grew up without a father in his house or a decent facsimile. He turned to his coaches, from high school to university to the only head coach he knew in the CFL, Michael Clemons, to help provide the life lessons he had missed growing up.

"This great man, this Canadian icon, is right here giving you the tools of life every day before practice," recalled Winters. "We wouldn't talk football or watch film. He would come in and talk about life. How to save money. How to treat your family. How to build relationships. How to become a better person. It was more about life as individuals than it was about football."

And Chuck listened. Here was a man who had come from the projects like him, was a man of faith like him, had a family and kids like him, and wanted the same things out of life. Chuck admitted to having filled fifteen to twenty notebooks with Pinball's quotes or thoughts, which he's kept all these years from his days as a player under Clemons. He credits these with making the transition from football to "normal life" an easy one.

"He was already paving the way."

John Williams Jr. had won the Grey Cup. Not alone, of course, and, if truth were told, he did not play a major role in the victory. But he was part of the family, stood shoulder pads to shoulder pads with his brethren in the special teams. He caught one kickoff that fell short to avoid the more serious deep threat waiting at the goal line. He was immediately tackled before he could even build up a head of steam. Most of what he did inside the game was swallowed in the madness of mass formations crashing wildly into one another during the exchange of possession. That was fine with him. He was in the game, he did his bit, and he got his ring. A special ring he had engraved with 72–04. The "72" represents the year his father, John Williams Sr., won the Grey Cup with the Hamilton Tiger-Cats. The "04" represents the year that he did. The first black father and son combination to have their names engraved upon the Cup.

That, in itself, is a family achievement.

Chapter Ten

A LASTING LEGACY: THREE PROFILES

Sometimes it felt like he'd been on the run his whole life. Running from poverty. Racism. Bigger kids. Drugs. Alcohol. The multiple sclerosis that stalked his family. And, on the gridiron, from the thunderous charge of large, armoured opponents whose task was to prevent him from doing what he was paid to do: run for his life.

There is no one in the history of the CFL who has run for more touchdowns on special teams — kickoffs, punts, or missed field goals — than Henry "Gizmo" Williams. Thirty-one touchdowns, twenty-six of those on punt returns. No one is even close. And that's where Henry liked to be: way out in front.

When Henry was five, his mother died of multiple sclerosis (MS). He didn't really know his father but he, too, would die a year later in a house fire. Henry went to live with his oldest brother, Edgar, who was only twenty-one when he took in Henry and five of his brothers and sisters. Including Edgar's wife and two kids, there were ten people living in a two-bedroom shotgun house in west Memphis, Tennessee, a tough, rough, poor part of town. Edgar and his wife took over the roles of mother and father for all the kids. Edgar got up at five o'clock every morning to go to work at Memphis Light, Gas and Water, and he made all the kids get up with him even though they didn't have to go to school until 8:00 a.m. He wanted to instill a sense of discipline in them. They were only going to get out of life what they put into it. Edgar was Henry's hero in life.

But Edgar didn't want the young Henry playing football. He was too small. He didn't want to see his little brother get hurt.

"We used to play this game called 'hot ball,'" Henry told me during our interview session at Commonwealth Stadium. "Hot ball was, you take the ball and you throw it up in the air, and every kid would try to catch it and run with it, everybody chasing and trying to tackle you. And when you play that game, you start off with probably about fifteen guys, and by the end of the day it's about a hundred kids playing this game."

And who was the kid at the centre, eluding his would-be tacklers the most? Henry Williams. This fact did not escape the attention of the principal, who then went to see the school football coach.

"You have to come see this little kid play," he told the coach.

And so the coach went to see the little hot ball hotshot play.

"You ever play football?" he asked Henry.

"Nah. I don't think my brother would let me play," Henry said. "The only way you can get me to play football is if you go talk to my brother."

The football coach at Henry's public school went to see Edgar Williams.

"Mr. Williams," he said respectfully. "Can you please let your brother Henry play football?"

This was Memphis, Tennessee, not Canada where health insurance is a given.

"I don't have no money for the insurance," replied his brother. In other words, if something happened to Henry during a game, Edgar wouldn't be able to pay for treatments.

"I'll never forget this," said Henry Williams. "The coach said, 'Don't worry about it, we'll take care of everything he needs.'"

Between the coach and the principal, they outfitted young Henry from head to toe: helmet, pads, cleats, the whole shebang. He never got to play the full four quarters in a game. The team was too good and Henry, in particular, was untouchable, sometimes scoring ten or eleven touchdowns a game. There were two plays: Henry right, Henry left. The coach took pity on the opposition and had to regularly bench Henry to keep the score down.

The legend of Gizmo was off and running.

* * *

Henry Williams never did hit a massive growth spurt. He topped out at five foot six, which turned off a lot of recruiters before they had even seen him play. He was drafted out of East Carolina University by the Washington Redskins in 1985 but chose to play for the Memphis Showboats of the United States Football League (USFL). That lasted one season before the league folded. But in that one year he did manage to pick up the nickname "Gizmo" from a teammate, future NFL Hall of Famer Reggie White. (Was he named for the mogwai in *Gremlins*, which had come out just a year earlier? Or because he was a small gadget that served any number of practical functions? Your guess is as good as mine.) Then he got a call from the Edmonton Eskimos of the CFL. He had never heard of Edmonton. He had never been to Canada, never seen a CFL game on television. Had no idea what awaited him. He came partway through the season. His first game was against B.C., where he was inserted into the lineup as a punt returner. The first punt he caught, he ran back for an eighty-nine-yard touchdown. A sign of things to come. He just had to remind himself there was no such thing as a fair catch in Canadian football. A man could get killed making that mistake.

There were other differences beyond the rules of the game that any first-year American player from the southern states, whether black or white, would have to learn.

"I was living in the Chateau Lacombe downtown … but I never forget that one morning when I got up and I looked outside. It was minus thirty-five degrees, snow was everywhere, and I was catching the LRT to get to the stadium. I didn't know that they were going outside to practise, because I never been in a blizzard or something before. And I'll never forget: [head coach and Eskimos legend] Jackie Parker came out and said, 'Everybody on the football field in ten minutes.' And I thought, *No way, no way*. I said, 'Ain't no way I can stay up here; this is too cold.' I'll never forget that day in practice. I didn't get nothing done. I could barely move. I think when they blew the whistle I was the first guy to the locker room. The first place I went with my clothes on was the steam room. It was cold."

Gizmo, or "the Giz," is perhaps most remembered for his return of a missed field goal in the 1987 Grey Cup game, played at BC Place against the Toronto Argonauts. The Eskimos would defeat the Argos on a last-second field goal, 38–36, in an exciting back and forth game between the Eastern and Western champions. But early in the game, Lance Chomyc of Toronto lined up to kick a forty-six-yard field goal. Henry Williams was the lone back waiting in the end zone. If the field goal was wide, he could either run it out or concede a single point. The ball sailed wide right. Henry caught the ball on the fly and took off running to his right before turning upfield. Watch it online and you can see an extra gear kick in. He hurdles a would-be tackler and then cuts toward the opposite corner of the end zone.

"I must have run about 200 yards. But it was fun, it was exciting."

Official record keepers have counted only 115 of those yards covered, the longest return in Grey Cup history. A decade later he would run a kickoff back for a ninety-one-yard touchdown run against the Toronto Argonauts during the Grey Cup dubbed "the Snow Bowl." The Eskimos would lose that day. All told, Henry played in five Grey Cups over his fifteen-year career with the Eskimos, winning two and losing three. He has career records no one will ever touch. It is unheard of for a kick returner to last as long as Gizmo did without suffering career-ending injuries or a huge drop-off in speed. If you're a kick-return specialist, the one thing you can't afford to lose is your speed. Many teammates had come and gone over his long career in Edmonton but one thing never wavered — his belief in them.

"I had a lot of guys on the football field who cared about me. Not just because I cared about football. I never said this, but I always felt like they'd never let anything happen to me. That's how much I trust my teammates. I always felt like when I'm running down the football field, they would never let nothing happen to me bad. They were always going to look after me."

He did give the NFL a try back in 1990 with the Philadelphia Eagles, but he hated it. He wasn't the coach's guy. Somebody else on the Eagles staff had brought him in. And in head coach Buddy Ryan's book, Henry could do no right. Buddy Ryan was the opposite of a Pinball Clemons; he wanted to control everything. Two games before the playoffs, Williams walked into Ryan's office and said, "You know what, release me."

"He couldn't believe I wanted to be released. He said, 'Why you want to be released? You're not happy here?' I go, 'I'm happy, I just feel like I need to.' And I know if I hadn't told him to release me, I probably would've done something stupid that I would've regretted. I just asked him to release me because I knew I had a home I could come back to."

And for Henry Williams that home was Edmonton.

"There's a lot of things that guys don't understand. When you play football in the CFL, you're playing because you love the game. You're not playing for the money, I can tell you right now. You're playing because you love the game. Because if I was playing because I loved the money, I would have been definitely trying to get a job back in the NFL."

Edgar Williams never got to see his little brother achieve fame and success as a professional on the gridiron. He never got to see Henry enter the Canadian Football Hall of Fame in 2002. Edgar Williams had to send Henry away to live with an uncle and aunt in Mississippi just as he was about to enter high school, because Edgar was sick with the MS that would ravage the members of Henry's immediate family. His mother died from MS, and so did his brother, Edgar. Of the ten siblings in the Williams family, seven of them died from MS. When Henry Williams turned thirty-seven years of age, he had already accomplished something none of those seven siblings could achieve: living past thirty-six. His last two brothers died from heart attacks brought on by drug and alcohol abuse. Of the twelve members of his immediate family, Henry is the only survivor. He is only fifty-six years old.

Today, Henry Williams works as a personal trainer, a high-school football coach, and a motivational speaker. He's in high demand in all these areas. He is also actively involved in a number of charities, including Kids with Cancer Society, Cystic Fibrosis Canada, and especially the Multiple Sclerosis Society of Canada. He is still a workout demon. Built like the proverbial brick you-know-what. Muscles bulging on muscles most people will never know exist. He may not still be running from MS, but he is fighting the possibility of attack by making an unassailable castle of his body.

Henry Williams is well aware that things aren't perfect for black people in Canada. Racism exists because racists exist. They can be anywhere. But freedom comes in many forms.

"I think a lot of guys when they come here they find themselves more relaxed. It's an equal opportunity for them to be whoever they want to be, to do whatever they want to do."

There is another kind of freedom for Henry and one that he says other Black Americans, especially those from the South, appreciate. Being in a place, in Henry's words, "where they ain't got to look over their shoulder all the time." If there's one experience Henry Williams knows something about it's the feeling of looking over his shoulder at whatever or whomever might be nipping at his heels.

"Growing up as a kid, I was always on the run. Move from here, go to here, going there. Edmonton is the only place I've really settled down and been able to find myself and know what I want to do with life now … and that's why I think the only way I'm going to leave Edmonton now is in a wooden box, head first. And I don't think I'm even going then."

On November 29, 2015, the Edmonton Eskimos defeated the Ottawa Redblacks on Investors Group Field in Winnipeg, Manitoba, for the 103rd Grey Cup. A piece of Canadian football history was made that night that might have gone unnoticed amid the celebrations for yet another Grey Cup for one of the most storied franchises in Canadian football: Ed Hervey became the first black general manager to win a Grey Cup.

Today, Ed Hervey is the general manager of the B.C. Lions. He came to the CFL as a receiver back in 1999 with the Edmonton Eskimos. He won two Grey Cups as a wide receiver with Edmonton. He went from the gridiron straight into scouting. He was never much interested in coaching. He was far more interested in the business side of operations, which included finding the talent worth signing. One of his mentors with the Eskimos organization was the president, Hugh Campbell, the man behind the signing of Eskimos legend Warren Moon. Campbell encouraged Hervey to pursue his ambitions. In 2009, Ed Hervey became the head scout for the Eskimos and, in 2012, the general manager, a position he held until 2016. One year later he took on the role of general manager with the Lions. That amounts to twenty years that Ed Hervey has given not only to Canadian football but to Canada itself.

Ed Hervey knows what it's like to live a double life. He spent his high-school years living undercover. Alert, wary, hiding the truth, retracing his steps, throwing off pursuers whether they existed or not. It was too dangerous to live without paranoia. Inhabiting a wardrobe of drab colours, varying shades of brown, grey, black. Nothing that might remotely grab attention or signal an association with the colours of a particular gang. That kind of mistake could get you shot.

That was life in Compton, California, a city of approximately 100,000 contained within Los Angeles County and a city more often associated with black gang violence than probably any city in the world. The main combatants were the Bloods and the Crips, of which existed any number of associated subsets throughout Los Angeles. Like Warren Moon had done twenty years earlier, Ed Hervey wanted to attend a high school outside his area, Compton High School, because of its athletic reputation. There was only one problem, one with possible deadly consequences: he would be living in an area dominated by Bloods while attending school in a neighbourhood under the influence of the Crips. Blood colours were red, the Crips' were blue. Best to eliminate either colour from one's wardrobe.

On Fridays at Compton High, the players got to wear their football jerseys on campus. Powder-blue home uniforms. There was no way he was ever going to bring that colour jersey home with him. He'd take it off and leave it at the school, then follow his convoluted path home as if traced by enemy agents.

"If they found out where I lived, whether I was involved or not, it wasn't about who you were but where you were from."

We spoke in the safety of the media room of the Eskimos' team facilities in Commonwealth Stadium. He admitted that the whole intrigue involved in his youthful double life was "silly." Not just in retrospect; he thought it was even then. An absurd pretend life, something out of a movie. But it was his reality.

"It was a world you had to live in and it was a world you had to survive in."

When he was fourteen, he'd look out the window of his house. It became something of a family routine. His mother would ask, "What's going on out there?"

"Oh, you know, a whole lot of people doing nothing," he'd respond.

"Good," she'd say. "I'm glad you see that."

But even though Ed Hervey dreamed of getting as far away from Compton as he could for all the obvious reasons like drugs, gangs, crime, guns, poverty, and oppression, he cannot simply dismiss that past. He knows that there are others like him who want more out of life, who have dreams and aspirations and may not have football as a passport out.

He remembers friends asking him when they were kids, "You want to go play pro football and leave the neighbourhood?" He'd answer with an emphatic "Yeah! Why would I want to stay here?"

"But all your friends are here."

"Hey, you guys will always be my friends. But there's something else that I've got to get away from."

"And what's that?"

How to express to his friends back then what he was able to tell a stranger years later?

"It's this fear of opening up and being who I really feel I am inside."

After high school, Hervey went to Pasadena City College, whose notable alumni include Jackie Robinson. At Pasadena, he played two seasons at quarterback, as a reserve in his freshman year before becoming the starter as a sophomore. After two years at Pasadena, he transferred to the University of Southern California. At USC, head coach John Robinson converted Hervey to a wide receiver. He was hampered by injuries in both his junior and senior years at USC, but he did make All-American in track in his senior year.

Hervey was drafted in the fifth round of the 1995 NFL draft by the Dallas Cowboys but he fractured his left fibula in a pre-season game. He was declared inactive for the rest of the season and was finally waived by the Cowboys. He spent three more years bouncing around NFL teams — Oakland, Denver, and then Oakland again. Nothing stuck. By this time, Ed Hervey just wanted to play football. He "burned" to play. His agent told him he could play in Canada. He was young enough that if he so desired he could prove himself up in Canada and NFL teams would be watching, and if there was an opportunity he could always return to the States.

"You know, all that stuff that agents sell you." Ed Hervey smiled.

He admitted it was a slow learning process but by the time his career started taking off and the NFL teams reached out to make contact, he had more or less made up his mind that he wanted to stay in Canada. He didn't see the point in trying to re-establish a career in the NFL when he already had an established career in the CFL. It wasn't an easy decision. The NFL had the draw of greater salaries. It comes down to "compensation" for many players. *What if I get hurt tomorrow? Will I be protected?*

"I felt like I was having too much fun to turn my back on a team that gave me the chance to play and gave me the opportunity to grow."

There was something else that Canada offered, and again it came down to the word "freedom." This was a different freedom from Henry Williams's version, that oppressive fear of looking over his shoulder. Hervey's freedom was all about the choice of wardrobe for a kid from Compton.

"It wasn't until I got to Canada that I put on a colour outside of black. It's just because I felt safer up here. Even then I felt uncomfortable because it wasn't something that I was accustomed to doing."

Ed Hervey remained very close with his grandmother, who lived in Sacramento.

"She never really wanted me to play football, but she was also thrilled that I was having so much success at it; she wanted to support her grandson."

At the end of every season she would ask Hervey the same question. Did you win the championship? And Hervey would sheepishly respond, "Not yet, Grandma, not yet. But we're close."

Then came 2002. The Eskimos made it to the Grey Cup game held that year in the Eskimos' own backyard, Commonwealth Stadium. Their opponents were the Montreal Alouettes. Both teams entered the game with identical season records of 13–5. Ed Hervey could not see the Eskimos losing the game. Certainly not before a hometown crowd primed to cheer their Eskimos to victory. The Alouettes, however, refused to co-operate with the desires of the thousands of Edmontonians shrieking their support for the Eskimos. The Alouettes won 25–16, giving Montreal its first Grey Cup in twenty-five years, a long time between Cups in the CFL.

Ed Hervey called his grandmother in the aftermath.

"Did you guys win?" she asked.

"No, we didn't win."

"Oh, you'll get it next year."

A subdued Hervey responded, "I hope so." He knew that his grandmother was not in the best of health and wondered whether he would ever have the opportunity again in her lifetime to give her the news she so badly yearned to hear.

The next year, 2003, the Grey Cup was held at Taylor Field in Regina, Saskatchewan. Once again the game featured Edmonton versus Montreal. This time the Eskimos came out on top. Ed Hervey's sister actually gave their grandmother the good news.

"Did they win?" his grandmother asked.

"Yes, they did," his sister replied.

Twenty-four hours later she passed away. His sister called to give Hervey the bad news just as he was preparing for the Grey Cup parade.

"Talk about something that levels you and grounds you. This is far greater than going back to Compton after a season's end and driving through the streets and seeing where you came from and realizing that you've got to keep working hard."

His sister told him that his grandmother had hung on long enough to hear the news that he had won.

"I gained some solace in knowing that she knew I had won."

At her funeral, Ed Hervey tucked his Grey Cup game jersey into his grandmother's hands. He wanted her to have something of his that meant so much to both of them. A reminder of a championship shared. A jersey he no longer felt obliged to hide for fear of something so elementary as its colour.

"People to this day ask me, 'Hey, where is your Grey Cup jersey?' And I say, 'My grandmother has it. She has it with her.'"

Henry Burris was born to play football. In fact, in Spiro, Oklahoma, the citizens refer to the hospital as the place "where football stars are born."

"When you're born in Spiro, pretty much the first question your parents are asked is 'What position is he going to play?'"

Spiro is one of those small Oklahoma towns that only draws attention to its existence every twenty years or so when a tornado touches down and obliterates everything in its path. Otherwise, it's business as usual. And that business is football.

Henry's father, Henry Burris Sr., was a baseball player. Henry figures he got his arm from his dad. When football coaches saw the way he threw the ball growing up, they made him the quarterback. But he got more than his arm from his father. From both parents he gained an awareness of the rewards of hard work.

"Both my parents worked hard, from sun-up to sundown, to make ends meet. I can honestly say I'm not one of those kids who came from a poor family. I came from a hard-working family. We kind of mixed the two worlds together where my family worked 9 to 5 but even before work and after work we were out there on the farm, baling hay, tending livestock, and things like that. I gained an understanding of what it meant to make ends meet, one. But also to earn your keep, two."

Our conversation took place in the press box high above the playing field at McMahon Stadium in Calgary. Neither of us knew it at the time, but it would be Henry's last year in Calgary where he had played for seven seasons. He was friendly and open and well-spoken, an interviewer's delight.

After high school he ended up going to Temple University in Philadelphia. Why didn't he want to play for one of the universities closer to Spiro that were courting him?

"Everybody thought I was going to either go to Texas Tech and go out there with the Red Raiders and hang out with the other farm boys and girls from rural Texas and Oklahoma. I wanted to achieve something different, experience something different. I grew up in a society where you're always judged. For some reason when I was in high school, going into my first year of playing high-school ball, our head coach at our football program at the time, he told me, 'You're not fast enough to play quarterback for me.' I looked at him, like 'Huh? Why should I run when the ball could get there quicker?'"

When he finished his four years of college ball at Temple, he held twenty passing records and ranked second all-time for passing yards in the Big East Conference. His team, the Temple Owls, did not share the same success. In his four years there, the Owls won only five games while losing an incredible thirty-nine times. The quarterback of a team that bad is not likely to attract much attention come NFL draft day. And that is exactly what happened to Henry Burris. He went undrafted. It was a bitter disappointment.

"I may not have been the biggest, tallest guy, the strongest guy, the fastest guy, or the prettiest guy, but I felt like I did enough to at least get an opportunity."

He remembered going for a tryout with the New York Giants, hoping to catch on as quarterback. An assistant coach was putting him through various drills and sprints.

"And the first statement that came to me was, 'Man, you'd make a great free safety.' I kind of looked at him and said, 'Free safety? I'm too busy torching those guys week in and week out to be one of them now.'"

But Calgary of the CFL was interested, and so Burris put his hopes for an NFL career on hold and came up to Canada. The first time he stepped on the larger Canadian football field he thought, *Wow, this field is huge.* His first pass from scrimmage during a pre-season game against Winnipeg was a wide-out route to the far sidelines.

"It felt like I almost threw my arm out. I threw it so hard, just to prove a point."

And that, it seems, has been the driving force behind his entire career. Proving a point. That Henry Burris could not be fit in a neat box of pre-conceived notions of what constitutes a quarterback. After he had attained a certain level of success in Canada, the NFL came calling. He spent a season with Green Bay as the third-string quarterback and playing on the practice squad. Then it was off to camp with the Chicago Bears, where he went into his first meeting with the coaching staff and the first words he heard were, "Man, you remind us of Michael Vick." Henry was stunned into silence. *Michael Vick? Have they seen me run?*

"I mean Michael Vick is a heck of a quarterback, but we're two different shapes and sizes. I'm a totally different package than what Mike brings to the table. But trust me, if coaches have you tagged already as being a certain type of player, it's hard to shake it, especially when other people are making the play calls."

After that season came to a miserable end, Henry could not wait to get back to Canada. In 2008, after the Calgary Stampeders had defeated the Montreal Alouettes 22–14 and Burris had been named MVP of the Grey Cup, the *Chicago Tribune* called him. He knew the purpose behind the call. They were looking for him to exploit his victory by trashing the Bears, a nice little revenge tale. *Not good enough for the Bears but now a champion!* That sort of thing. But Henry wasn't buying into it. He declined the interview, telling them, "I just want to enjoy the moment and not look at all the negatives but the positives. What the CFL game has given me, what the city of Calgary has done for my family … I'm definitely thankful for that and I'm not looking back at all."

In the 2016 Grey Cup, Henry Burris led the Ottawa Redblacks to a Grey Cup victory against the overwhelming favourites, the Calgary Stampeders, at the ripe old age of forty-one, and then announced his retirement. Known as "Smilin' Hank" for that 1,000-watt smile he flashed anyone who entered the chromosphere of his presence, he also had a less flattering nickname for a perceived inability to deliver in the big game: "Bad Hank." But if you have been around long enough and played in enough big games and had more than your share of negative outcomes, the media requires a label they can slap on your image. Thus, victory is turned into vindication. A loss is a vindication of sorts as well; it proves the media were right to label you a loser in the first place. Henry Burris had heard it all in his long and storied career.

"When I saw Damon Allen, the first time I watched a CFL game, it was the Memphis Mad Dogs playing against the Shreveport Pirates," Burris told me. This was during the lost years for many CFL fans, '93 to '95, when the CFL experimented with expansion into the United States. Perhaps the greatest highlight of this era was when a Las Vegas lounge singer, Dennis Parks, tasked with singing both national anthems before a Las Vegas Posse game, lost his musical path during the presentation of "O Canada" and began singing the lyrics to the tune of "O Tannenbaum." Priceless. "And to see Damon Allen out there just putting on a show I'm like, 'How come this guy isn't playing in the NFL?' Football is football, the last time I checked. You either make the right decision as a quarterback or you make the wrong decision. And the bottom line to me is some quarterbacks make their teams better and some quarterbacks are only as good as their team can make them."

Henry Burris played twenty years of professional football and never once was he unemployed. He threw for over 60,000 yards in the CFL. He won three Grey Cups, two with Calgary and one with Ottawa, and was twice named MVP of the Grey Cup game. He won the Schenley Award twice, first in 2010 and again in 2015, when he was forty years old. He topped that when he quarterbacked the Ottawa Redblacks to a Grey Cup victory over Calgary and was named the game's MVP at forty-one.

Burris is not only a student of the game but a student of its history. He is especially proud of the black pioneers who cleared the way for players like him to follow in their footsteps.

"I knew a lot about Johnny Bright 'cause I grew up in Oklahoma. They don't teach you a lot about that down in Oklahoma. They try to keep it more underground. You know, when it comes to Black History Month, you learn pretty much the basics of black history. But just having a father like I had he taught me the whole story about Johnny Bright and how Oklahoma basically had a bounty on his head in that game.… What I had to deal with was nothing compared to that. I mean, just what they had to go through to give me the opportunities that I have today. I'm truly thankful for it."

Henry and his family recently gained permanent residency in their journey to attain Canadian citizenship. They want to stay as so many others who came before them remained. And so, like most Black American players who came to Canada to ply their trade and remained, Henry feels a deep sense of owing to the past, as well as to those yet to come, the kids of today without access to opportunities. Henry Burris, Damon Allen, Henry Williams, Chuck Winters, Michael Clemons, John Williams Jr. — the list goes on and on — all speak, teach, give clinics, and contribute to the communities where they live in ways that demonstrate a deep attachment and commitment to their adopted country.

"That's why, whenever it comes time to celebrate any occurrence of black history, I'm always a person putting my front foot forward and lending a helping hand," said Burris. "Because I definitely want to help those out who went through the hardships and perils they went through to get me to where I am today. If it weren't for them, who knows where I'd be."

Henry Burris understands that for many black athletes who came here to play football, whether they stayed or whether they returned to their first home, Canada was more than just a country. It was and remains a state of mind. There is no need anymore for a true "underground railroad," shepherding shackled souls north to freedom. But there is something to be said for those who chose to cross the borders in their lives and in their minds that tried to keep them from reaching their true potential. In the case of Johnny Bright, Bernie Custis, Bruce Smith, Henry "Gizmo" Williams, Chuck Winters, Warren Moon, Condredge Holloway, Henry Burris, Ed Hervey, John Williams Sr., John Williams Jr., and so many others, past and present, that underground railroad of the human spirit happened to run right through the frozen football fields of Canada. And those who have followed that path know what it is to stand on the shoulders of champions.

ACKNOWLEDGEMENTS

I really must begin by acknowledging my partners at Strongwall Productions in Toronto, who were there through the difficult process of getting the film *Gridiron Underground* made: William (Bill) Armstrong, who shot and edited most of the film, and Gina Binetti, who production-managed, handled business, oversaw the editing and post-production of the film, and kept her two partners grounded when they got "too football-y." Our fourth partner at Strongwall, Marta Nielsen, never lived to see the finished film. She was set to direct but had to withdraw because of ongoing treatments for the cancer that eventually took her life in 2014. It took years to make the film, as there were times when we all had to take other work while we waited for further financing, and throughout it all, she remained our guiding spirit. The film was dedicated in her memory.

Back in 2006, Marta, Gina, and I made a film for Global TV, called *Shattered Dreams*, about disadvantaged black youth in Toronto. That's when we met the "Pastor of Bay Street," former defensive tackle with the Hamilton Tiger-Cats and Toronto Argonauts, Bruce Smith. I had already hooked up with an old film-school friend, Bill Armstrong, who had come to me with an idea for a film about Black Americans in the CFL. He even had a title: *Gridiron Underground*. I thought it was one of the greatest titles I had ever heard. (Thank you, Bill!) We teamed up with Marta and Gina and were introduced to this extended family in Hamilton consisting of Bruce Smith, Bernie Custis, John Williams Sr. — all former Tiger-Cats — and John Williams Jr., who was still playing for the Argos. Bruce was John Jr.'s godfather and Bernie was like an uncle to him. We suddenly realized that we had the core of our film.

I want to thank all the interview subjects who contributed to the film and/or this book, three of whom are no longer with us: Bruce Smith, Ulysses Curtis, and Bernie Custis. They will be missed. As for the others — Warren Moon, Condredge Holloway, Ed Hervey, Henry "Gizmo" Williams, Henry Burris, Chuck Ealey, Dave Buchanan, Tony Gabriel, Ed Jones, Hector Pothier, Tom Wilkinson, Dr. Marianne Miles, Brett Miles, Joan Mayfield, Mark Brown, Herb Trawick Jr., Chuck Winters, John Williams Sr., and John Williams Jr. — your patience and openness were greatly appreciated and will be remembered.

There are so many others I could thank here regarding the making of the film, but they have received on-screen thanks in the credits, so I will leave it at that. Just know that I care.

(But I would be remiss if I didn't mention our corporate champions at KPMG, David Zych and Marc Burchett, as well as the Canadian Football League and former commissioner Jeffrey Orridge for coming through when I needed them.)

The books I used in my research are listed in the bibliography, but two saw more action than others. Graham Kelly's *The Grey Cup: A History* was enormously helpful whenever I needed to check facts, figures, and insights pertaining to Grey Cup games. And, of course, Woody Strode's *Goal Dust* was a lively read, even if you couldn't always rely on Woody's memory of events.

To list every website I gazed upon however briefly would be an exercise in excessive futility, therefore I'll restrict my acknowledgments to a select few: Newspapers.com was particularly useful in finding game reports, quotes, and media viewpoints from sixty years ago. I also made substantial use of the digital archives at Macleans.ca, particularly for Trent Frayne's piece on Herb Trawick. I also discovered a wonderful site on Western Canada Baseball at attheplate.com. That's where I discovered the amazing story of the Indian Head Rockets.

Thanks to the Edmonton Eskimos, Calgary Stampeders, Hamilton Tiger-Cats, Toronto Argonauts, Montreal Alouettes, Winnipeg Blue

Bombers, Saskatchewan Roughriders, B.C. Lions, and Ottawa Redblacks for keeping Canadian football alive and well.

Thanks to Cassandra Rodgers, my agent at The Rights Factory, who enthusiastically helped me develop the shape and focus of the book so that it might find a home somewhere. And it did at Dundurn Press. Mighty thanks to acquisitions editor Scott Fraser, for believing in the importance of the subject matter. And while I'm on the subject of Dundurn, I would like to thank everyone I have met (mostly by Skype), exchanged emails with, or spoken to over the phone. Their continued support and availability has been a godsend. The Dundurn team: Kathryn Lane, editorial director; Elena Radic, project editor; Dominic Farrell, developmental editor; Michelle Melski, publicity manager; Tabassum Siddiqui, senior publicist; Kathryn Bassett, marketing associate; and Laura Boyle, senior designer.

Of course, I'm saving a special thanks for my editor on the book, Jess Shulman, who made the process of editing a pleasurable learning experience for me. I thank you from the bottom of my heart.

Once again, a shout-out to Bill Armstrong (an Argos season ticket holder for many years) who has been on call, it seems, forever in case I need a name, a place, a film clip, or a fact. Cheers, my friend.

And finally, I would like to acknowledge the enormous sense of gratitude I feel for the continued love and support I receive from my partner and bestie in life, Cynthia, and our children — Simone, Alex, and Julia — who, despite their own busy adult lives, never fail to show interest and a certain pride in whatever project their old man is working on. Means a lot.

Thank you all.

BIBLIOGRAPHY

Barrett, Warrick Lee. *Johnny Bright, Champion*. Lincoln, NE: iUniverse.
com, 2000.

Clemons, Michael. *All Heart: My Story*. Toronto: HarperCollins, 1999.

Cosentino, Frank. *A Passing Game: A History of the CFL*. Winnipeg:
Bain & Cox, 1995.

Ducey, Brant E. *The Rajah of Renfrew: The Life and Times of John E.
Ducey, Edmonton's "Mr. Baseball."* Edmonton: The University of
Alberta Press, 1998.

Freeman, Samuel G. *Breaking The Line: The Season in Black College
Football That Transformed the Sport and Changed the Course of Civil
Rights*. New York: Simon & Schuster, 2013.

Kelly, Graham. *The Grey Cup: A History*. Red Deer, AB: Johnson Gor-
man, 1999.

Lefko, Perry. *Pinball: The Making of a Canadian Hero*. Mississauga, ON:
John Wiley & Sons Canada, 2005.

Marc, David. *Leveling the Playing Field: The Story of the Syracuse 8*.
Syracuse, NY: Syracuse University Press, 2015.

Moon, Warren. *Never Give Up on Your Dream*. Philadelphia: De Capo
Press, 2009.

Rampersad, Arnold. *Jackie Robinson: A Biography*. New York: Alfred A.
Knopf, 1997.

Richardson, Jael Ealey. *The Stone Thrower: A Daughter's Lessons, A Father's Life*. Markham, ON: Thomas Allen, 2012.

Robinson, Jackie. *I Never Had It Made*. New York: HarperCollins, 1995.

Slade, Daryl. *Sugarfoot*. Calgary: Daryl Slade, 2018.

Strode, Woody. *Goal Dust*. Lanham, MD: Madison Books, 1990.

Film

The Color Orange: The Condredge Holloway Story. ESPN Year of the Quarterback presents in association with Souls Shine Films, a Tackle Box Films Production, a Kenny Chesney and Shaun Silva Film, 2011.

Gridiron Underground. Toronto: Strongwall Productions, 2016.

Audio

Oral History, Paul Morrison #2. Drake University Digital Collections, 2015.

INDEX

Reeves, Daniel, 37–38
Regina Caps, 99, 101–2
Renfrew Park, 102
Rice, Grantland, 69
Rich Stadium, 170
Richard, Maurice "Rocket," 21
Rickey, Branch, 22, 26, 39
Riefenstahl, Leni
   Triumph of the Will, 34
Rita, Adam, 219, 222
Robinson, Jackie, 21–24, 26–28,
   32–35, 38–39, 140, 244
   I Never Had It Made, 22
Robinson, John (coach), 244
Robinson, John (photographer),
   91, 93
Rogers, Buck, 47
Rollins, Sonny, 31
Rose Bowl, 35–36, 124–25,
   162–63, 165, 186, 192
Rowland, Chris, 161
Royal York Hotel, 43
Rozelle, Pete, 134
Rue de la Montagne, 31
Rue Saint-Antoine, 31
run-and-shoot (offence), 187–88
Ryan, Buddy, 240–41

Sam Houston University, 122–23
Samuel Walker Houston High
   School, 120–21
Sarnia Imperials, 15, 60
Saskatoon Star-Phoenix, 101
Sazio, Ralph, 134–35, 140, 151–52,
   155, 187, 200, 216
Schenley Award, 104, 143, 189–

92, 194
Schmidly, David, 111
Schwartzwalder, Floyd Burdette
   "Ben," 70–72, 142
Scioto River, 114, 132
Scott, Tom, 174, 177–78, 191
Screen Actors Guild, 44
Screen Extras Guild, 44
Seabiscuit (film), 44
Seattle Post-Intelligencer, 161–62
Seattle Slew, 163
Sheets, Kory, 108
Sheridan Bruins, 85
Shreveport Pirates, 249
Sidat-Singh, Wilmeth (Wilmeth
   Webb), 68–69
Simmons, Oze "Ozzie," 90
Sioux City Journal, 89
Skrien, Dave, 148
Smith, Bruce, 117–23, 125–31,
   137–40, 146, 151, 154–57, 200,
   205, 251
Smith, Waddell, 177, 191
Smith, Wilbanks, 90–93, 95, 97,
   111–12
Snow College, 204
Snyder, Dan, 25
Solem, Ossie, 90
Songin, Edward "Butch," 80–83
Southeastern Conference, 181,
   183
Southern Conference, 133
Southern Intercollegiate Athletic
   Conference, 51
Southern Saskatchewan Baseball
   League, 99

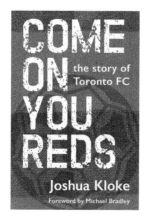

Come On You Reds: The Story of Toronto FC
Joshua Kloke
Foreword by Michael Bradley

From Toronto FC's inception, the club and their fans did things their own way. When Danny Dichio scored the first goal in franchise history, fans at BMO Field threw their seat cushions onto the field in ecstasy. It looked as though TFC had a bright future ahead of it, but what followed instead was eight seasons of poor results, mismanagement, and misery. Still, TFC fans never wavered, building the most unique atmosphere in Toronto sports. When it seemed TFC was destined to become an afterthought in a city crowded with teams, the club carved out a niche by creating a winning culture unlike anything Toronto had ever seen, bringing a championship to the city in 2017.

Come on You Reds takes fans behind the scenes, from the inception of TFC, through the team's lowest years, and finally, to the story of how management arguably built the best team in Major League Soccer history.

Blue Monday: The Expos, the Dodgers, and the Home Run That Changed Everything
Danny Gallagher
Foreword by Larry Parrish

Blue Monday: one of the most unforgettable days in Canadian baseball history.

Danny Gallagher leads readers up to that infamous day in October 1981 when Rick Monday of the Los Angeles Dodgers hit a home run off of Montreal Expos pitcher Steve Rogers in the ninth inning, giving the Dodgers a berth in the World Series. Readers will be taken back to 1976 when a five-year plan for winning the National League championship was set in place by the Expos with the hiring of experienced manager Dick Williams. Gallagher examines old narratives about Blue Monday and talks to all the key players involved in the game, unearthing secrets and stories never before told.

Hockey 365: Daily Stories from the Ice
Mike Commito

A hockey history moment for every day of the year!

A few seconds can make a game, even a season, and behind each play is a piece of history. Mike Commito marks every day of the year with a great moment in hockey and shows how today's game is part of an ongoing story that dates back to its origins on frozen ponds.

From the National hockey League's first games in 1917 to Auston Matthews's electrifying four-goal debut for the Maple Leafs in 2016, *Hockey 365* has something for everyone and is sure to give you a better appreciation for the sport we all love.

Book Credits
Project Editor: Elena Radic
Editor: Jess Shulman
Proofreader: Patricia MacDonald

Designer: Laura Boyle

Publicist: Tabassum Siddiqui

Dundurn
Publisher: J. Kirk Howard
Vice-President: Carl A. Brand
Editorial Director: Kathryn Lane
Artistic Director: Laura Boyle
Production Manager: Rudi Garcia
Publicity Manager: Michelle Melski
Manager, Accounting and Technical Services: Livio Copetti

Editorial: Allison Hirst, Dominic Farrell, Jenny McWha, Rachel Spence,
Elena Radic, Melissa Kawaguchi
Marketing and Publicity: Kendra Martin, Elham Ali,
Tabassum Siddiqui, Heather McLeod
Design and Production: Sophie Paas-Lang

dundurn.com   dundurnpress
@dundurnpress   dundurnpress
dundurnpress   info@dundurn.com

FIND US ON NETGALLEY & GOODREADS TOO!

DUNDURN